THE
CYBRARIAN'S
WEB

AN A–Z GUIDE TO 101 FREE WEB 2.0 TOOLS AND OTHER RESOURCES

CHERYL ANN PELTIER-DAVIS

Foreword by Stephen Abram

facet publishing

© Cheryl Ann Peltier-Davis 2012

Published by Facet Publishing
7 Ridgmount Street, London WC1E 7AE
www.facetpublishing.co.uk

Facet Publishing is wholly owned by CILIP: the Chartered Institute of Library and
Information Professionals.

First published in the USA by Information Today, Inc.
This UK edition 2012.

British Library Cataloguing in Publication Data
A catalogue record for this book is available from the British Library.

ISBN 978-1-85604-829-3

Text printed on FSC accredited material.

Mixed Sources
Product group from well-managed
forests and other controlled sources
www.fsc.org Cert no. SA-COC-1565
© 1996 Forest Stewardship Council

FSC

Printed and made in Great Britain by MPG Books Group, UK.

To Andre and Antonio

Contents

Foreword, by Stephen Abram xi

Acknowledgments xiii

About the Website xv

Preface xvii

Introduction xxi

1. AbiWord | productivity tool 1

2. About.com | search engine 5

3. Academic Earth | video sharing service 9

4. Amplify | social network 14

5. Animoto | video production and sharing service 17

6. Audacity | audio production, recording, and editing service 21

7. Aviary | productivity tool 25

8. Bing | search engine 30

9. Blio | ebook reader 34

10. Blogger | blog publishing service 40

11. Bloglines | news and feed aggregator 45

12. BusinessCard2 | productivity tool 50

13. CiteULike | social bookmarking service 54

14. Connotea | social bookmarking service 58

15. CuePrompter | productivity tool 62

16. Delicious | social bookmarking service 65

17. Digg | social news service 70

18. **Dogpile** | search engine **75**

19. **Doodle** | productivity tool **79**

20. **Drupal** | content management system **83**

21. **Ecademy** | social network **87**

22. **Facebook** | social network **91**

23. **FaxZero** | productivity tool **97**

24. **Flickr** | photo and video hosting service **101**

25. **Foursquare** | social network **106**

26. **GIMP** | productivity tool **112**

27. **Google Analytics** | productivity tool **116**

28. **Google Books** | digital library **121**

29. **Google Docs** | productivity tool **126**

30. **Google Reader** | news and feed aggregator **131**

31. **Google Sites** | productivity tool **135**

32. **HathiTrust** | digital library **139**

33. **Hulu** | video hosting service **143**

34. **Internet Archive** | digital library **149**

35. **iTunes U** | audio and video hosting service **155**

36. **Jing** | productivity tool **160**

37. **Justin.tv** | live video broadcasting service **164**

38. **Khan Academy** | video sharing service **168**

39. **LibGuides** | content management system **172**

40. **Library Success** | wiki **176**

41. **LibraryThing** | social cataloging service **180**

42. **Library 2.0** | social network 186

43. **LinkedIn** | social network 189

44. **LISWiki** | wiki 194

45. **LISZEN** | search engine 198

46. **Livemocha** | social network 201

47. **LucidChart** | productivity tool 205

48. **Lulu** | online publishing service 209

49. **MARC21 in Your Library** | online cataloging webinar 213

50. **Meebo** | instant messaging service 217

51. **Mikogo** | web conferencing service 221

52. **Moodle** | course management system 226

53. **Movable Type** | content management system 230

54. **Myspace** | social network 234

55. **Ning** | social network 239

56. **OpenID** | productivity tool 243

57. **OpenOffice.org** | productivity tool 246

58. **Orkut** | social network 250

59. **PBworks** | wiki 254

60. **PDF-to-Word** | productivity tool 258

61. **Photobucket** | photo hosting service 262

62. **Picasa** | photo hosting service 266

63. **Podcast Alley** | podcast service 270

64. **Prezi** | productivity tool 274

65. **Project Gutenberg** | digital library 279

66. **Qwika** | search engine 285

67. **Readerjack.com** | online publishing service 288

68. **Remember the Milk** | productivity tool 292

69. **Rollyo** | search engine 296

70. **Rondee** | productivity tool 300

71. **Scour** | search engine 304

72. **Second Life** | 3D virtual world 308

73. **Shelfari** | social cataloging service 312

74. **Skype** | productivity tool 317

75. **SlideShare** | productivity tool 322

76. **SortFix** | search engine 327

77. **Spybot-Search & Destroy** | productivity tool 331

78. **StatCounter** | productivity tool 335

79. **StumbleUpon** | social bookmarking service 339

80. **SurveyMonkey** | productivity tool 344

81. **Technorati** | search engine 349

82. **TripIt** | travel planning service 354

83. **Twitter** | social network/microblogging service 358

84. **TypeFaster** | productivity tool 364

85. **Ustream** | broadcasting service 368

86. **Vimeo** | video hosting and sharing service 374

87. **VuFind** | open source ILS 379

88. **Widgets** | programming code service 383

89. **Wikipedia** | wiki 387

90. Wikis by Wetpaint | wiki 394

91. Wolfram|Alpha | search engine 399

92. Wordle | visualization tool 404

93. WordPress.com | blog hosting service 407

94. WorldCat.org | next-generation online union catalog 412

95. XING | social network 418

96. Yahoo! Answers | question-and-answer service 422

97. YouSendIt | file hosting and sharing 427

98. YouTube | video hosting and sharing service 431

99. Zoho | productivity tool 436

100. Zoomerang | productivity tool 443

101. Zotero | productivity tool 447

Appendix I: Tips and Teaching Tools for Keeping Up-To-Date
         With Web 2.0 Technologies 453

Appendix II: Web 2.0 Tools and Other Resources:
         A Glossary 457

Appendix III: Referenced Websites 465

About the Author 475

Index 477

Foreword

by Stephen Abram

I once lamented that what Library 2.0 needed was its own Yellow Pages—but with only the good stuff there. My prayers have been answered.

Cheryl Peltier-Davis has taken her considerable skills and created an up-to-date guide that offers a roadmap for learning about the opportunities for libraries in Web 2.0 applications. The bulk of the work is in the carefully curated tools. Each is well catalogued and offers real world examples of what actual libraries are doing with these ubiquitous 2.0 tools today. Cheryl's librarian's sensibility has selected those Web 2.0 tools that have applicability to library service strategies. And these apply to all types of libraries. Cheryl's decision to limit the directory to those Web 2.0 sites that are free or low cost fits very nicely into today's library budgetary situation. There are few excuses to avoid innovation and improving the user experience when 101 resources are listed here for pilots, trials, and experimentation at your library.

There has been much debate in librarianship about whether there is a Library 2.0 strategy founded in the opportunities afforded by free or inexpensive Web 2.0 applications. Cheryl's guide puts the lie to these worries for those library leaders who recognize that the biggest impact of the web on libraries has been that the majority of our users now experience the library virtually. They see that the opportunity for the biggest impact is the improvement of the virtual experience to complement our on-site services. And these changes increase the scale of library service immeasurably. Web 2.0 tools are essentially social tools that engage users in social interaction with information—recommendations, learning, community sharing, and more. Libraries, as social institutions, can achieve benefits from learning from and about these tools by trying small experiments and rolling them out gradually.

I've read *The Cybrarian's Web*, and I consider myself a fairly aware librarian who keeps his eye on developments in tools that will assist librarians in meeting our mission. Cheryl has identified and described

101 tools here that far exceed my knowledge and awareness. This is fabulous! I look forward to playing with as many of them as possible soon. Cheryl's cataloguer's eye is evident in her excellent categorization of these tools. You can see her recommendations of what 2.0 tools are worth considering in the library environment as well as being inspired by the actual libraries who have piloted these tools in real life situations. And this is a modern guide. Don't neglect to visit the companion website, which makes linking easy and will keep things up-to-date in the constantly changing 2.0 world. Pay particular attention to Cheryl's sage advice on tips for keeping up-to-date with Web 2.0 technologies in Appendix I.

This book belongs on every library innovator's bookshelf. This isn't just for the techies and, indeed, it would be a shame to limit its use to techies. Web 2.0 is first and foremost about the end-user experience, and so, for every reference librarian, trainer, director, web content writer, blogger and library leader, review the opportunities in this guide as part of your strategic planning process. You'll be glad you did!

Play, enjoy, and share.

Stephen Abram,
vice president,
Cengage Learning

Acknowledgments

This book would not have been possible without the network of cybrarians I have befriended and worked closely with during my professional life. Thank you all for your diligence and dedication to the profession, and for your commitment to using leading-edge technologies to build what have been described as the storehouses of knowledge for present and future generations. To the developers of the resources covered in this book, your innovations provided the groundwork required for the extensive research that went into putting this book together.

To James Broderick and Darren Miller, your book, *Consider the Source: A Critical Guide to 100 Prominent News and Information Sites on the Web* (Medford, NJ: Information Today, Inc., 2007), was indeed a source of inspiration and a perfect model to follow in writing the book chapters. Thanks to Stephen Abram for his advice and willingness to write the Foreword for this book. I would also like to extend my gratitude and acknowledge the thorough review of my book by my colleagues Rich Ackerman, Arlene Batson-George, and Deborah Tritt, who voluntarily took time out from their busy schedules to meticulously go through every chapter. Thanks to John Bryans, editor extraordinaire, imbued with extreme patience and support of fledging writers, and to Amy Reeve, managing editor, who tirelessly and patiently responded to my queries and requests for last-minute changes.

Finally, thanks to my two sons, Andre and Antonio, for their support and understanding during the long hours spent in researching and writing this book.

About the Website
www.cybrariansweb.com

As with any publication of this nature that attempts to provide a comprehensive list of resources on the ubiquitous but unpredictable internet where websites are not static and may change often, I have taken precautions and created a companion website. This companion website lists URLs to all Web 2.0 tools and other resources covered in this book and provides summaries of new sites and resources. It also contains a link to my blog and space for your comments and recommendations. The addition of this companion website ensures that readers are kept up-to-date with developments in this highly dynamic and fast-moving target. To access it, go to www.cybrariansweb.com. Please feel free to email your comments, changes, or additions to cybrarianweb101@gmail.com.

Disclaimer
Neither the publisher nor the author make any claim as to the results that may be obtained through the use of this webpage or of any of the internet resources it references or links to. Neither publisher nor author will be held liable for any results, or lack thereof, obtained by the use of this page or any of its links; for any third-party charges; or for any hardware, software, or other problems that may occur as the result of using it. This webpage is subject to change or discontinuation without notice at the discretion of the publisher and author.

Preface

Where can I find these Web 2.0 resources? When can I start using these new Web 2.0 technologies? How can I keep up given my busy schedule? These are questions I often hear after attending a conference or workshop presentation on Web 2.0 technologies. In *The Cybrarian's Web: An A–Z Guide to 101 Free Web 2.0 Tools and Other Resources*, I attempt to provide answers to these questions and much more.

Each chapter features in-depth summaries of cutting-edge Web 2.0 technologies and the practical applications of these resources in libraries and allied communities. Coverage includes blog publishing services, wikis, RSS feeds, photo and video sharing services, folksonomies (tagging and tag clouds), podcast services, instant messaging, mashups, virtual worlds, productivity tools, social networks, social bookmarks, and social cataloging.

Whether it is your intent to create a book review blog, social bookmark a reference collection, create subject-specific RSS feeds, develop a policy-driven wiki, record a podcast, create a tutorial using digital video, attract fans on a Facebook page, or provide regular tweets on upcoming events in your library, you will find this guide invaluable for promoting your services in an increasingly virtual world and attracting even the most tech-savvy patrons. You may discover dozens of sites that hitherto have remained hidden, or rediscover sites that you may have used and found helpful.

During what can best be described as tumultuous times—mainly in the economy, but certainly in our careers and organizational roles—I hope that this book will serve as a valuable research tool and provide practical lessons for librarians and other information professionals, working in all type of libraries, wishing to harness the potential of the Web 2.0 technologies. My fervent wish is that these chapters will provide the leverage needed to develop the cutting-edge skills required to deliver highly customized, value-added services at your workplace.

For lecturers and students in library schools, where Web 2.0 and its practical usage in libraries have been integrated into the core curricula, this book can augment recommended reading material. In fact, any reader with a passing interest in learning about new technologies and innovations and learning how to apply these within a specific community will find information that can be immediately used and beneficial.

How This Book Is Organized

Choosing which resource to include in each chapter was by far my greatest challenge. My main goal was to provide exhaustive coverage of each resource, giving the reader as much information as possible about structure, content, and usefulness. The length of the book was also an important consideration and in the final revisions, manageability and ease of use won over long-winded and superfluous coverage.

My lengthy tenure and skills developed as a cataloger who willingly and easily catalogs all things—tangible and intangible—are reflected in the categorization and arrangement of individual resources. Each Web 2.0 technology mentioned is reflective of the application's origins and falls into one of several broad groupings such as blog publishing service, wiki, podcasting service, photo hosting service, video sharing service, social network, social bookmarking service, search engine, productivity tool, and question-and-answer service.

As readers will discover, the 101 resources are arranged alphabetically in an A–Z list for readability and ease of use. Chapters are autonomous, allowing readers to jump immediately to their resource of interest. Each chapter also includes illustrative screenshots, which show the resource in action and help readers to visualize its main features. Entries are organized as follows:

> Name of the Web 2.0 resource

> Categorization of application (blog publishing service, wiki, podcast service, photo hosting service, video sharing service, social network, etc.)

> Static URL of the website where the resource can be found on the internet (for example, www.zotero.com)

> Overview of the site's origin, development, and functions, focusing on questions such as who created the resource, why, and when it was created

➤ Important features, which gives readers a clear and concise explanation of the resource's main features, functionality, design, and usability

➤ "How Cybrarians Can Use This Resource," which provides innovative real-world examples of how libraries and librarians are using Web 2.0 tools (This section can be viewed as valuable for practitioners in the field wishing to observe Web 2.0 technologies at work in libraries. For library administrators, this section will provide concrete evidence of libraries that are using these technologies to enhance their online presence, showcase innovative services, and increase patronage.)

➤ FYI (For Your Information), where readers will find fun factoids or interesting snippets of information on the resource, like awards received, trends to watch, and usage statistics

➤ Appendix I, which features tips and teaching tools to help cybrarians on their never-ending quest to keep up-to-date with new technologies

➤ Appendix II, an annotated glossary of each resource covered in the book

➤ Appendix III, a list of websites referenced in the book

Criteria Used in Choosing Web 2.0 Tools and Other Resources

At the time of this writing, the majority of the software applications included in this book were free. Some may have a minimal subscription fee attached to using the service, and this is disclosed to readers.

The selection of all resources was based on independent review and personal analysis, and the following factors weighed heavily in the decision-making process and greatly influenced the inclusion of resources in the ensuing chapters:

➤ What is the relevance of the features, function, and organization of the resource? For example, is the content useful to librarians and information professionals? Can it add immediate value to current services provided? Can it be easily implemented by less tech-savvy users? Is it organized for ease of use?

➤ Is the resource well-known and established? For example, is there constant chatter and buzz in blogs, eforums, and other discussion groups about its reputation?

➤ Does the site have longevity as evidenced by the time it was created and its current iteration?

➤ Has the resource received good reviews from consumers?

➤ Is there evidence of technical support?

Final Comment

Readers, I encourage you to plunge ahead and read about the limitless selection of new, and in many instances, freely available tools in the Web 2.0 digital universe. I am certain that you will discover that many of these social tools have already touched and shaped some aspect of your life—work, research, education, entertainment, or social activities. I hope you enjoy the journey and learn something new along the way.

Cheryl Ann Peltier-Davis
Learn, Experiment, Share

Introduction

Why Use Web 2.0 Resources in Libraries?

Web 2.0, a term associated with the O'Reilly Media Web 2.0 conference held in 2004, refers to a perceived second generation of web-based services (such as social networking sites, wikis, communication tools, and folksonomies) that emphasize online collaboration and sharing among users. Library experts have used simpler and somewhat common terms to describe the Web 2.0 phenomenon: the read/write web where users are both consumers and producers of online content; an interactive two-way web; a place where everyday folks with internet access can create and edit stuff. Some have even ventured to draw the distinction between Web 1.0 and Web 2.0 by describing the former as *a place to go and get*, and the latter as *a place to be and do.*

Embedded Web 2.0 technologies are commonplace in high user volume social networking sites such as YouTube, Delicious, Myspace, Facebook, Second Life, LibraryThing, Ning, Flickr, Twitter, Meebo, WorldCat.org, Wikipedia, and others. Stephen Abram[1] does a good job of identifying key technologies and social software tools that serve as the foundation of Web 2.0. These include:

➤   Blog publishing services

➤   Wikis

➤   RSS (Really Simple Syndication) feeds

➤   User-added reviews, ratings, and summaries

➤   Instant messaging

➤   Podcasts and vodcasts

➤   Folksonomies, tagging, and tag clouds

➤   Social bookmarking

➤   Social networking sites

- ➤ Streaming audio and video

- ➤ Community photo services or photo sharing

- ➤ Community book services (publishing)

The widespread popularity and almost obsessive need to participate and connect with one's family, friends, colleagues, and community on mobile and nonmobile devices (smartphones, MP3 players, laptops, tablets, PCs) and social- and community-oriented networking sites is evidenced in a recent Pew report. The Pew Internet and American Life project, "Adults and Social Network Websites," shows that within a span of four years (2005–2009), the share of American adult internet users who have a profile on an online social network site has quadrupled from 8 percent to 35 percent, but this figure is still much lower than the 65 percent of online American teens who use social networks.[2]

Given this statistical data, it is not surprising that the potential benefits of Web 2.0 technologies, which allow us to easily create, contribute, communicate, and collaborate with each other in new and exciting ways, have not gone unnoticed within the library community. There has been widespread consensus that these cutting-edge tools should be immediately adopted, in a bid to retain core library users and cajole new users into the library. Five immediate benefits of using these Web 2.0 tools, which ultimately enhance the library's online presence and the library user's experiences, include:

1. *Delivery of highly customized, value-added services to tech-savvy clients.* Librarians can augment their roles as educators and community leaders by teaching constituents how to use and how to value using these social tools. Many library patrons are already proficient in using tools such as blogs, wikis, RSS feeds, and podcasts as an integral part of their daily regimen. Sites that embody Web 2.0 characteristics, like YouTube (video hosting and sharing), Flickr (photo and video sharing), Twitter (microblogging), LibraryThing (social cataloging), and Facebook (social networking), attract millions of users every day. Any attempt to serve up library services to these tech-savvy clients must be an aggressive customer-driven effort. Cybrarians should be proactive, learning more about these tools and pushing library services

and content to users where they need it the most—in effect, invading their social worlds.

2.   *Overcoming economic turmoil by integrating Web 2.0-driven services into the library's economic recovery efforts.* As budget woes, staff layoffs, and cuts in services continue unabated at libraries and allied companies in the information industry, many administrators have been assigned the bitter task of stepping back, reflecting on, and reassessing existing services. Fortunately, during these tough economic times, forced frugality and stymied efforts to increase library budget allocations have ignited a spirit of innovation and creativity among library administrators and staff. In a united team effort, both groups have come together to reevaluate and reposition library policies, advance networking and collaboration efforts, and become more creative in using scarce resources. This show of unity and originality has prompted many observers to comment that the economic downturn should be described as both the best of times and worst of times for libraries. As will be shown by using live library examples, some libraries have been more adept and successful than others in harnessing and implementing Web 2.0-driven services at a lower cost with increased patronage.

3.   *Building alliances with patrons and improving communications with staff.* Social networking tools can advance a library's external dialogue with its patrons and improve internal communication and knowledge sharing with staff. For example, a library wiki can be developed as an online knowledge base, a tool to maintain best practices as well as policy and procedures manuals.

4.   *Instant implementation and democratization of the web.* Putting content on the web is no longer the exclusive right of experts with knowledge of HTML and web programming languages. With the social software available for creating blogs, wikis, podcasts, vodcasts, and social networking sites, anyone—even those of us with limited technological expertise—can add online content. All you need is access to a computer and an internet connection.

5.   *Survival in a competitive landscape.* Cybrarians[3] are not only challenged to get ahead of the Web 2.0 wave, but cautioned that once there, it is imperative that they stay on board and continue to lead the way. This becomes more crucial with the arrival of a new iteration dubbed *Web 3.0* or the *semantic web*, as evidenced by increased chatter in the blogosphere about the web being on the cusp of another wave of change.[4] If there is hesitation or unwillingness to adapt to changes, other rival information services will do the job for us. Google, who by its own admission wants "to organize the world's information and make it universally accessible and useful,"[5] is already at the forefront, creating unique web applications to make it simpler for people to share information and get things done together. Google Books is an example of one such application that provides access to the full text of books that have been digitized and stored in a digital database. The relative success and widespread usage of Google Books among web searchers has already initiated stormy debates about the future and seemingly relegated role of libraries as storehouses of mainly print information.

Libraries have always been at the forefront of, and benefited from, adopting innovative approaches to improve services. It would now seem inevitable that Web 2.0 technologies could be added to the list of innovations and that librarians could gain recognition as early adopters. In fact, as readers will discover, most of the resources given in-depth treatment in individual book chapters have already been successfully integrated into existing library services and offered through library portals.

As beneficial as free and inexpensive Web 2.0 options can be for libraries with scarce resources, some words of caution should be heeded before rushing headlong into early adoption. As is the norm when implementing any new product or service, a period of critical evaluation and review (of current needs and product effectiveness) and intense consultation (with staff, clients, and vendors) is required. When these perfunctory first steps have been taken, only then can the right decision be made.

This book is a good starting point toward product evaluation. As you read each chapter, please consider sending your comments and contributing new resources to the accompanying book website at www. cybrariansweb.com.

Endnotes

1. Stephen Abram, "Social Libraries: The Librarian 2.0 phenomenon," *Library Resources & Technical Services*, 52 (2008): 20.

2. Amanda Lenhart, "Adults and Social Network Websites," Pew Internet and American Life Project, January 14, 2009, www.pewinternet.org/Reports/2009/Adults-and-Social-Network-Websites.aspx (accessed August 10, 2011).

3. *Cybrarian* is a shortened form of *cyberlibrarian*, coined from the terms *cyberspace* and *librarian* to refer to a librarian whose work routinely involves information retrieval and dissemination via the internet and the use of other online resources. "Cybrarian," Online Dictionary for Library and Information Science, www.abc-clio.com/ODLIS/odlis_c.aspx (accessed August 10, 2011).

4. *Semantic web* is a term coined by World Wide Web Consortium (W3C) director Tim Berners-Lee. It describes a group of methods and technologies to allow machines to understand the meaning—or *semantics*—of information on the World Wide Web. "Semantic Web," Wikipedia, en.wikipedia.org/wiki/Semantic_Web (accessed August 10, 2011).

5. "Google Company Overview," Google, www.google.com/corporate (accessed August 10, 2011).

1

AbiWord
productivity tool
www.abisource.com

Overview

AbiWord is a free word processing program, similar to Microsoft Word and WordPerfect, which can be used for a wide variety of word processing tasks. Originally conceived as an open source project by the SourceGear Corporation, AbiWord's source code has been released and adopted by a thriving developer community that continues to make improvements and enhancements to the software. The software was initially released in December 1998, and its latest stable iteration (version 2.8.6) was released in July 2011.

Similar to Microsoft Word and rival open source word processing products, AbiWord supports basic word processing features such as creation of mailing lists and tables, mail merge, multiple page views, spell and grammar checking, and support for footnotes and endnotes as well as page headers and footers. Its unique distinction among other word processors is its ability to run on cross platforms operating systems including UNIX, Windows (95 and later), and MacOS X.

As a wholly volunteer project, AbiWord is licensed under the GNU General Public License. On its main website (www.abisource.com) there is an open call for contributors to assist in areas such as beta testing, bug triaging, translation, and coding.

Features

> ➤ The software from the main website (www.abisource.com/ download) downloads relatively easily. AbiWord 2.8.6 (latest stable release) is available in multiple languages and support

1

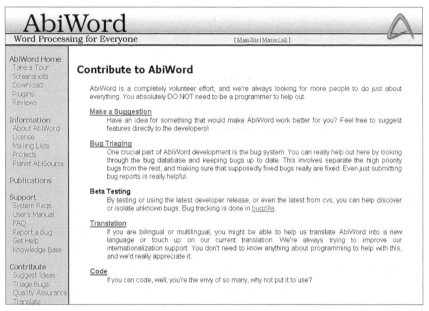

On the AbiWord developers' page, there is an open call for contributors to assist in beta testing, bug triaging, translation, and coding.

is provided for Microsoft Windows and Linux operating systems.

➤   The following features are highlighted on the Take a Tour (www.abisource.com/tour) link on the homepage:

• Interoperability: AbiWord provides support for reading and writing standard documents such as OpenOffice.org, Microsoft Word, WordPerfect, Rich Text Format (RTF), and HTML webpages.

• Advanced document layout: Layout options include access to tables, bullets, lists, images, footnotes, endnotes, and formatting styles.

• Support for multiple languages: AbiWord dictionaries are available for more than 30 languages. Support is also provided for right-to-left, left-to-right, and mixed-mode text. Thus, in addition to supporting European languages, AbiWord supports other languages like Hebrew and Arabic.

- Extensible Plugin Architecture: Plugins and tools (www.abisource.com/wiki/PluginMatrix) are available for users wishing to extend AbiWord functionality. This exhaustive list includes document and image importers, tools for creating document summaries, and a thesaurus and grammar checker.

➢ For first time users of the software, the AbiWord User's Manual (www.abisource.com/support/manual) is available in three languages (English, French, and Polish). An FAQ wiki addresses general questions posed by new users and the developers of the software. Technical support is provided via a Report a Bug page, a user's mailing list, and an online chat room.

➢ AbiWord's Reviews page (www.abisource.com/reviews) provides updated summaries on other users rating of the current release, its compatibility with rival software, usefulness of new features, and basic functionality.

➢ A publications page (www.abisource.com/papers) provides up to date information on lectures, articles, conference papers, and other miscellaneous publications contributed by the AbiWord Team.

How Cybrarians Can Use This Resource

Productivity Tool for Basic Word Processing Tasks

As a free, open-source, cross-platform word processor, AbiWord can be considered as a noteworthy alternative to proprietary (and sometimes expensive) products. This is an example of software that Cybrarians can promote via continuing education workshops or on a productivity tools resource page to library patrons seeking a functional inexpensive word processing application.

Here are some advantages that can be highlighted while promoting this resource:

➤ A user-friendly interface that is similar in layout, features, and function to other word processing software such as Microsoft Word and WordPerfect

➤ Quick access to tools required for writing, editing, formatting, and reading documents

➤ Compatibility with Microsoft Word for opening and saving documents although the program has its own proprietary file format

➤ Integration with the AbiCollab.net web service (abicollab.net), which allows users to store documents online, collaborate with multiple users simultaneously in real-time, share online documents with friends and colleagues, and perform format conversions on the fly

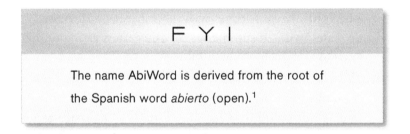

F Y I

The name AbiWord is derived from the root of the Spanish word *abierto* (open).[1]

Endnote

1. "AbiWord," Wikipedia, www.en.wikipedia.org/wiki/AbiWord (accessed September 7, 2011).

2

About.com
search engine
www.about.com

Overview

About.com was acquired in 2005 by the New York Times Company, a leading media company whose publications include the *New York Times, International Herald Tribune, Boston Globe,* and 15 other daily newspapers. On the homepage (www.about.com) the service is described as a valuable resource for content that helps users solve the large and small needs of everyday life. The majority of users redirected to About.com from search engines are information seekers searching for solutions in response to an immediate need.

Help is proffered by a seemingly robust network of about 800 experts or guides who have written more than 70,000 articles on topics such as cooking, health care, hobbies, parenting, politics, technology, travel, jobs and careers, sports and recreation, and much more. Expert advice and practical solutions to everyday problems are offered by way of these original handcrafted articles, product reviews, videos, and tutorials.

By its own estimates, the website attracts an average of about 40 million unique visitors in the United States every month and adds more than 6,000 pieces of new content each week.[1]

Features

➢   The caption at the top of the prominently placed search box on the About.com homepage reads: "What can we help you accomplish today?" The service's willingness to provide guidance and assist users in finding information to solve a

About.com has four search options: Browse Categories, Explore Topics, Editors' Picks, and a keyword search.

problem, learn something new, or make a decision is supported by the four options available for searching the resource:

1. Users can Browse Categories, which cover diverse subjects such as business and finance, computing and technology, education, entertainment, health, jobs and careers, news and issues, parenting and family, religion and spirituality, sports and recreation, and travel.

2. Users also have the option to Explore Topics, an A–Z list of specialized topics covering areas such as American history, blogging, career planning, freelance writing, low calorie cooking, reality TV, smartphones, and the U.S. economy.

3. The Editors' Picks and Guide Tweets connect searchers to buzzworthy trending topics.

4. For the experienced web searcher there is the option to construct a search query by entering keywords into a single search box.

➤ About.com is marketed as a trusted information source. Toward this end, much is made of the fact that all of the content is written by a network of expert writers (guides) and contributing authors. These experts are real people who are selected by using exacting standards and who qualify for the job based on their professional experience in the subject area, educational background, and writing ability. Contributions by guides are accompanied by in-depth biographies and photographs.

➤ Content for all topics on About.com is posted on guidesites or websites, written and updated by guides and contributing authors. These guidesites are well organized and somewhat consistent in content, offering articles, commentaries, links to pertinent resources related to the topic, and links to the author's blog and discussion forum.

How Cybrarians Can Use This Resource

One-Stop Reference Source

As one of the leading producers of original content on the web with an unerring focus on delivering high-quality, credible content on a broad range of topics, About.com can serve as a one-stop reference shop for cybrarians wishing to tap into an established network of experts for those difficult reference questions. The site's experts and guides are knowledgeable on topics and provide content that is succinct and easily digestible for beginners and experts alike.

Workshop and Training Support

Staff at the Lebanon Branch of the Russell County (VA) Public Library posted the URL link on its library blog to the Computer Beginners Handbook[2] available on About.com. The link to this resource was of value to patrons who were unable to attend a basic computer skills course offered by the library. The online handbook covered topics such as hardware, file management, computer gaming, MS Windows basics, and software applications such as MS Word, PowerPoint, Excel, and Access.

Publishing

Cybrarians can harness a potential publishing opportunity by applying to be a guide or contributing writer for About.com (beaguide.about.com). As a freelance writer, you can reap immediate benefits such as working online, setting your own schedule, earning compensation, and writing on topics relevant to libraries. All potential guides go through a rigorous two-part online training program that teaches editorial standards, while writing articles and blog posts and publishing these on a test site with support from About.com's publishing tools. A list of available topics is updated regularly and the application process can be completed online.

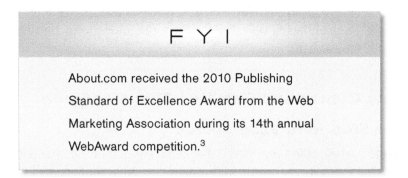

F Y I

About.com received the 2010 Publishing
Standard of Excellence Award from the Web
Marketing Association during its 14th annual
WebAward competition.[3]

Endnotes

1. "Who We Are," About.com, www.advertiseonabout.com/Who_We_Are (accessed August 10, 2011).

2. "About.com: The Computer Beginner's Handbook," Russell County Public Library Blog, www.ruscolib.blogspot.com/2009/05/aboutcom-computer-beginners-handbook.html (accessed August 10, 2011).

3. "About.com Press Releases," About.com, www.advertiseonabout.com/Press_Release/55/ (accessed August 10, 2011).

3

Academic Earth
video sharing service
www.academicearth.org

Overview

As more and more educational content becomes freely available online, Academic Earth is a researcher's goldmine. The site offers free access to video courses and academic lectures from leading colleges and universities in one centralized educational repository. The parent company (which carries the same name as the resource, Academic Earth) is led by entrepreneur Richard Ludlow and is headquartered in San Francisco, California.

Its stated goal is to "give everyone on earth access to a world-class education."[1] This somewhat lofty goal seems easily achievable, given that all of the video content has been harvested from prestigious universities such as MIT, Stanford, Berkeley, Columbia, Harvard, Michigan, NYU, Princeton, UCLA, and Yale.

Visitors to the site can watch the same full-length lectures that registered undergraduate students from these universities would attend. Subject areas are diverse and include astronomy, biology, chemistry, computer science, economics, engineering, English, entrepreneurship, history, law, mathematics, medicine, philosophy, physics, political science, psychology, and religious studies.

As of this writing there are more than 1,500 videos available for viewing. New videos are added every day. Some of these are grouped into courses, which may contain from four to 50 lectures.

Features

> For the first-time user of this resource, registration and creating login credentials to view videos are optional.

9

However, users wishing to save videos to their favorites list should register on the homepage (www.academicearth.org) and create a profile.

➤ Academic Earth's online interface is easy to navigate. Courses can be browsed using four categories: subjects (broad subject areas), universities, instructors, or playlists. Playlists are thematic collections of lectures from different speakers selected and compiled by the site's editors, including offerings such as You Are What You Eat, Laws of Nature, Understanding the Financial Crisis, and First Day of Freshman Year. Using the advanced search feature, users can filter searches by course ratings, university, and subject. Search results can be sorted by relevancy, title, and rating.

➤ In addition to full courses, the site also features guest lectures on leadership, entrepreneurship, technology, and policy from luminaries such as Google co-founder Larry Page, Facebook founder Mark Zuckerberg, *New York Times* columnist Thomas Friedman, and others.

➤ Online course videos are viewable within the same interface. If a download option appears, a QuickTime version of the lecture can be downloaded. Videos can be shared with friends on social networks such as Facebook and StumbleUpon, bookmarked in Delicious, embedded in a blog or website, and subscribed to as an RSS feed or podcast.

➤ According to a posting on the FAQ page, all lectures start out with a grade of B.[2] From this point on, the final grade is an average of the grades that all users collectively assign. Course grades are based on the ratings given to the individual lectures in that course. Highly rated content shows up first in the browse results and in the Top Rated section of the homepage.

➤ For each course viewed online, there is a comprehensive course description and a list of lectures offered. Some lectures have accompanying photographs of the lecturers.

➤ For serious researchers, there is a link to bibliographic citations. At the bottom of each page there is a Contact link to provide feedback on design and content or to post a question.

How Cybrarians Can Use This Resource
Simplifying the Patron Search Experience

Described in some forums as the Hulu of education (the way Academic Earth manages academic content is similar to how Hulu [www.hulu.

Academic Earth online course videos can be
downloaded or shared with friends on social networks.

com] manages television content; see Chapter 33), Academic Earth sets the bar high as a model of how free online education resources, taught by some of the world's best scholars, can be easily organized into a centralized platform. This resource offers new opportunities for librarians to simplify the customer search experience, connecting end users with quality research.

Reference and Research Assistance

For undergraduate and postgraduate students struggling with algebra, physics, or history coursework and assignments, reference librarians can save these students the time and effort it takes to scour the internet for answers by guiding them to this easily accessible repository of academic video courses and guest lectures. Faculty and other educators can also be guided to the resource to study the teaching methods of other instructors. For lifelong learners, there is the opportunity for personal enrichment and access to a world-class education. The large collections of business, computer science, and engineering lectures can be utilized by professionals and job seekers.

Engaging Faculty

Academic librarians can engage faculty and foster new alliances by working with the academic community to develop the infrastructure needed to create videos, record live video feeds, and post relevant video courses and lectures to the Academic Earth educational repository.

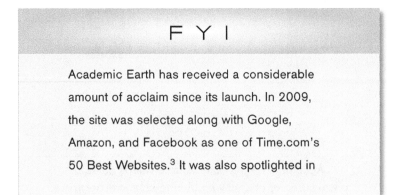

F Y I

Academic Earth has received a considerable amount of acclaim since its launch. In 2009, the site was selected along with Google, Amazon, and Facebook as one of Time.com's 50 Best Websites.[3] It was also spotlighted in

the 2010 Annual Letter of the Bill and Melinda
Gates Foundation in which Bill Gates
described his personal use of the site and
endorsed it as an online educational tool.[4]

Endnotes

1. "Mission Statement," Academic Earth, www.academicearth.org/about (accessed August 10, 2011).

2. "Academic Earth FAQ," Academic Earth, www.academicearth.org/pages/faq#6 (accessed August 10, 2011).

3. "50 Best Websites 2009," Time.com, www.time.com/time/specials/packages/completelist/0,29569,1918031,00.html (accessed August 10, 2011).

4. Bill Gates, "2010 Annual Letter from Bill Gates," www.gatesfoundation.org/annual letter/2010/Documents/2010-bill-gates-annual-letter.pdf (accessed August 10, 2011).

4

Amplify
social network
www.amplify.com

Overview

Amplify is a social blogging and curation service created for users wishing to engage in conversations about news, current events, and original ideas they want to share. As described on the website Top Tools for Learning, Amplify should attract Twitter users as "not all conversations can be had in fewer than 140 characters, so while Twitter is an amazing place for keeping up with what's going on in the world, Amplify is the place to talk about it."[1]

Using Amplify's proprietary browser add-on and web clipping technology, users can easily clip, share, and add comments on excerpts from articles, photos, videos, and webpages. Additionally, they can add their original ideas by writing blog postings directly on Amplify and post these directly to social networks such as Twitter, Facebook, Google Buzz, Flickr, WordPress, Blogger, FriendFeed, and more.

In June 2011, the service introduced Amplify Mobile with support for the iPhone, iPad, and Android phones. Founded in 2009, Amplify is based in New York City.

Features

> To start using the service, you can sign up for a free account on the homepage (www.amplify.com) by completing the web-based form with your full name, username, email address, and password; you must also complete a verification process to prevent spam. Users also have the option of signing in using an existing Twitter or Facebook account.

➤   Like Twitter, Amplify provides two input boxes: What Do You Want to Talk About (40-character limit) and What Do You Want to Say (1,000-character limit) for posting original thoughts or sharing interesting news found on the web. Posts can be categorized into one of several broad subject categories provided.

➤   Users have the option of enabling automatic postings simultaneously to supported social networks including Twitter, Facebook, Google Buzz, WordPress, and Blogger.

➤   Amplify provides tools for customizing Amplogs (personalized dashboards) by adding background or header images and changing font colors.

➤   Users can search for and import friends from Twitter, Facebook, and Gmail.

➤   Support is provided for adding Google Analytics to monitor statistics on user traffic.

➤   Amplify users have the option of installing an Amplify bookmarklet (www.amplify.com/bookmarklet) to a web browser or obtaining the Amplify Firefox add-on or Google Chrome extension. Once installed, this bookmarklet enables automatic clipping and sharing of information discovered while browsing the web.

➤   Access to Mingle (an open forum) initiates discussions with other Amplify users.

How Cybrarians Can Use This Resource

Current Awareness Service

Amplify is another example of a social networking service that was developed with the goal of providing 2.0 users with a platform to talk about events and ideas that hold their interest. Cybrarians can use this meta-dashboard to fulfill their information sharing needs and keep library patrons up-to-date and informed about innovative services, new library collections, current events, training opportunities, systems

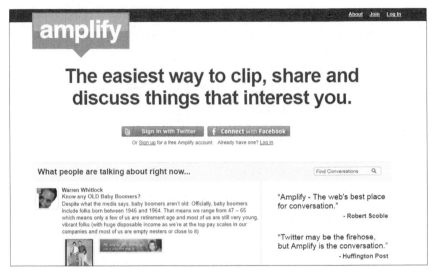

Amplify is a social blogging service created for users
wishing to engage in conversations about news, current events,
and original ideas they want to share.

alerts, changes in library policy, exhibits, book sales, library statistics,
and links to evaluating new eresources.

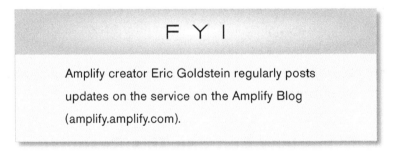

F Y I

Amplify creator Eric Goldstein regularly posts

updates on the service on the Amplify Blog

(amplify.amplify.com).

Endnote

1. "Top Tools for Learning: Amplify," Center for Learning and Performance
Technology, www.c4lpt.co.uk/Top100Tools/amplify.html (accessed August 10,
2011)

5

Animoto
video production and sharing service
www.animoto.com

Overview

With the click of a button, Animoto produces videos by using images, video clips, and music that users select during different stages of the creative process. Utilizing the patent-pending and somewhat closely guarded Cinematic Artificial Intelligence technology, the developers of this resource claim that videos created using Animoto are unique, have the visual energy of a music video, and the emotional impact of a movie trailer.[1]

Statistics show that users buy into this marketing strategy; they have been craving this unique experience since the site's launch in August 2007. By November 2010, 2 million users had registered to use the Animoto service.[2] Creating an Animoto 30-second video is free. To create full length videos, you must purchase an annual subscription, which ranges from $30 to $499. If you are an educator, you can apply for a free Animoto all-access pass to produce unlimited full-length videos in the classroom (www.animoto.com/education).

Animoto has offices in New York City and San Francisco. The robust infrastructure that supports the application is built on top of Amazon's web-based cloud computing services.

Features

A sophisticated video creation platform is available on the Animoto homepage (www.animoto.com) to create, view, and share videos by following these steps:

➤   You must first decide whether you will use the free or fee-based version of the platform.

➤   Once you have reconciled the cost factor, you must then determine if your computer has the software components required to support the application, such as a web browser that supports JavaScript and Flash 10.

➤   Start the process of creating your videos (it takes about 3 minutes to render 30 seconds of video). Animoto's behind-the-scenes technology is intuitive and adaptive to users' needs and will prompt you through the procedures required to create a video:

  • Upload images and video clips (photos can be selected from your computer or third-party applications like Flickr, Facebook, Picasa, and Photobucket).

  • Choose music (select from Animoto's extensive library collection or you can upload your own MP3 files).

  • Finalize your video creation by adding text for the title, a brief description, and producer information. It is during this finalizing stage that Animoto makes extensive use of its acclaimed Cinematic Artificial Intelligence technology to process, analyze, and render your video with the same sophisticated postproduction skills and techniques that are used in television and film.

  • Once created, videos are saved for future viewing in the Animoto database and can be emailed, downloaded, or embedded on blogs, websites, and social networks like Facebook, Myspace, Twitter, and YouTube.

How Cybrarians Can Use This Resource

Library Branding

Brand your library in a creative way by making a free, professional 30-second video that showcases your collections and services. Staff at the

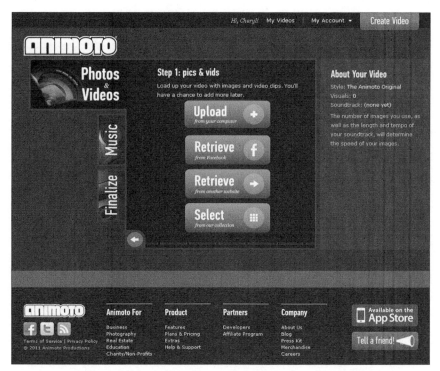

Using Animoto, users can upload photos, video clips, and
music to create customized web-based video presentations.

Penn State University Libraries used Animoto's stock video and music
to create a "Getting Connected to the PSU Libraries" video.[3]

Outreach Services

As part of your outreach services, collaborate with a teacher or lecturer
at your institution and apply for a free Animoto all-access pass for educators (animoto.com/education) to produce full-length videos for
instructional courses. Viewable case studies of this resource at work in
the classroom, benefiting both teachers and students, are available on
the Animoto for Education website (www.animoto.com/education).

F Y I

Animoto has received a number of awards including the 2009 Crunchies Award for best design of the year and the 2010 and 2011 Professional Photographer Hot One Awards.[4]

Endnotes

1. "About Animoto," Animoto, www.animoto.com/company (accessed August 10, 2011).

2. Jennifer Van Grove, "Animoto Grows to 2 Million Users," Mashable, November 3, 2010, www.mashable.com/2010/11/03/animoto-2/# (accessed August 10, 2011).

3. mlpatrick, "Adding Spice to Library Instruction," PaLa, www.crdpala.org/2011/07/25/adding-spice-to-library-instruction (accessed August 10, 2011).

4. "Press Coverage and Buzz," Animoto, www.animoto.com/about/buzz (accessed August 10, 2011).

6

Audacity
audio production, recording, and editing service
www.audacity.sourceforge.net

Overview

Audacity is a free, open source (the source code is available for anyone to study or use), audio editor and recorder. In a competitive IT environment, where audio recording and editing often require professional input, Audacity's free sound-editing program redefines this task, making it less complex. This ease of use has prompted users to describe Audacity as the word processor for audio files.

Using the easily navigable program interface, users can record and play sounds; import and export multiple file formats such as WAV, AIFF, Ogg Vorbis, and MP3; edit sounds using cut, copy, and paste (with unlimited undo); mix tracks together; and apply special effects to recordings.

Audacity has been marketed as an application that is tailored to a global audience, given its ability to work seamlessly with operating systems such as Mac OS X, Microsoft Windows, and Linux. A core group of volunteers are assisting in efforts to translate the Audacity software and provide tutorial support in different languages. The software was released in 2000, and is licensed under the GNU General Public License (GPL).

Features

➤ On Audacity's homepage (www.audacity.sourceforge.net), there are tabs that provide the information required for new

21

Google™ [   ] [Search]

◉ this site ○ Wiki/Forum/Team site ○ Web

AudacityStore.com
All sales directly benefit the Audacity Developer Team

| Home | About | Download | Help | Contact Us | Get Involved |

The Free, Cross-Platform Sound Editor

Audacity® is free, open source software for recording and editing sounds. It is available for Mac OS X, Microsoft Windows, GNU/Linux, and other operating systems. Learn more about Audacity... Also check our Wiki and Forum for more information.

The latest release of Audacity is 1.3.12 (Beta). This is our active "work in progress" version with our latest features. Documentation and translations into different languages are not quite complete. We recommend this version for more advanced users, and for everyone on Windows 7, Windows Vista and Mac OS X 10.6. See New Features in 1.3 for more information about the 1.3 Beta series.

Audacity 1.2.6 is our main release, complete and fully documented, but no longer under development. You may install Audacity 1.2.6 and 1.3.12 on the same machine.

Download Audacity 1.2.6

for Windows® 98/ME/2000/XP/Vista

Download Audacity 1.3.12 (Beta)

for Windows® 98/ME/2000/XP/Vista

Read about provisional support for Windows 7

Other downloads

April 01, 2010: Audacity 1.3.12 released, and Audacity book release from PACKT Publishing

The Audacity Team is pleased to announce the release of Audacity 1.3.12 (Beta) for Windows, Mac and Linux/Unix. There are some important bug fixes and improvements, especially for dragging and synchronization of labels.

We continue to recommend the ongoing Beta series for Windows 7, Windows Vista and Mac OS X 10.6, rather than 1.2. Please help us test 1.3.12 and let us know of any problems you find. Advanced users are encouraged to test our subsequent changes as we make them by downloading our Nightly Builds. Please subscribe to receive news of all our future releases.

Summary of Changes in 1.3.12:

Bug fixes for:
- Cutting or deleting a region in the waveform and label track did not move the labels in advance of the cut
- Incorrect behavior snapping to labels and boundaries with Snap To enabled
- Projects froze if files imported via On-Demand were no longer available
- *(Windows 7)* Clicking in a file open or save dialog caused files or folders to disappear from the list, and file filtering was broken
- Other import/export, effects and crash fixes

Changes and Improvements:
- A hover tooltip is now provided if the Mixer Toolbar input selector cannot control the system slider for the selected input
- More intuitive behavior when moving and resizing labels by dragging
- Export Multiple: new option to use a numerical prefix before existing label or track names
- New Equalization preset "Inverse RIAA", with new button to invert other curves
- New Preferences choice for "System" language which is used on first run instead of asking user to choose language

Please see Changes in Audacity 1.3.12 for more on 1.3.12 and the Beta series. **Note:** This release supports Windows 98/ME, and we recommend users on those systems to upgrade from the previous 1.3.7 release.

Also this month: PACKT Publishing release a new book about Audacity "Getting started with Audacity 1.3" by Bethany Hiitola. PACKT operate an Open Source Royalty Scheme, and every sale of the new Audacity book will directly benefit our project. You can find the new book and others on our Books about Audacity page.

Users can click on tabs for information on downloading the software, technical support, and volunteering for the Audacity project.

users to start using the software. The Download tab links to the current version of the software, which can be easily downloaded to supported operating systems. The Help tab links to technical support, user documentation, a user-editable wiki, and tutorials. There is also a Get Involved tab, which is an undisguised plea for volunteers (developers, translators, donors to support development, testers for latest codes) to be part of the open source project.

➤ Of interest to the novice user is the laundry list of features and functions on the Audacity website (www.audacity.source forge. net/about/features), under the following categories:

- Recording: Audacity can record live audio through a microphone or mixer, and digitize recordings from cassette tapes, vinyl records, or minidiscs. With some sound cards, it can also capture streaming audio.

- Import and Export: The software can import and edit sound files and combine these with other files or new recordings. Recordings can be exported in several common file formats (WAV, AIFF, AU, MP3, Ogg Vorbis).

- Editing: Audacity's easy editing functions include cut, copy, paste, delete, undo, redo, and access to the drawing and envelope tools.

- Effects: Built-in effects include echo, phaser, wahwah, reverse, remove noise, alter frequencies, and adjust volumes.

- Sound Quality: The software can record and edit 16-bit, 24-bit, and 32-bit (floating point) samples. Recordings can be done at up to 96 kHz.

- Plug-ins: Audacity supports VST (Virtual Studio Technology) and LADSPA (Linux Audio Developers Simple Plug-in API) plug-in effects.

- Analysis: A spectrogram mode is available for visualizing frequencies. Plot Spectrum command can be used for detailed frequency analysis.

How Cybrarians Can Use This Resource

Support for Research and Multimedia Projects

At the Interactive Media Center at the University Libraries, University at Albany, SUNY (library.albany.edu/imc), the Audacity software is used to support the creation of multimedia projects and the digital design of presentations, publications, and websites. Students, faculty, and staff who visit the media center have access to Audacity tools to support their research, instruction, and publication needs. These tools can be used to create digital recordings, edit audio files, and convert analog audio to digital.

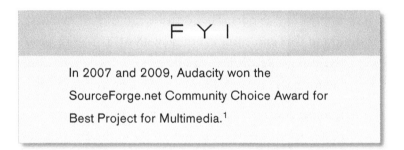

F Y I

In 2007 and 2009, Audacity won the SourceForge.net Community Choice Award for Best Project for Multimedia.[1]

Endnote

1. "Audacity news," Audacity, www.audacity.sourceforge.net/about/news (accessed August 10, 2011).

7

Aviary
productivity tool
www.aviary.com

Overview

The staff at Aviary, a privately held company headquartered in Long Island, New York, hold strong in their conviction that everyone in the world should have access to powerful creation tools. The company's mission to "make the world's creation accessible"[1] to everyone, and its provision of a free suite of online editing tools to artists of all genres, readily vindicates this belief.

This creative online editing suite—coincidentally, the Aviary suite carries the same name as the company—is power-packed with web applications that work together to empower users to create and market their work within a socially creative network. Using the freely available design and editing tools and templates, users can create, retouch, and share images; design logos, business cards, and letterheads; develop multimedia presentations and projects; and record podcasts.

The company's motto "creation on the fly,"[2] led to the bird metaphor being inevitably applied to the holistic approach in naming all of its products. These products include Phoenix (image editor), Toucan (color editor), Peacock (visual laboratory for creating visual effects), Raven (vector editor), Roc (music creator), Falcon (markup editor), Myna (audio editor), and Talon (Google Chrome and Mozilla Firefox extensions that allow users to perform screen captures).

Features

> There is quick and easy access to a full suite of creation tools on the homepage (www.aviary.com), which at first glance can

seem a daunting task to someone with little or no experience in using online design and editing software. Cognizant of this, Team Aviary has provided a plethora of learning resources to make the tasks as enjoyable and seamless as possible. All tools are accompanied by video tutorials. Other support tools include community-created documentation in a wiki format, blogs, discussion forums, and a FAQ page.

➤ The Discover Creations tab on the website guides users to content created by the Aviary community that is stored in an online database within the application. In the database, users can limit searches to popular creations, undiscovered creations, and designated Hall of Fame creations and Staff Picks. There is also an option to enter keywords into a search box in order to search all creations in the database.

➤ Aviary stores the artistic creations within its internal file cloud (code named Rookery), and this is redundantly backed up on the Amazon web services platform, thus rendering files safe, secure, and available from any computer with internet access.

➤ Currently, all editing tools are available online in most browsers, but the company has plans to beta test and release separate standalone versions of the applications for students and educators.

➤ The site states that users own the full rights to all works created. There is the stipulation on the FAQ page that, "Aviary only retains a license to display any works you make viewable to the public within Aviary and in any external publication provided it's in a way that promotes Aviary."[3]

➤ Developers have access to Aviary APIs (developers.aviary.com), which provide the creative tools required to enhance the end users' experience when visiting a website, blog, or mobile application. Popular APIs include the Effects API (allows bulk processing of photos) and Suite API (allows creation of original projects or access to preloaded templates).

➤   In November 2010, Aviary launched Feather, an HTML5
photo editor (www.aviary.com/html5)—in contrast to the
majority of its previous web apps, which were built in
Flash—that can be easily embedded in third-party websites
and used with HTML5-compatible browsers such as Chrome,
Firefox, and Safari.

Aviary has a suite of browser-based design tools where users can create
and add effects to images, design presentations, and record podcasts.

How Cybrarians Can Use This Resource

Promoting Access to a Web-Based Suite of Design Tools

Aviary is easily one of the best web-based suites of design tools one can access free of charge, packed with features that are comparable to fee-based desktop editors. The Google Apps marketplace (www.google.com/enterprise/marketplace/home), which offers products and services designed for Google users, currently lists Aviary under the category of productivity applications on the website. Here one can find a detailed summary of the usefulness of this tool, demonstrating how cybrarians can use this resource to create, modify, and share essential digital assets in their libraries. The list includes:

➤ Phoenix Image Editor: Useful for basic image retouching or complex graphic effects in business cards, letterheads, PowerPoint slides, and labels.

➤ Falcon Markup Editor: Crops, resizes, and marks up images and webpages captured from your browser; useful for PowerPoint slides, screen captures, adding arrows/text, and annotating images.

➤ Raven Vector Editor: Creates fully scalable vector art; useful for making logos, designing T-shirts, and creating icons.

➤ Myna Audio Editor: Remixes music tracks and audio clips, with sound effects and voice recording features included; useful for mixing podcasts, recording audio, audio filter effects, and remixing music.

F Y I

Team Aviary also created Worth1000.com (www.worth1000.com), an online community of 500,000 talented digital artists who compete daily in creative online competitions.

Endnotes

1. "Aviary Frequently Asked Questions," Aviary, www.aviary.com/faq (accessed August 10, 2011).

2. Ibid.

3. Ibid.

8

Bing
search engine
www.bing.com

Overview

In a search engine market where Google is considered king, there are a number of challengers who are vying for that coveted second-place position. Microsoft Bing is one such competitor. When unveiled by Microsoft in May 2009, Bing was billed as a decision engine with a matching tagline, "Bing and Decide."

According to Microsoft CEO Steve Ballmer, "Bing is an important first step forward in our long-term effort to deliver innovations in search that enable people to find information quickly and use the information they've found to accomplish tasks and make smart decisions."[1]

This current line of thinking has led Microsoft into developing a somewhat innovative marketing strategy, one that hinges on touting a consumer-friendly approach that concentrates on popular topics such as travel, entertainment, news, maps, weather, and shopping.

Since launching Bing, Microsoft has made steady gains on Google, largely due in part to its decision to partner with Yahoo!. In what has been considered by many industry insiders a bold move, in July 2009 Microsoft and Yahoo! announced a deal in which Bing would power Yahoo! Search.

So far, this altruistic alliance seems to be working well enough. According to market research firm comScore (www.comscore.com), as of November 2010 Bing was third in search engine rankings and had cornered 11.8 percent of the U.S. core search market, with Google owning the lion's share at a staggering 66.2 percent and Yahoo! second with 16.4 percent.[2]

A strategically placed search box invites users to Bing and decide.

Features

In order to gain more traction in a marketplace where choice of search engine is often driven by habit, Microsoft implemented a number of unique features within Bing in an effort to differentiate it from its closest competitors:

➤ In addition to the strategically positioned search box on the main page (www.bing.com), which allows for keyword searching, there are a number of guided searches on the left navigation bar. These include images, videos, shopping, news, maps, travel, entertainment, and search history.

➤ Background images change daily. These images may be of familiar world-renowned landmarks or photographs of animals, people, sports, and recreational activities. Each image is accompanied by snippets of factual information about the elements shown in the image.

➤ On the results page, in addition to returned searches, users can navigate related searches, search history, and gain access to extended previews of webpages found.

➤ In video search, video thumbnails are viewable on the results page and these videos automatically start to play when the mouse hovers over the thumbnail.

➤ A Preferences tab on the main page allows searchers to apply general settings to all searches. General settings include safe search for filtering adult content from search results, setting current location (city and state) to find search results relevant to your area, choosing a language for the display and layout of Bing, limiting the number of search results to display on a single page, and the option to show search suggestions as you type.

➤ A Popular Now list on the main search page shows current trending topics on the internet.

➤ Recognizing that Twitter is a virtual treasure trove of timely and socially relevant information, Bing has followed an emerging trend of integrating real-time content from Twitter into its search results. Microsoft has also partnered with the computational knowledge engine Wolfram|Alpha to allow more in-depth searching into areas such as diet and nutrition.

How Cybrarians Can Use This Resource

Reference and Research Instruction

The explosive growth of online content has continued unabated, and cybrarians are challenged daily to keep up with new search tools to help patrons easily navigate the information overload that has come to characterize many of today's search experiences. In such an environment, it makes sense that these researchers should be taught about search engines such as Google, Bing, and Yahoo!, which offer quick and simple ways to readily access information on the internet.

It should be noted, however, that care must be taken by library instructors to provide information on other authoritative resources available within the library collections. This comparison of authoritative vs. nonauthoritative resources can be particularly useful in library instruction classes, adding fuel to an already lively debate about the benefits and limitations of undergraduate and postgraduate students' sometimes inappropriate use of search engines instead of the library subscription online databases.

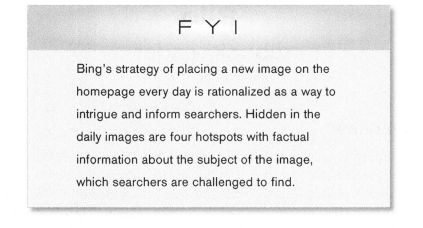

F Y I

Bing's strategy of placing a new image on the homepage every day is rationalized as a way to intrigue and inform searchers. Hidden in the daily images are four hotspots with factual information about the subject of the image, which searchers are challenged to find.

Endnotes

1. "Microsoft's New Search at Bing.com Helps People Make Better Decisions," Microsoft News Center, May 28, 2009, www.microsoft.com/presspass/press/2009/may09/05-28newsearchpr.mspx (accessed August 10, 2011).

2. "comScore Releases November 2010 U.S. Search Engine Rankings," comScore, December 15, 2010, www.comscore.com/Press_Events/Press_Releases/2010/12/comScore_Releases_November_2010_U.S._Search_Engine_Rankings (accessed August 10, 2011).

9

Blio
ebook reader
www.blio.com

Overview

According to a report by market research firm In-Stat, in 2009 stand-alone ereaders were identified as one of the more popular devices in the consumer electronics world. This trend continued into 2010, and the firm predicts that the market for ebook readers will most certainly have tripled from 12 million units in 2010 to 35 million units in 2014.[1] This demand will steadily increase in ensuing years, despite the threat of increasing competition from the Apple iPad and a new wave of tablet computers. In such a lucrative market, it is not surprising when one learns that there is much jostling and positioning among well-established players in the dedicated ereader market—Amazon Kindle, Barnes & Noble Nook, and Sony Reader—to try and hold onto a shrinking piece of the pie by offering newer enhanced features and lower price points to consumers.

And then Blio enters the fray, and it may well jump ahead of the competition, because it is currently being marketed as a *free* ebook reader with high expectations of setting the standard for digital reading. Blio, when downloaded to a PC or other supported device, delivers ebooks that purportedly mimic the printed version—in full color (if the book has color illustrations), as laid out originally by the publisher—and with all of the features consumers would expect from a fully functional ereader.

At the core of the development process in creating this innovative tool is Ray Kurzweil, well-known inventor of the flatbed scanner and character-and-speech-recognition technologies, and founder of K-NFB Reading Technology company, which developed Blio. Kurzweil says of the device: "By providing a full-color, flexible, and interactive experience,

Blio redefines the boundaries of the ebook, opening up entirely new categories of multimedia content and, as a result, engaging new groups of readers of ebooks."[2]

Kurzweil has high hopes of living up to this hype. The first move involved partnering with Baker & Taylor (one of the world's largest distributors of print and digital books) to offer access to top best sellers, videos, slideshows, and audio-enhanced content via the Blio bookstore.

At the launch of the service in September 2010, Blio's bookstore consisted of more than 1 million paid and free titles with expectations that this number would be augmented daily. Currently, Blio supports English, French, and Spanish, with Italian, German, and Asian language options to follow. At the time of this writing, Blio can be immediately downloaded from the site's homepage (www.blio.com/downloads), to Windows-based, iOS, and Android devices.

Features

As listed on its Meet Blio page (www.blio.com/meet_blio) the ereader has a host of functions that increase its flexibility and ease of use. Highlights include:

> The unique ability to reproduce color, layout, and original fonts, thus mimicking the printed version of a book. This feature is particularly useful for genres such as children's books, travel guides, cookbooks, and textbooks, where readers want a close or exact approximation of the original text. The software is able to do this by using files in XPS format, which allow digital-surrogate books to stay true to their original print version. Blio also supports EPUB-formatted books.

> Advanced text-to-speech technology integrated into the device. Using the Nuance Vocalizer, readers can download two lifelike voices (Samantha and Tom), which facilitate using the ereader hands-free. Blio also provides synchronized highlighting of the words being read.

> Personalization and customization through the insertion of notes, text, or images into digital pages (which can be saved and exported), the ability to highlight sections and look up

Blio can be downloaded from the site's
homepage for reading both paid and free ebooks.

references on external websites from within the ebook.
Multiple reading views are also included: text-only mode,
single page, dual page, tiled pages, or 3D "book view" for
realistic page turning.

➤   A built-in bookstore within the ereader's interface to
purchase new or download free titles.

➤   Storage of all downloaded Blio titles in a personal virtual
library, enabling flexible access to content. This library can be
accessed and easily synced to up to five devices, thus allowing
users to begin reading their book on a home PC, then pick up
where they left off on a netbook or laptop.

How Cybrarians Can Use This Resource

Using Ereaders to Transform Library Collections and Services

The release of Blio and other ereaders has fueled speculation on the impact of these devices on the readership and patronage of libraries. It is still early in the game to make any definitive statement about how ereaders are going to transform libraries. What is certain is that if widely adopted, these devices do have the potential to impact how cybrarians store, circulate, and allow patrons to access econtent.

The following libraries have already taken the proverbial leap of faith and are experimenting with using these devices to offer innovative services to consumers who—research has shown—are accustomed to accessing most of their content online.

Ereader Loan Program

In the spring of 2010, Duke University Libraries (www.library.duke.edu/ereaders) introduced a pilot project to loan ereaders to patrons as a way for patrons to interact with emerging book and information technologies, to increase access to high-demand titles in the collection, and to experiment with more patron-driven acquisitions. The libraries initially purchased 12 Kindle DX wireless ereaders, which circulated for a two-week loan period from both the Perkins and Lilly libraries. The response by patrons was overwhelmingly positive and the libraries have since added the rival Barnes & Noble ereader Nook to their collection.

Downloading Library Ebooks to Ereaders

Here is a list of select libraries offering ebook downloads to a supported device:

- ➤ Charlotte Mecklenburg Library, Charlotte, North Carolina, www.tinyurl.com/31t5ywa

- ➤ Fairfax County Public Library, Virginia, www.tinyurl.com/4438585

- ➤ Free Library of Philadelphia, Pennsylvania, www.tinyurl.com/4ydyqow

> Broward County Library, Florida, www.tinyurl.com/3lotb2g

Partnerships With Ereader Vendors

In September 2010, Sony announced the names of libraries participating in the inaugural Reader Library Program (ebookstore.sony.com/library-program).[3] Key components of this program include:

> In-house training sessions for participating library staff developed by Sony, covering such areas as digital reading formats, overview of sources for digital materials, and training on Sony's Reader digital reading device.

> Distribution of educational materials and bookmarks to provide patrons with background information on digital reading devices.

> Scheduling of biannual update sessions designed to keep participating libraries and their staff current with the latest developments in digital reading content, formats, and devices.

F Y I

Since its launch in September 2010, Blio has maintained a Twitter page (www.twitter.com/blio reader) to keep users updated with information about enhanced features, press releases, and user feedback.

Endnotes

1. "Despite Potential Threat From Tablet Devices E-reader Unit Shipments to Reach 35 Million by 2014," In-Stat, September 14, 2010, www.instat.com/press.asp?Sku=IN 1004757ID&ID=2851 (accessed August 10, 2011).

2. "K-NFB Launches Free E-Reader Software That Revolutionizes Digital Reading Experience," Blio, September 28, 2010, www.blio.com/news/2010/09/28/knfb-

launches-free-ereader-software-that-revolutionizes-digital-reading-experience (accessed August 10, 2011).

3. "Sony Announces Inaugural Participants in Reader Library Program," Sony Press Room, September 27, 2010, news.sel.sony.com/en/press_room/consumer/computer_peripheral/e_book/release/58621.html (accessed August 10, 2011).

10

Blogger
blog publishing service
www.blogger.com

Overview

Blogs (a truncation of the term *weblog*) are modern-day forms of online journals. It is rare these days to find someone who has not read a post on a blog, posted a comment on a blog, or created a personal blog. The relative ease with which you can use a blog to give advice on a topic of your choosing, post updates to friends and family about your personal life, discuss your political views, or evaluate a product or service has led to the widespread usage and popularity of this informal type of commentary.

Technorati, a blog search engine that regularly reports on growth and trends in the blogosphere, reports that it currently indexes more than 1 million blogs.[1] Google's Blogger is just one of a growing number of blog publishing platforms available free on the internet.

The negligible cost, and the ease with which one can use the service to create blogs (in a matter of minutes you can start posting text, photos, videos, and more to your blog), has led to Blogger being tapped as one of the more trendy blog publishing tools available. Blogger is currently available in multiple languages, including English, French, Italian, German, Spanish, Dutch, Portuguese, Chinese, Japanese, and Korean.

Two great advantages that may account for the popularity of this resource are (1) you can host multiple blogs with the same account name, and (2) the blogs you create can be hosted free on www.blog spot.com. For bloggers wishing to retain their own domain, there is a custom domain option available.

Blogger's intuitive-driven interface allows users to create blogs in three steps: create an account, name your blog, and choose a template.

Features

➤ Blogger features an intuitive-driven interface (www.blogger.com), which empowers users to create blogs in three steps:

1. Create an account (if you already have an account with other Google services such as Gmail, Google Groups, or Orkut, you can use the same account).

2. Name your blog.

3. Choose a template.

➤ Once your blog is set up, Blogger has a basic WYSIWYG (What You See Is What You Get) editor, which lets you fully customize the look and feel of your posts by changing fonts, bolding or italicizing text, and adjusting text color and alignment. As each new blog post is composed, it is automatically saved. A spell-check feature checks for unwanted spelling errors and each post can be categorized for search and retrieval later by adding labels or keywords.

➤   The drag-and-drop interface allows further customization of the blog's design by allowing users to add gadgets such as slideshows, user polls, or AdSense ads. Similarly, adding photos or videos to your blog is achieved with the click of an image icon on the editor toolbar. Photos are hosted on Google's Picasa Web Albums account, and videos uploaded through Blogger are hosted on Google Video.

➤   There are myriad external options for posting to your blog. These options include sending posts from your mobile phone, configuring Blogger with a secret email address so you can email your posts to your blog (Mail-to-Blogger email address), or using the Blogger Post Gadget from the iGoogle homepage.

➤   For bloggers who are interested in earning revenue, money can be made directly by using AdSense, Google's content-targeted advertising program. Google's servers determine what your posts are about and display the most relevant ads to your readers. For example, if you blog about painting, there might be ads for art supplies. If the blog is about baseball, there may be baseball memorabilia. The amount earned depends on your subject matter and the popularity of your blog.

➤   The Google Toolbar has a feature called BlogThis, which allows toolbar users with Blogger accounts to post links directly to their blogs. Google Docs (a free, web-based word processor, spreadsheet, and presentation service) has direct publishing integration to Blogger. There are also third-party applications that can be added to your blog. Feedburner, Flickr, Photobucket, and Wikispaces are a few noteworthy mentions.

➤   In July 2010, Blogger introduced integrated web statistics for its users. This new resource is clearly no rival to the more robust Google Analytics, but it is simpler to manage (no code to install or configuration required) and provides updates in near real time, giving Blogger users greater insight into statistics such as visitor traffic, top posts visited and viewed, referral data, keyword searches, and audience (page views by country, page views by browsers, and page views by operating systems).

How Cybrarians Can Use This Resource

In social media, it is often said that the content is the conversation. Blogs are media that librarians can use to initiate and continue conversations and to receive feedback from the communities they serve. Here are some innovative uses of blogs that can be readily adopted and integrated into existing library services:

> Library Director Blog (Ann Arbor District Library, Michigan), www.aadl.org/aboutus/directorsblog

> Ohio University Libraries Subject Blog on Business, www.library.ohiou.edu/subjects/businessblog

> Readers' Advisory Blog (Pasco County Library System, Florida), www.pclsreaders.blogspot.com

> Book Club Blog (Roselle Public Library, Illinois), bloggerbooksclub.roselle.lib.il.us

> Current Events and News Blog (Greensboro Public Library, North Carolina), www.greensborolibrary.wordpress.com

F Y I

Blogger was initially launched by a small start-up company based in San Francisco called Pyra Labs in August 1999. It holds the distinction of being one of the earliest dedicated blog publishing tools. Google acquired the company in 2002 for an undisclosed sum of money.

Endnote

1. "About Technorati," Technorati, www.technorati.com/about-technorati (accessed August 10, 2011).

11

Bloglines
news and feed aggregator
www.bloglines.com

Overview

When new subscribers access the Bloglines homepage, its logo—a rolled-up newspaper—is prominently displayed and immediately gives subscribers a sense of the type of service offered. Bloglines is a free web-based news aggregator service, or RSS feed reader. When subscribed to Bloglines and similar services like Google Reader (Chapter 30), users can add URLs of the syndicated feeds to which they wish to subscribe, and Bloglines will post these feeds on a personalized webpage that can be viewed and read at the subscribers' convenience.

Since the development of the service in 2003, Bloglines has been heralded as a pioneer in bringing RSS feeds and rich content to mainstream internet users and has been rewarded for excellent service in the form of awards and accolades around the world. In late 2010, the survival of the service was in doubt with an announcement by its parent company, Ask.com, that the service was going to be shut down. Competition from rival service Google Reader and the impact of real-time news stream from social networks Twitter and Facebook were factors contributing to the service's decline.

Fortunately for Bloglines subscribers, MerchantCircle (www.merchant circle.com/corporate), an online marketing network for small business owners, stepped in and reached an agreement with Ask.com to assume control of the service, pledging to rejuvenate, reinvest, and enhance the platform for the benefit of its 2.7 million users.[1]

Features

➤ Bloglines subscribers wishing to migrate old accounts to the new system can do so by logging in with their existing Bloglines username and password, accepting the new terms of service, and auto-importing existing feeds into the new platform. There is an import/export feature available to manually import feeds that cannot be automatically transferred to the new service.

➤ A video tutorial on the newly designed homepage (www. bloglines.com) demonstrates the migration process and provides a brief overview of the service's new features. New features include drag-and-drop functionality, an option to search for and add popular widgets to personal dashboards, access to three new feed views (list, graphical mosaic, and widget), more options to share articles with friends by creating a public page, and Facebook and Twitter integration.

➤ For new or existing subscribers, the options available within Bloglines to search for, add, track, and manage feeds remain the same. To subscribe to a feed, subscribers can click on the Add Content option on the main navigation bar, and in the box provided enter the feed address or website URL for the resource they wish to subscribe to. Bloglines will attempt to locate the appropriate feed. Feeds are automatically added to personalized dashboards and can be read in easy-to-navigate viewing panes.

➤ Further assistance in searching for and adding content to an existing account is provided by the Bloglines Team that regularly creates updated lists of feeds, podcasts, events, and other applications arranged for browsing in broad topical categories such as business, lifestyle, news, sports, shopping, tools and technology, and travel.

Bloglines subscribers can migrate old accounts to the
new service by following a few simple steps.

How Cybrarians Can Use This Resource

Innovative Library Services Using RSS Feeds

There has been some debate about the waning popularity of RSS feeds, with some bloggers going so far as to predict that RSS is slowly dying.[2] The reason for this lack of interest has been attributed to a general change in news consumption patterns by consumers. Consumers are now looking toward real-time news streams from social networks like Twitter, Facebook, Digg, and StumbleUpon and are less reliant on blog-like news feeds via an aggregator such as Bloglines.

This reality was borne out in a recent survey on online tools usage conducted by WebJunction for its members in academic and public libraries. Survey results showed that nearly half of the respondents (49 percent) use email listservs daily. One-third of the respondents (35 percent) use professional or social networking sites daily. A quarter or less of the respondents use the following daily: online news or magazines (21 percent), blogs (14 percent), RSS feeds (14 percent), bookmarking sites (10 percent), wikis (9 percent), employment sites (6 percent), and online courses (3 percent).[3]

In the midst of this debate, there is still a need for cybrarians to continue to provide innovative library services with RSS feeds as the core technology. Many libraries have used RSS feeds to develop current awareness services for new materials and recently cataloged titles, have created RSS user-driven feeds for users to track updates to the library's website, have offered native and customized RSS feeds for catalog search results, and have used RSS feeds to display library events. The librarian's one-stop shop for great ideas, the Library Success: A Best Practices Wiki, has created a webpage highlighting the innovative use of this technology (www.libsuccess.org/index.php?title=RSS).

F Y I

The average Bloglines user tracks more than
20 news feeds.[4]

Endnotes

1. "MerchantCircle to Take Over Operations of the Popular Bloglines Platform," MerchantCircle Blog, November 4, 2010, blog.merchantcircle.com/2010/11/merchant circle-to-take-over-operations.html (accessed August 10, 2011).

2. M. G. Siegler, "Twitter and Facebook Really Are Killing RSS (at Least for TechCrunch Visitors)," TechCrunch, January 3, 2011, techcrunch.com/2011/01/03/techcrunch-twitter-facebook-rss/# (accessed August 10, 2011).

3. "Library Staff Report Their Use of Online Tools," WebJunction BlogJunction, July 6, 2010, blog.webjunctionworks.org/index.php/2010/07/06/library-staff-report-their-use-of-online-tools (accessed August 10, 2011).

4. "Bloglines FAQ," Bloglines, www.bloglines.com/help/faq (accessed August 10, 2011).

12

BusinessCard2
productivity tool
www.businesscard2.com

Overview

BusinessCard2 is a marketing platform for networking and exchanging business cards on the internet. In an age where an online presence is deemed imperative for generating job leads, building relationships with new customers, and engaging in social conversations, BusinessCard2 offers professionals a quick option for creating a truncated profile, easily accessible and digestible by others.

The features of the service, which continue to attract its growing user base, are the seamless integration with social hubs such as Twitter, Facebook, YouTube, Blogger, StumbleUpon, WordPress, Delicious, Digg, Flickr, and LinkedIn; online access to a free hosting platform for saving contact information; and the ability to use the service with minimal designing or programming skills.

Professionals using the service create profiles that provide quick access to personal information including name, address, telephone numbers, email addresses, URLs for personal websites, logos, photographs, online documents, and video clips. This information is saved to a searchable database and can be shared online via email and popular social networks by sending a direct URL link to the profile page created or embedding the virtual business card to a personal blog or website.

BusinessCard2 is the creation of Workface Inc. (www.workface.com), a privately held, venture-backed company currently based in Minneapolis, Minnesota. The company was founded in 2006 with a stated mission of creating a social business platform that connects business professionals on the internet.[1]

Features

➤ New members can register for a free account on the homepage (www.businesscard2.com/signup). Building an online profile can be accomplished in a short amount of time as registered users are guided to add the following profile information:

- General information (full name, company, job title, work industry, profile image, assigned URL of virtual business card page created—for example, johndoe.businesscard2.com)

- Contact information

- Business sales pitch including an online billboard image and any special business offers and discounts

- Live streams to be added from a growing list of social networks including Blogger, Delicious, Digg, Facebook, Flickr, StumbleUpon, and Twitter

- External website links to personal or business websites, blogs, YouTube videos, and RSS feeds

- Files including PDF documents, spreadsheets, presentations, and images

➤ Members have the option to upgrade existing accounts to premium status, gaining access to additional features like live chat and customizable skins.

➤ The BusinessCard2 Resource Center (www.business card2.com/resources), maintained by the BusinessCard2 team, is available to all members and serves as a valuable source of information on such issues as marketing and branding.

➤ Registered BusinessCard2 members have access to advanced statistics tools that automatically record and track information such as the number of times the business card was accessed and downloaded.

BusinessCard2 users must first register
with the service to create an online business card.

How Cybrarians Can Use This Resource

Creating Virtual Business Cards

In today's digital age it seems natural that cybrarians would consider using virtual business cards (vCards) instead of traditional business cards. The latter, more often than not, are easily lost or stored in a place that is not readily accessible from both home and work offices. Creating a vCard using a service such as BusinessCard2 offers the following advantages:

> ➤ Cost-effective way to create a business card

> ➤ Quick method to share your information with your professional and personal network

> ➤ Fully customizable service offering seamless integration with third-party email services, social networks, personal websites, and blogs

> ➤ Ability to add virtual business card profile to email signatures or download the information and print it to a physical business card

➤ Storing data online in one place with no fear of this data being lost

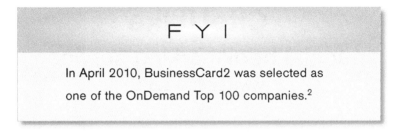

F Y I

In April 2010, BusinessCard2 was selected as one of the OnDemand Top 100 companies.[2]

Endnotes

1. "About Us," BusinessCard2, www.businesscard2.com/company (accessed on August 10, 2011).

2. "Workface, Developer of BusinessCard2, Selected by AlwaysOn as an OnDemand Top 100 Winner," Businesscard2 Press Releases, www.businesscard2.com/press-releases#ondemand (accessed on August 10, 2011).

13

CiteULike
social bookmarking service
www.citeulike.org

Overview

CiteULike is a free service created to help researchers store, organize, and share scholarly papers and other publications they are currently reading. If there is an article on the web that interests you, you can bookmark this article with one click, using the CiteULike button (installed on your browser). CiteULike automatically extracts and saves the citation details (author, title, publisher, page numbers, etc.) and the article's URL to a personalized MyCiteULike Library, eliminating the need to manually type the citations. This personalized "library" is stored on the service's external servers and can be accessed anywhere, anytime, and shared with friends who have similar research interests.

Given this function of collating, managing, and linking to scholarly resources, one can readily surmise that this tool is a boon for scholars, students, and researchers alike. In fact, when CiteULike creator Richard Cameron was asked why he developed this software, he offered this rather frank assessment of the current research environment in the following words: "I was slightly shocked by the quality of some of the tools available to help academics do their job. I found it preferable to start writing proper tools for my own use than to use existing software. Collecting material for a bibliography is something which appeared to require an amazing amount of drudgery."[1]

The service has been on the web since October 2004 and is heralded as the first web-based social bookmarking tool designed specifically for the needs of scientists and scholars.

Features

➤ CiteULike works from within your web browser so there is no need to install any software on your computer. Once you create your account and sign in on the homepage (www.cite ulike.org), there are three ways you can add articles to your MyCiteULike Library:

1. You can manually enter the URL of an article in the Post URL page, which you can find within the MyCiteULike menu.

2. You can bookmark new articles and papers by clicking on the CiteULike button or bookmarklet easily installed in your browser.

3. You can also copy articles from other users' libraries into your own. First, search for an article using the Search link at the top of the CiteULike main page. Click on an article of interest and then select Copy to add the article to your own library.

➤ Users who create MyCiteULike personal libraries have access to the following functions:

- Add tags or keywords to later search and retrieve your article.

- Flag the article saved as one of your publications if you are the author of the article.

- Rate your priority to read the article.

- Set your posting settings to public or private.

- Add attachments such as PDFs or images.

- Add notes or comments to the article saved.

- Write a review of the article.

- Find related articles on your topic saved by other CiteULike users.

- Import or export records saved in either BibTeX or RIS format.

- View the citations saved in one of 16 standard citation formats. This list includes popularly used formats such as ACS, APA, APS, Chicago, Harvard, MLA, Oxford, and Turabian.

- View an abstract or the full text (PDF) of the saved article. Full-text views are only available if the article is not copyright protected.

- Create groups (communities of users with shared libraries) or join existing groups.

On the CiteULike homepage, users can sign up in order to begin bookmarking scholarly articles to the MyCiteULike Library.

How Cybrarians Can Use This Resource

Research and Publishing

For cybrarians working in libraries where publishing is a requirement for tenure and promotion, CiteULike is useful for working collaboratively with colleagues on articles and other publications. You can easily:

➤ Store and share resources (books, journal articles, websites) you find online and later compile these into a bibliography using one of the standard citation styles provided by CiteULike.

➤ Discover new resources for the collaborative work by searching other CiteULike members' libraries, bookmarking these, and storing them online for easy access anywhere, anytime.

➤ Use the automated article recommendations based on your previous selections to keep you up-to-date with current research in your specified field.

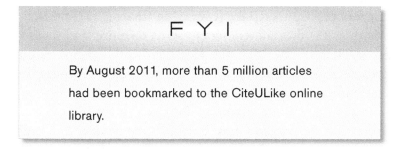

F Y I

By August 2011, more than 5 million articles had been bookmarked to the CiteULike online library.

Endnote

1. "CiteULike Frequently Asked Questions," CiteULike, www.citeulike.org/faq/faq.adp (accessed August 10, 2011).

14

Connotea
social bookmarking service
www.connotea.org

Overview

Connotea is a free online reference management service modeled on similar services like CiteULike (covered in Chapter 13) and Delicious (see Chapter 16) that allows users to store, organize, and share references or bibliographic citations to their favorite online resources. References created are stored within a personalized Connotea library, and these can be accessed from any computer.

Saving bibliographic citations for your favorite resources in Connotea is comparable to most bookmarking services. You begin by saving the URL link for the resource (from articles, websites, and other online resources). Connotea will, whenever possible, recognize the reference and automatically add in the bibliographic information for you. Users can assign keywords (or tags) to references saved and share references online with colleagues.

Although the service has been heavily marketed for use by scientists, researchers, and clinicians, its popularity has led to it garnering support from user communities throughout other academic disciplines. Connotea was created by the Nature Publishing Group (www.nature.com/npg_/index_npg.html), and the software has been made available as an open source distribution under the name Connotea Code.

Features

➢ New users can sign up to use this tool from the homepage (www.connotea.org). There is a short video tutorial

(2 minutes, 41 seconds) on the homepage with narration and screen shots on how the service works. There is also a fair share of support documentation to get users started.

➤ Adding references to a Connotea library has been simplified to three steps: Find, Save, and Customize.

1. First you need to find a reference to add to your personalized Connotea library (for example, a scholarly PDF article in your favorite database, an Amazon product page for a book, or a newspaper editorial).

2. Save the reference or link to the resource by clicking on the Connotea Browser button (which can be installed in any web browser without technical support). Connotea automatically fills in the title and URL for the resource, and also adds in bibliographic information such as author, title, publication name, publication date, and number of pages.

3. Customize the reference by adding keywords or tags so that it can be easily accessed later. You can share references saved with your colleagues by emailing them the URL link to the page.

➤ Although you can add any article on the web to your Connotea library, it is to users' benefit if this is an academic or scholarly article from a list of Connotea's supported websites. This list is maintained on a regularly updated webpage (www.connotea.org/guide#autocollection) and includes sources like PubMed, Nature.com, Wiley Interscience, and *D-Lib* magazine. For these types of articles, Connotea will automatically import all bibliographic details. It is also possible to manually enter bibliographic citations for pages not recognized by Connotea.

➤ Connotea also provides RSS feeds, allowing users to keep track of articles posted under tags created to support their research interests or by users with similar interests.

➤   Connotea's community pages (www.connotea.org/wiki),
     maintained as a wiki any user can edit, provide access to
     articles on how to use the site, an FAQ page, a list of
     requested features, and reports of possible problems
     encountered using the service.

➤   Connotea's personal library (My Library), includes the
     following functions:

     • Add a display title.

     • Add tags.

     • Add a brief summary and comments.

     • Indicate if you are the author or one of the co-authors of
       the work saved.

Connotea My Library allows users to add details, comment on
and summarize entries, share bookmarks with others, and
import/export references to other reference managers.

- Choose to share a bookmark with other users or keep the bookmark reference private.

- Add a date to release the saved reference publicly.

- Import and export references or links from your library, in formats supported by Connotea (RIS, BibTeX, MODS XML), to other reference managers such as EndNote.

How Cybrarians Can Use This Resource

Research and Publishing

➤ Quickly save and organize links to your references for an article or book.

➤ Easily share references with your colleagues for a collaborative work.

➤ Discover new publishing leads in your subject field by exploring other Connotea users' libraries just as easily as you can navigate your own.

F Y I

The Connotea Blog (blogs.nature.com/connotea) provides regular updates on upcoming changes, integration with third-party applications, and useful tips for using the service.

15

CuePrompter
productivity tool
www.cueprompter.com

Overview

When you are in the midst of a live conference presentation, it can sometimes be difficult to remember your main talking points when you are in front of a large, attentive audience. CuePrompter is a free online teleprompter/autocue service that allows you to turn your computer's web browser into a teleprompter that keeps you on track as you give that all-important speech or record a podcast or videocast.

Using CuePrompter does not require technical skills. All you need to do is copy and paste your prepared text in a form on the homepage, add some customization (screen size, font size, speed), and click Start Prompter, and your computer screen is transformed immediately into a giant teleprompter, similar to teleprompters used by news broadcasters.

CuePrompter is free for both commercial and noncommercial use. One disadvantage of note is that each prompter session is limited to 2,000 characters, thus restricting the use of the service to short presentations.

Features

➤ There is no need to create login credentials to start using CuePrompter. The service does advise, however, that to use all of its functions, users may need to change browser security settings by adding the URL www.cueprompter.com/prompter.php as a trusted zone to your computer.

➤ After inputting the prepared text or script, which can be created in an external text editor, to the online form or blank

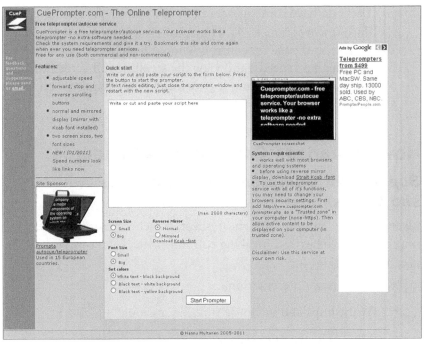

Write or cut and paste text into the CuePrompter
online form and click the Start Prompter button to start the service.

screen on the homepage (www.cueprompter.com) you can
further customize CuePrompter by choosing the
following options:

- Small or big screen size

- Small or big font size

- Colors (white text on black background, black text on
  white background, or black text on yellow background)

- Settings for reverse mirror

➤ Once your customization is complete, press the Start
Prompter button. CuePrompter launches in a new window
with the displayed text on the screen, displaying the font size
and background you selected.

➤ Users do have some measure of control over the scrolling text once the program starts. They can select stop, forward, reverse, and page up controls; choose from nine different scrolling text speeds; and view the scrolling full-screen text in normal or mirrored mode (mirrored mode requires you to download the Strait Kcab-font).

How Cybrarians Can Use This Resource

Support for Conference Presentations and Workshops

Likened to an online giant cheat sheet, which can prove useful for impromptu or rehearsed speaking commitments, CuePrompter can be used by cybrarians for:

➤ Conference presentations

➤ Workshops and in-house training sessions

➤ Library instruction classes

➤ Recording podcasts and videocasts

FYI

CuePrompter was voted Web App of the Week by the online technology news website Maximum PC in April 2010.[1]

Endnote

1. David Murphy, "Web App of the Week: CuePrompter," Maximum PC, April 18, 2010, www.maximumpc.com/article/web_exclusive/web_app_week_cueprompter (accessed August 10, 2011).

16

Delicious
social bookmarking service
www.delicious.com

Overview

Are you having a difficult time keeping track of all the interesting webpages you find? Would you like to bookmark all your favorite websites and access these bookmarks from any computer? Do you ever wonder what the hot trending topic on the web is right now? Or are you looking for the most popular websites on a specific topic? Delicious (formerly del.icio.us, pronounced delicious), the social bookmarking service, is the solution to all of these issues.

Delicious allows users to tag, save, and manage all their bookmarks (favorite resources) online, access these bookmarks from any computer, share the bookmarks with friends, and discover what hot topics other people on the web are bookmarking. Using the service is intuitive, not unlike bookmarking services CiteULike and Connotea, covered in previous chapters.

Once you have registered for the service, you are required to add a Bookmark on Delicious bookmarklet (button) to your browser toolbar. While browsing the web, if you find a webpage you wish to bookmark, click on the bookmarklet. The bookmarklet uses its one-click functionality to automatically extract data from the webpage and save it as an online bookmark in Delicious. Personalize this bookmark by modifying the title extracted from the saved webpage, adding tags or descriptive terms to group similar links together, or adding extended notes for yourself or for others who have access to your bookmark.

Considered by many to be the standard by which other social bookmarking services should be measured, Delicious has been actively in service since 2003, and it was acquired by Yahoo! in December 2005. In

May 2011, Delicious was acquired by Chad Hurley and Steve Chen, the founders of YouTube, who were reported to be "committed to running and improving Delicious going forward and providing a seamless transition for users."[1] Yahoo! continued operating the service through July 2011. Delicious is headquartered in Sunnyvale, California.

The Delicious homepage for registered users is organized into four main sections: Home, Bookmarks, People, and Tags.

Features

➤ The simplistic (not many bells and whistles) and relatively easy-to-navigate Delicious interface (www.delicious.com) may well account for the longevity of the service. This basic design supports three user functions: to bookmark any site on the internet and have these bookmarks synchronized on any computer, to share bookmarks, and to discover useful and interesting bookmarks on the web.

➤ Registered users can sign in and access a personalized page, which is organized into four main sections: Home, Bookmarks, People, and Tags.

- Home Tab: By clicking on the Home tab you can immediately view "fresh" or recently added bookmarks by all Delicious users, access a "hotlist" of the most popular bookmarks being saved across multiple areas of interest, and "explore" tags or keywords Delicious users have used to describe their bookmarks.

- Bookmarks Tab: Click on the Bookmarks tab to view all the bookmarks saved to your account and the number of people who have bookmarked the same resource. A search box allows you to search and find saved bookmarks by tags. Under the Bookmarks tag, you can also edit or delete a bookmark, create an RSS feed, sort bookmarks by date or alphabetical order, and display the number of bookmarks per page.

- People Tab: Under the People tab you can create a network (friends, family, co-workers) to connect you to other Delicious users.

- Tags Tab: Click on the Tags tab to quickly view all tags you have added as a cloud. There are options to rename tags, delete tags, manage tag bundles, and sort tags by size or in alphabetical order.

➤ Users have the option of saving bookmarks to their Delicious account by using bookmarklets installed to supported web browser toolbars. Support is currently provided for Firefox, Safari, Internet Explorer, Chrome, and Opera. Regardless of the browser chosen, once users click the Bookmark on Delicious bookmarklet, the following fields are presented in an online form to be populated with data:

- URL: The URL field is simply the address of the page you have bookmarked. This URL is automatically extracted and added to the field.

- Title: The title is also automatically provided and can be edited and modified if required.

- Notes: Add a summary or short annotation to describe the page added.

- Tags: Enter one or more tags or keywords separated by spaces. Tagging is optional, but if added they can make bookmarks easier to organize and navigate in order to find similar concepts.

- Send: Use this line to add names and email addresses of other Delicious users or social networks such as Twitter you wish to share your bookmark on.

- Message: Record a message that will appear with your Twitter, email, or Delicious posting. This is limited to 116 characters.

How Cybrarians Can Use This Resource

Sharing Web Resources

Delicious as a social bookmarking tool is useful for libraries because it facilitates the discovery, saving, and sharing of web resources of interest to patrons in the library community. As a social networking service it exemplifies the collaborative and social aspects of Web 2.0 tools.

PennTags is an example of an innovative social bookmarking tool developed by librarians at the University of Pennsylvania for locating, organizing, and sharing online resources (tags.library.upenn.edu).

F Y I

The Delicious Blog (blog.delicious.com)

provides regular updates on new features,

imminent changes, service alerts, and useful

tips and tricks for using the service.

Endnote

1. "YouTube Founders Acquire Delicious," Delicious Blog, May 11, 2011, blog.delicious. com/blog/2011/05/youtube-founders-acquire-delicious.html (accessed August 10, 2011).

17

Digg
social news service
www.digg.com

Overview

Launched in 2004, Digg has grown to be one of the more popular sources of information for valued web content, and it is currently promoted as a place for readers to discover and share content found on the web as viewed through the lens of the collective community. In fact, the creators of the service view it as a successfully democratizing, one-of-a-kind digital medium; it changes the way people consume information online. This is true to some extent, as all content on Digg—articles, images, online videos—is submitted, voted on, and rated by its community of users.

If Digg users discover content online that they determine may be of value to others, they can submit this to Digg (www.digg.com). This submission will immediately appear in Upcoming Stories, where other members can find it, and if they like it, rate it highly (Digg It). If the submission receives enough Diggs (great reviews), it becomes popular and is promoted to the front page in its topic category. If it becomes one of the most popular submissions, it qualifies as a Top 10. If a submission does not receive enough Diggs within a certain time period, it eventually falls out of the Upcoming section. Both the promotion and burying of stories submitted by active users are managed by algorithms developed by Digg.

Headquartered in San Francisco, the service, launched in 2004, was originally an experiment in social news aggregation by its founder Kevin Rose. Rose resigned from the service in March 2011 but will continue in an advisory role on the Board of Directors.[1]

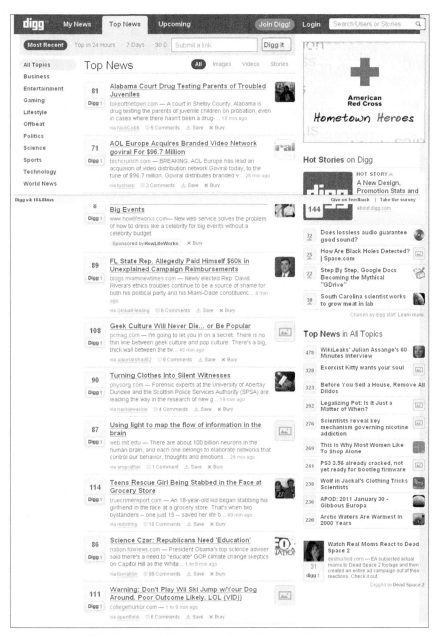

Digg is a social news service where readers can
discover and share content found on the web.

Features

➣   To take full advantage of the opportunity to submit, share, save, bury, or comment on Digg content, users must first register on the homepage (www.digg.com) by filling in the provided online form with an email address, username, and password.

➣   Once registered there are several options available for discovering content (news stories from newspapers, blogs, magazines, videos, podcasts) on Digg:

   • From the left navigation bar on the homepage, browse groups or categories on designated topics (business, entertainment, gaming, lifestyle, offbeat, politics, science, sports, technology, world news) and immediately view the top trending stories in each individual category.

   • Browse the expansive Top News section described as the "global zeitgeist of popular content on the web as voted by the Digg community."[2] Alternatively, users can browse the Upcoming section for stories that have not been promoted to the front page.

   • Browse the newly created My News section. Here Digg users can access personalized news or recommended articles—filtered by friends who are also on Digg—with existing Facebook, Twitter, or Google accounts and from news sources (publishers, bloggers) they trust for content.

➣   To Digg a story, sign in and simply click on the thumbs up icon next to the story, and in real time the numerical value assigned to the story immediately goes up by one. Registered Digg users can also add comments, bury a story, save it as a favorite, or share with friends using Facebook, Twitter, or email.

➣   To submit a story, users type the URL in the input box provided at the top of the homepage, add a title, select a category, and write a short summary or description.

➤ Digg can be easily integrated into an existing website or blog by adding Digg widgets, buttons, and badges (about.digg. com/publishers). These tools are beacons that encourage readers to submit the stories posted on these portals to Digg. Developers have access to APIs (application programming interfaces) that return Digg data in a form that can be easily integrated into other third-party applications and websites.

➤ The Digg blog (about.digg.com/blog) is fairly active and provides constant updates on the service for its community of users. As a social news aggregation service that openly solicits content with no restrictions on who can post a news story, Digg does advance a list of stringent community guidelines (about.digg.com/community-guidelines), including warnings to members to submit only original stories, to avoid copyright infringement, to be respectful to other community members, and to maintain unique single accounts.

➤ There are several mobile options available for on-the-go Digg users. A mobile version of the site (m.digg.com) is accessible, and there are apps for the iPhone, iPod Touch, iPad, and Android smartphone.

How Cybrarians Can Use This Resource

Current Awareness Service and Interacting With Library Patrons in Their Social Spaces

Social news aggregation services like Digg, and its main competitor Reddit (www.reddit.com), are considered innovative and democratizing, heavily impacting the way news is distributed and consumed by avid readers online. Cybrarians can use these aggregators to keep up-to-date with trends in real-time news as it relates to their subject areas, and at the same time provide outreach services to patrons by guiding them to these services as potential news sources to tap into and keep current in their fields of endeavor.

There is also the opportunity to become active members of these communities, hanging out where potential library users are spending their time, invading their social spaces, and while there, adding quality content that will attract even the most disillusioned user.

Integrating the Digg button (about.digg.com/publishers) in your main library portal or gateway to information is one proactive move for driving traffic to that portal. This allows visitors to Digg library-endorsed postings and submit these ratings to Digg, which purportedly attracts more than 1 million visitors every day.

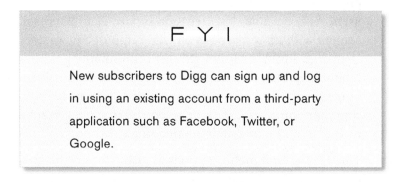

F Y I

New subscribers to Digg can sign up and log

in using an existing account from a third-party

application such as Facebook, Twitter, or

Google.

Endnotes

1. Michael Arrington, "Kevin Rose Resigns From Digg, Closing Round on New Startup," TechCrunch, www.techcrunch.com/2011/03/18/kevin-rose-resigns-from-digg-closing-round-on-new-startup (accessed August 10, 2011).
2. "Digg Frequently Asked Questions," Digg about.digg.com/faq (accessed August 10, 2011).

18

Dogpile
search engine
www.dogpile.com

Overview

Given the number of disparate search engines covered in various chapters in this book, it may be difficult for dedicated web searchers to determine which search engines to target in their attempt to find information. Google, for most searchers, is the obvious choice as it is undeniably the king of search. But, what if it was possible to have one resource that aggregates the most relevant searches from the leading search engines and delivers the result set in a convenient search-and-retrieve interface? Dogpile does this.

Powered by metasearch technology, Dogpile returns all the best combined results from industry leaders Google, Yahoo!, Bing, and Ask.com, as well as lesser-known websites like Fandango, allowing searchers to quickly find what they are looking for. Dogpile utilizes its own algorithm to evaluate the search results, decides which are most relevant to the search query, eliminates duplicates, and compiles the final web-search results in a single window.

InfoSpace, the developer of this metasearch engine, makes no secret of the fact that search results returned are a combination of sponsored and nonsponsored results for any given search term. To InfoSpace's credit, all sponsored results are always clearly identified with a "Sponsored: Ads by Google," or similar designation. The company, which has been in existence since 1996, believes that its mission—to make the discovery of information faster, easier, and more relevant—is philosophical and attractive enough to contend evenly in a competitive search engine market.[1] The time-saving philosophy of the service—compiling and presenting the best results in one easy-to-access interface—inspired the name

Metasearch engine Dogpile returns all the best combined
results from industry leaders Google, Yahoo!, Bing, and Ask.com.

Dogpile and the mascot Arfie who is quick to "fetch and deliver"
results.

Features

➢   Dogpile is relatively easy to access and use from the
homepage (www.dogpile.com). Search queries are entered in
a centrally placed search box and submitted by clicking the
Go Fetch button. Searches can be filtered by using specific
categories such as web, images, video, news, yellow pages, and
white pages. An advanced search option is available for
independent searchers.

➢   A Preferences tab links to a page where customized search
preferences can be set. These preferences include search filters
(choice of moderate or heavy), options to bold search terms
and set the number of results displayed, and the choice of
opening the search results in a separate window.

➢   Spelling correction offers suggested spellings for words that
may be misspelled and automatically corrects commonly
misspelled keywords.

➤ The statistics bar shows how many results were returned for the search term entered.

➤ The Are You Looking For … ? feature offers a list of other search keywords that are relevant and related to the original search term.

➤ The Recent Searches feature keeps track of the most recent searches. This list resets when the browser is closed.

➤ Results can be shared using social networks Facebook, Twitter, Delicious, Myspace, and StumbleUpon.

➤ The Dogpile toolbar is a free application that can be downloaded and offers a convenient way to search for internet content within any browser.

How Cybrarians Can Use This Resource

Promoting the Benefits of Using Metasearch Engines

Recognizing the immediate benefits of providing access to one resource that allows patrons to enter their search criteria only once and access several search engines simultaneously, BLINN College Library located in Brenham, Washington County, Texas, created a webpage devoted exclusively to metasearch engines (www.blinn.edu/library/find/internet/Meta_Search_Tools.htm). The webpage is well organized and begins by offering researchers a Wikipedia definition of metasearch engines. Also included on the webpage is a list of metasearch engines (including Dogpile) currently available on the internet, a comparison chart listing each metasearch engine identified and its capabilities, as well as the type of searches offered by each search engine in the following categories: online help, audio, government, health, images, multimedia, news, and shopping.

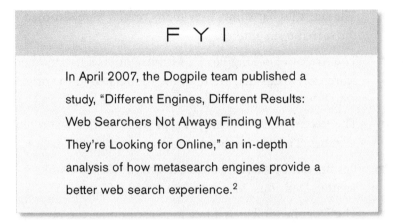

F Y I

In April 2007, the Dogpile team published a study, "Different Engines, Different Results: Web Searchers Not Always Finding What They're Looking for Online," an in-depth analysis of how metasearch engines provide a better web search experience.[2]

Endnotes

1. "InfoSpace: Our Story," Infospace, www.infospaceinc.com/ourstory (accessed August 10, 2011).

2. Dogpile.com, "Different Engines, Different Results: Web Searchers Not Always Finding What They're Looking for Online," www.infospaceinc.com/onlineprod/Overlap-DifferentEnginesDifferentResults.pdf (accessed August 10, 2011).

19

Doodle
productivity tool
www.doodle.com

Overview

For many cybrarians, scheduling meetings (ad hoc or recurring) can be a laborious, time-consuming task. The most common method for scheduling meetings is that of emailing invitees en masse with agendas attached. Doodle, an online scheduling service, makes the task of polling attendees to match the right date and right time for an event much more efficient and productive. Doodle administrators can schedule a meeting or conference call in less than five minutes for a diverse group by using a very simple process.

The first step is to create a Doodle poll list of suitable dates and meeting times, then to send the URL link to the poll to attendees (Doodle can send links automatically as well), and finally, to allow attendees to fill in the blanks, noting when they are available. There is no limit to the number of polls created or number of participants invited. There are more advanced options available for polling a range of dates or exporting results as a PDF document or Excel spreadsheet.

The basic version of Doodle (Standard Doodle) is free and does not require users to register to use the service or install software. MyDoodle is offered as a free account for potential power users who, once registered, can connect (sync) their personal calendars on Google and Outlook and keep track of all meeting requests.

Doodle was launched in March 2007 and is currently based in Zurich, Switzerland. Due to widespread popularity, the service began offering premium accounts (Premium Doodle), with advanced functionalities, greater customization, and no advertising. Doodle From Anywhere is an

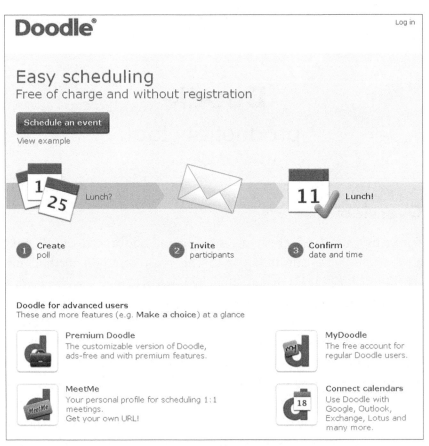

The Doodle homepage offers free Standard Doodle
and MyDoodle, as well as paid Premium Doodle.

added service for iGoogle, XING, and Google Apps users. Access is also
provided to a mobile version of the service (www.doodle.com/mobile).

Features

➤ With three quick steps, Doodle eliminates the difficulties
encountered when trying to find the right date and time for a
group of people to meet.

  • Scheduling an event (Step 1): Users can create a poll by
  clicking on the Schedule Event link on Doodle's homepage

(www.doodle.com); in the online form presented, add a title, location, your name, email address, and proposed dates and times for a conference call or board meeting. Registering to perform this task is optional. Events scheduled can be personal- or business-related. The Doodle menu offers a choice of multiday and multitime appointments, time zone support, and optional settings such as hidden polls and limiting the number of participants.

- Voting using Doodle's poll table (Step 2): After setting up a meeting, you can send a URL link to the participants to cast their vote online, choosing a date and time of the event using the poll table. Participants can be invited directly from the Doodle website or by using Outlook and/or Google contacts. There are available options to edit or delete a vote, add a comment, view and print the poll as a PDF document, embed a summary of the poll to a webpage or blog, subscribe to email notifications for the poll, and upload files (100 MB maximum).

- Closing the poll (Step 3): Administrators have rights to close the poll, choose an appropriate date, and inform participants about the final decision.

How Cybrarians Can Use This Resource

Online Scheduling Tool

It has been proven that Doodle as an online scheduling tool alleviates the pain and frustration of finding suitable dates and times for a diverse group of people to meet. Use Doodle to schedule work-related events such as reference meetings, collection development meetings, board meetings, and conference calls. Doodle can also be used for scheduling family-related group events such as a family reunion, movie nights, and vacations. Cybrarians have the added flexibility of syncing Doodle with other personal calendars maintained in Google or Outlook, and in this way can access, manage, and maintain all appointments and events in one place.

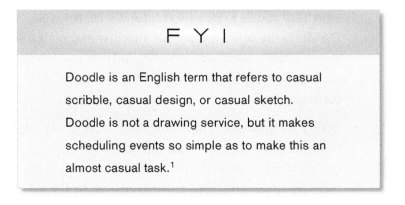

F Y I

Doodle is an English term that refers to casual scribble, casual design, or casual sketch.
Doodle is not a drawing service, but it makes scheduling events so simple as to make this an almost casual task.[1]

Endnote

1. "Doodle FAQ," Doodle, www.doodle.com/about/faq.html#doodlename (accessed August 10, 2001).

20

Drupal
content management system
www.drupal.org

Overview

Distributed under the GPL (GNU General Public License), Drupal's content management platform can be likened to a true open source platform success story. Thousands of volunteer developers, businesses, and nonprofit organizations have worked together to build and support this flexible, feature-rich application used by individuals, an active community of users, and business enterprises to build and manage content on dynamic websites.

This indeed was the intent of founder Dries Buytaert, who developed the Drupal project in 2001 as a test bed for emerging social technologies on the web: "The core idea behind Drupal is to give everyone the power to create compelling community-driven websites without sacrificing power."[1]

For web developers, web administrators, and library managers, Drupal offers a broad range of features and add-on modules to support the creation of a wide range of web projects such as personal, corporate, community or social networking websites, discussion forums, resource directories, and intranet and ecommerce applications. Integrated system features include user administration rights, flexible publishing workflows, support for chat and news aggregation, metadata creation using controlled vocabularies, and XML publishing for content sharing and built-in security.

Large well-known corporations, academic institutions, and libraries have used Drupal to build user-friendly web portals. The list (www. drupal.org/cases) includes Warner Brothers Records, AOL Corporate, Yahoo! Research, Portland State University, and Penn State University.

Features

➤   Contributors are Drupal's most valuable asset and the sole
driving force behind improvements to the platform.
Drupal.org, the official website of Drupal, is host to a number
of resources to provide support for this wide network of
volunteers and active users.

➤   New users can get started by clicking on the Download tab on
the homepage (www.drupal.org), and downloading the latest
release of Drupal core files. These new releases are bundled
with the required modules and themes to give users a good
starting point to begin building websites. Drupal core files
include basic community features like blogs, forums, and
contact forms, and these can be easily extended by
downloading other user-contributed modules and themes.

➤   A Support tab links to training resources, documentation,
and user-moderated discussion forums to help users get a
head start on building their websites.

➤   For technical problems, bug fixes, and useful tips on
installation and maintenance, users can click on the Forum
tab and search forums maintained by the Drupal community
of users.

➤   A Contribute tab links to an appeal for monetary donations
to support the project. It also links to information on how to
volunteer in areas such as writing documentation for APIs,
tutorials, creating multimedia screencasts, developing
modules and patches for the core infrastructure, writing
translations, testing usability, designing applications and
themes, and marketing.

How Cybrarians Can Use This Resource

Building Content-Rich Web Portals

For cybrarians wishing to use this free and incredibly flexible resource
to create content-rich web portals for library patrons, consider Drupal
analogous to a Lego kit. Skilled developers have already made the

The Drupal homepage hosts a wide range of resources to provide support for its network of volunteers and active users.

building blocks—in the form of contributed modules—and all you need to complete the infrastructure is to customize the application.

There are two valuable online resources for cybrarians wishing to implement Drupal at their institutions:

1. Groups.drupal.org serves the Drupal community by providing a place for groups to meet, organize, plan, and work on projects. One of these groups serves as a forum for librarians (groups.drupal.org/libraries) and maintains a comprehensive Libraries Using Drupal list (groups.drupal.org/libraries/libraries). Libraries that have successfully implemented Drupal are encouraged to add their names to this regularly updated list.

2. Drupalib (drupalib.interoperating.info/library_sites), dubbed as a "place for drupallers to hang out," is another portal created for Drupal implementers in libraries to share ideas, configurations, themes, and collaborate to develop modules that enhance commonly desired functionality in library websites. Drupalib features a blog, a forum, and a listing of Drupal sites maintained by libraries. Examples of library sites listed at Drupalib include Western Washington University Libraries, Miami University Libraries, Keene Public Library (New Hampshire), Simon Fraser University Library, Library at California State University-San Marcos, New City Library (New York), and Hoover Public Library (Alabama).

F Y I

In 2010, Drupal won the Infoworld Bossie
Award for the best open source application.[2]

Endnotes

1. "Drupal 6.0 Released—Bringing Greater Simplicity, Performance and Style To This Open Source Social Publishing Platform," Drupal, www.drupal.org/press/drupal-6.0/en (accessed August 10, 2011).

2. "Drupal Awards," Drupal, www.drupal.org/about/awards (accessed August 10, 2011).

21

Ecademy
social network
www.ecademy.com

Overview

Community, Conversations, and Commerce are the three taglines that underpin the goals of Ecademy, a shared community that was created in 1998 as a network for business professionals. Visitors to this site connect online to share knowledge, build their network, and grow their business. Ecademy is similar in intent and purpose to the more popular professional network LinkedIn (see Chapter 43).

Both services are marketed on the premise that having a powerful online presence will help professionals to position themselves as experts in their fields of endeavor, become more visible in the online marketplace, and establish credibility and leverage for their products and services.

Advertised as 50 percent social and 50 percent business, Ecademy members, using the tools and resources that Ecademy has developed, can create an online profile and connect with others to make new contacts, find employment, get business support and advice, and meet with other entrepreneurs at a business networking event. The company is based in Grayscott, United Kingdom.

Features

➤ Potential users must complete an online registration form accessible from the homepage (www.ecademy.com) to join Ecademy. New members have the choice of registering for any of three levels of membership—a free membership service, and two fee-based services, Blackstar and PowerNetworker.

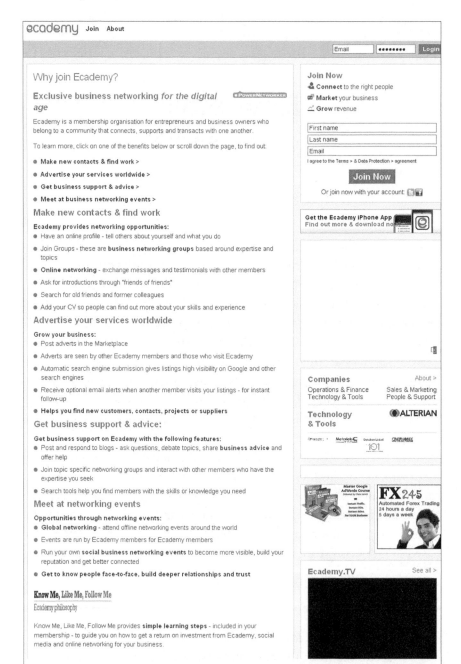

Ecademy is a social network for professionals who are encouraged to become part of Community, Conversations, and Commerce.

➤ The free subscription features offered are basic, but this is enough to provide access to the tools and resources needed to start building personal networks. These features include:

- Creating a profile (business or individual)

- Rating other members' updates (limited to 3 per day)

- Accessing NetNews website feeds to show all personal internet content and leave messages for friends on the network

- Building a social network quickly by searching, finding, and inviting new contacts

- Following favorite contacts (limited to 20 contacts)

- Searching and replying to messages

- Starting forum threads (limited to 2 per day) and posting forum messages (limited to 5 per day)

- Searching and posting comments on blogs

- Registering to attend meetings and events

- Searching for events and meetings on the network

- Searching the online marketplace to find relevant products and services

How Cybrarians Can Use This Resource

Creating a Professional Social Network

Using the tools and resources that Ecademy has developed, cybrarians can quickly and effectively find the right kind of people to connect to for community, conversations, and professional development. Other benefits include:

➤ Making new business contacts and finding a job

➤ Advertising professional services globally

➤   Accessing professional support and advice

➤   Gathering important leads at conferences and other networking events

F Y I

Registered members regularly post their recommendations and reviews of the service on Ecademy's testimonial page (www.ecademy. com/node.php?id=4155).

22

Facebook
social network
www.facebook.com

Overview

It is nearly impossible in this cyberage to not have heard about Facebook, or "fb" as it is commonly known by its users. Facebook, founded by Harvard student Mark Zuckerberg, started out in 2004 as a social networking site created for college students, and subscription was available by invitation only. Now, with membership open to all since 2007, Facebook is a social and cultural phenomenon attracting users from across the globe. Statistics on the service's fact page point to more than 750 million active subscribers—much more than the registrants recorded by its closest rival, Myspace. Facebook is now the undisputed leader among social networking sites.[1]

As a social network, the central figure is "you," the user (individual, school, university, library, business), forging connections with friends, relatives, colleagues, and acquaintances who work, study, and live around you. This, in fact, is Facebook's stated mission: "To give people the power to share and make the world more open and connected."[2] Registration is required to join the network and create a profile. Profiles allow users to upload an unlimited number of photos, share links and videos, read and add comments, link to blogs and web applications, and generally learn more about the people they meet.

One major factor accounting for the service's continuing popularity and widespread usage by all age groups is the company's stated adherence to an open development philosophy that enables outside developers and programmers to integrate their third-party applications using Facebook APIs. The upside for these developers is immediate access to millions of users through this social graph. Facebook applications developed by third-party clients include WorldCat.org, Animoto videos, Apple's iPhone, Windows Live Messenger, Scrabble, Pandora, Yahoo!, Twitter, TripAdvisor, SlideShare, JSTOR, LibGuides, and Delicious. Facebook's main headquarters is in Palo Alto, California.

Features

➤ Creating a Facebook account is free; users do, however, have the option of purchasing Facebook credits, which can be used to send gifts or to purchase applications or games. From the sign-up page (www.facebook.com) potential members are asked to provide their full name, email address, password, gender, and date of birth. After completion of the sign-up form, Facebook sends an email to the address provided. Clicking on the confirmation link completes the sign-up process.

➤ Facebook's simplified navigation gives members easy access to the site functions and applications. The Profile, Friends, and Messages pages—core to the user experience on

Facebook encourages potential users to sign up
and join a community of more than 750 million subscribers.

Facebook—all have a prominent place at the top of a member's profile page.

- Profile: Add basic information about yourself such as current city, hometown, gender, birthday, personal interests, political and religious views, biodata, favorite quotations, likes and interests, information about education and work, and contact information. You can also add a profile picture and indicate relationship status (single, engaged, married, divorced). In December 2010, Facebook's profile page was enhanced with more visual elements and now includes a quick summary of personal information right at the top of each profile and a row of recently tagged photos.

- Friends: Use Facebook Search to find a person you know and then click on the Add as Friend button to the right of the search listing. A friend request will be sent to that person. Once the person has confirmed that he or she would like to be your friend, that person will show up on your Friends list.

- Messages: All incoming messages from friends in your network or messages you have sent are stored in the Messages Inbox.

➤ Other Facebook applications—Photos, Notes, Groups, and Events—are displayed on the left-side navigation bar, along with any third-party applications that members have added to their account.

➤ Chat is one of the more popular features on Facebook and useful for initiating online conversations with friends. Members can see which friends are online by clicking the Chat menu at the bottom right of any Facebook page. A green dot will appear next to a friend who is online and available to chat, and a moon will appear next to a friend who is currently idle. When you send someone a chat message, your message will appear in a new Chat conversation at the bottom of your friend's browser. Your friend can chat back by typing in the same window.

➤　Facebook has built interactive applications for smartphones on many platforms (iPhone, Palm, Sony Ericsson, INQ, Blackberry, Nokia, Android, Windows Phone, and Sidekick). Many of the main features of the native site (www.facebook. com) are also accessible on the Facebook mobile web interface (m.facebook.com).

➤　Third-party applications on Facebook are designed to enhance members' experience on the service. Some applications are built by Facebook developers, but most applications are built by outside developers who use Facebook's APIs and abide by Facebook's somewhat rigorous Developer Principle and Policies (developers.facebook.com/ policy). Applications available allow members to play social games, set reminders, share similar taste in movies, and send virtual gifts to friends. All resources for potential developers have been centralized and are available on the Facebook website (developers.facebook.com).

How Cybrarians Can Use This Resource

Connecting With Communities

Integrating social networking software into existing services is a new approach for some academic and public libraries. Many embark on such a project in order to make libraries not only "cool" in the public's eyes, but also to foster the image of a third space where potential library users can participate and exchange ideas with library staff and other library users. Many academic and public libraries have created Myspace or Facebook pages in an attempt to promote and extend their library services and to capitalize on the benefits alluded to above:

➤　Libraries Using Facebook Pages (online forum), www.facebook.com/group.php?gid=8408315708&ref=ts

➤　Librarians and Facebook (online forum), www.facebook.com/group.php?gid=2210901334

➤   Libraries with Facebook pages:

- Alvin Sherman Library, Research and Information Technology Center, Nova Southeastern University, www.facebook.com/AlvinShermanLibrary

- Dublin City Public Libraries, Ireland, www.facebook.com/DublinCityPublicLibraries

- Department of Library and Information Studies, University of the West Indies, Mona, Jamaica, www.facebook.com/pages/Kingston-Jamaica/Department-of-Library-and-Information-Studies-UWI-Mona/86794320112

- The Houston Public Library, www.facebook.com/houstonlibrary

- Manchester Library and Information Service (U.K.), www.facebook.com/manchesterlibraries

- National Library of Scotland, www.facebook.com/pages/Edinburgh-United-Kingdom/National-Library-of-Scotland/14754995380

- Worcester Polytechnic Institute Gordon Library, Massachusetts, www.facebook.com/pages/Worcester-MA/WPI-Gordon-Library/6392256246

F Y I

Here are some select Facebook statistics[3]:

- Half of Facebook's active users log on to the service on any given day.

- An average user has 130 friends.

- More than 30 billion pieces of content (web links, news stories, blog posts, notes, photo albums, etc.) are shared each month.

- More than 70 translations are available on the site.

- About 70 percent of Facebook users are outside the United States.

Endnotes

1. "Statistics," Facebook, www.facebook.com/home.php?#!/press/info.php?statistics (accessed August 10, 2011).

2. "Facebook," www.facebook.com/facebook?v=app_7146470109 (accessed August 10, 2011).

3. "Statistics," Facebook.

23

FaxZero
productivity tool
www.faxzero.com

Overview

Using FaxZero, anyone can send a free fax to any fax machine in the United States (including Puerto Rico) and Canada. Users are allowed two free faxes per day, and there is a stipulation that only a maximum of three pages can be faxed per day. All free fax transmissions include a FaxZero-branded logo on the cover sheet.

Documents currently supported include PDF, Microsoft Word (.doc, .docx, or .rtf), and Excel spreadsheets (.xls or .xlsx formats). There is no need for a fax machine, as the fax is sent from within a web browser. What is required is a valid email address, which the service will use to send acknowledgment that the fax has been sent.

Sending faxes in this way is relatively easy. An online form must first be completed by filling in information about the sender and the receiver. Users have the option of typing the text of the fax or attaching a file from their computer. Click the Send Free Fax Now button to complete the process.

The service also facilitates sending faxes to international countries at a relatively inexpensive rate and offers a premium fax subscription service.

Features

➢ A web-based form is available on the main FaxZero page (www.faxzero.com) to send free faxes following these steps:

- Add sender information (name, company, fax number, email address), and receiver information (name, company, fax number).

- Type the text of your fax or attach a file.

- Carefully type the confirmation code provided on the screen. This is usually a combination of letters and

To send free faxes in FaxZero, complete this online form and click on the Send Free Fax Now button.

numbers and is used to verify that data is being entered by a human and not spam.

- Click the Send Free Fax Now button. A confirmation message will be sent to your email address. Click the URL in that message. This is required, as the fax will not be transmitted until you click the link. If using spam filters, users should add support@faxzero.com to the nonspam list. FaxZero will then attempt to deliver the fax to the receiver. Successful faxes are confirmed with a message sent to your email address. Users will also be notified of unsuccessful faxes.

How Cybrarians Can Use this Resource

Productivity Tool

For cybrarians working in smaller libraries, FaxZero can be a workable solution if there is no need to maintain a dedicated fax machine because there are not many incoming and outgoing faxes every day, and if there is even less justification for spending money on ongoing machine maintenance costs. FaxZero can be used to send two free faxes per day. For libraries wishing to send more than two faxes per day, there is the option to upgrade to the premium service to send up to 15 pages per day, with no ads on the cover page.

F Y I

In 2010, FaxZero was named one of "52 Incredibly Useful Sites" by PC World.[1]

Endnote

1. Robert Strohmeyer, "52 Incredibly Useful Sites: The Full List," PCWorld, April 25, 2010, www.pcworld.com/article/194735/52_incredibly_useful_sites_the_full_list. html (accessed August 10, 2011).

24

Flickr
photo and video hosting service
www.flickr.com

Overview

"Share your life in photos" is the lead-in tagline to welcome users to the most popular online photo management and sharing application on the internet. With the growing popularity of digital cameras, especially on mobile devices, comes the expectation that users should become experts at organizing and managing the vast number of photos taken or videos shot, at home, work, or leisurely events. This has not necessarily proven to be the case, and to some, photo and video management is cause for concern and continues to be an exercise in futility.

Flickr was created to provide such hapless users with a place in cyberspace to store, sort, search, and share photos and videos online with family, friends, and colleagues. Flickr's appeal to users, and the service's unrelenting ability to rule supreme in the photo sharing competitive sphere, can be attributed to a number of factors: a user-friendly, easily navigable interface; a myriad of tools to help users organize and display their photos and videos; and the empowerment of users to enhance their pictures with rich descriptions such as titles, tags, locations, and names in order to add contextual metadata to photos. Other factors include the flexibility of sharing photos with others and allowing them to choose favorites, make comments, and add notes; and the security and comfort of posting and sharing photos online knowing you have access to well-managed privacy controls.

There have been recent attempts by rivals to duplicate the services offered by the Flickr prototype—Photobucket, Picasa, Webshots—but none have been able to attain the global popularity of Flickr and its community of followers. Flickr reports that it now hosts more than 5 billion of the world's photos.[1] As is the case with Web 2.0 services, Flickr started off as a free beta service, but with popularity and widespread usage, it surreptitiously added a subscription service, the Flickr Pro account.

Four options are available on the Flickr website for uploading photos and videos.

Features

➤ There are currently four options available on the Flickr website (www.flickr.com/tools) for uploading and managing photos and videos:

1. Upload from a browser using Flickr's Basic Uploader tool.

2. Manage uploads from your desktop using Flickr's desktop application Desktop Uploadr.

3. For users of mobile devices, photos can be uploaded on the go with Flickr's iPhone and Blackberry applications. For email users, there is the option of creating a unique email address to forward photos.

4. A number of third-party photo applications allow users to upload photos directly to Flickr.

➤ Sharing Photos is an enhanced feature with the added capability of allowing contacts (family, friends, and colleagues) to add comments, notes, tags, and favorites to photos.

➤ Using Flickr's search box, content can be searched on the service by selecting one of the following filters: Everyone's Uploads, Your Photostreams, Your Contacts' Photos, Groups, and Flickr Members. To use this feature, users must be logged in to the service.

➤ There is built-in privacy to protect who sees users' photos, by designating these viewers as Family or Friends. In this way, users can restrict viewing of any photo to only those they trust. Public photos are accessible to everyone.

➤ Users can connect their Flickr account to other social networks by sending real-time updates to Facebook when uploading public photos on Flickr, uploading to Flickr and Twitter simultaneously, tweeting a photo from a Flickr photostream, or adding postings from Flickr directly to blogs by setting up a connection between Flickr and the user's blogging service.

➤   Users can organize photos by dragging and dropping them into sets, and grouping sets into collections using the Flickr Organizr tool (www.flickr.com/photos/organize). Use this tool to quickly search an entire collection and edit batches of photos on the fly.

➤   Flickr's community of users can view and explore other photos and videos posted on Flickr in various ways, such as choosing a specific timeline, browsing Galleries (user-selected and posted photos with abstract themes), and using a map of the world to explore the universe through millions of geotagged photos.

➤   Flickr Groups are forums created to share content and conversation. There are hundreds of groups available to help users connect with others who share the same interests. For example, the Libraries and Librarians forum (www.flickr.com/groups/librariesandlibrarians), hosts more than 3,000 members. Groups can either be public, public (invite only), or completely private. Every group has a pool for photos and/or video and a discussion board for posting conversation threads.

➤   The Flickr Blog (blog.flickr.net/en) keeps users up-to-date with daily postings on new applications, revisions, and milestones reached on the service.

➤   The Flickr App Garden (www.flickr.com/services) is the staging place where Flickr's developer community can showcase some of the applications they have developed using the Flickr API.

How Cybrarians Can Use This Resource

Publicizing Archived Photo and Video Collections

Cybrarians can explore the Commons (www.flickr.com/commons), hosted by Flickr, to view innovative and pioneering ways other libraries are using Flickr applications. The Commons was launched on January 16, 2008, when the Library of Congress initiated a pilot project with Flickr (www.flickr.com/photos/library_of_congress) to host more than 3,000 photos from two of its popular collections. Visitors to this photostream can tag, comment, and make notes on the images.

Other libraries have followed this model and opened their archives on Flickr to increase access to and publicize photographic collections, and also to provide an avenue for the general public to contribute information and knowledge they have about the collections. These institutions include: the Smithsonian (www.flickr.com/photos/smithsonian), the New York Public Library (www.flickr.com/photos/nypl), and the U.S. National Archives (www.flickr.com/photos/usnationalarchives).

Outreach Programming

Using Flickr to develop outreach programs for the community is another innovative way of using this resource. For example, your library could sponsor a workshop on the practical applications of Flickr in generating employment leads and connecting with friends online (www.slideshare.net/apeoples/flickr-workshop).

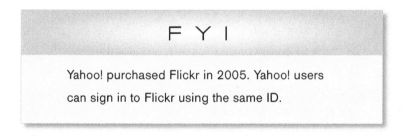

F Y I

Yahoo! purchased Flickr in 2005. Yahoo! users can sign in to Flickr using the same ID.

Endnote

1. Flickr homepage, www.flickr.com (accessed August 10, 2011).

25

Foursquare
social network
www.foursquare.com

Overview

Foursquare is a mobile location-based social network for finding and connecting with friends. Since the application was launched in 2009, by co-founders Dennis Crowley and Naveen Selvadurai, it has gained a large following mainly based on the perception that it offers much more than the typical social network functions of finding and connecting with friends. Instead, the service is viewed as a social city guide, giving users the opportunity to quickly access and explore more interesting city sites and local neighborhoods, and as a social game that challenges users to compete in a friendly arena and rewards them for doing so.

Once registered with the service, users must download the Foursquare application to their mobile device. Members can immediately Check In to the place they are currently located, such as parks, bars, museums, restaurants, airports, and libraries. By using this method of checking in, your friends are alerted to where you are. Points, badges, and special appointments (mayorship for the user who has checked in the most to the same venue) are awarded based on participation.

Foursquare has taken social networking a step further, showing the potential financial benefits of location-based services by partnering with many local businesses that offer specials (discounts and prizes) to loyal members who Check In to their venue. Foursquare records an average of 3 million Check Ins per day.[1] Its headquarters is in New York City.

Foursquare is viewed as a social city guide to explore interesting places and as a social game arena to compete for rewards.

Features

➢ Registration to the service can be completed in a series of simple steps:

- From the Foursquare homepage (www.foursquare.com), click on the Join Now tab.

- Enter personal data including first name, email, telephone, location, gender, birthday, and password in the web-based form provided. Alternately, Facebook users can log in with their Facebook account and elect to have the service automatically add their list of friends from Facebook. Twitter users have the same option.

- Download the Foursquare application to a mobile device and Check In from a current location. Applications are presently available for the iPhone (available from the Apple Store), Android, Blackberry, Nokia, Windows, and Palm smartphones. Members without smartphones can Check In using a mobile browser (m.foursquare.com).

➤ Most Foursquare Check Ins will earn members points. More points are added for frequent traveling, visiting a new location, or adding a venue. Frequent Check Ins to the same venue are rewarded with a mayorship, and friends can compete for this prize by being listed on a weekly Leaderboard.

➤ Badges are rewards that members earn for doing something considered adventurous or checking in to interesting places: superstar badge (achieved for Check Ins to 50 locations), local badge (Check Ins at the same place three times in one week), super mayor badge (achieved by holding 10 current mayorships), and crunked badge (achieved by Check Ins four-plus times in one night).

➤ Members have access to a tips and to-do system. Tips, as the name suggests, are generally recommendations (shown as a pop-up window) that members leave for others after a Check In. To-dos are notes to self about interesting sites visited or tasks to complete.

➤ Specials are rewards that venues give out just for Foursquare users. The rewards can range from in-store discounts to free admission to museums. Members can unlock specials in different ways (depending on the venue), including being the mayor, having a certain number of Check Ins, or simply showing up as a first-time visitor to a specific venue.

➤ New members have access to Foursquare support (support.foursquare.com/home), including an online searchable knowledge base and a FAQ page to search for answers and vote on answers considered useful.

➤ Similar to other social networks, Foursquare has an API that allows developers to build their ideas on the Foursquare platform. Developers have already used this API to build new Check In functionality, games, and interesting data visualizations. These applications are available in the Foursquare app gallery (www.foursquare.com/apps).

➤ Registered members have immediate access to personal statistics tied to their login, and these statistics can be filtered weekly or monthly. Statistics maintained include days Checked In, number of Check Ins, average Check Ins, percentage of Check Ins at a new venue, and new places discovered. For businesses, there is the opportunity to gain real-time venue statistics, including most recent and frequent visitors, the time of day members Check In, total number of unique visitors, gender breakdown of visitors, and the percentage of Foursquare Check Ins broadcasted to Twitter and Facebook.

How Cybrarians Can Use This Resource

Integrating Location-Based Social Networks Into Library Services

Foursquare works like other social networks covered in previous book chapters. The main difference is that this service is largely location-based and tied to mobile devices. Foursquare currently dominates the field in the development of location-based social networks and has been successfully embraced by businesses, academic institutions, and news agencies. Libraries are also getting on board, valiantly attempting to adopt this technology and integrate it into current services. David

Lee King[2,3] shares some interesting ideas for using Foursquare in libraries:

➤ Adding your library as a Foursquare location for registered members to Check In, and promoting Foursquare's playful atmosphere by awarding weekly prizes to the person nominated as mayor

➤ Using Foursquare to add tags relevant to your library—thus promoting unique services

➤ Adding tips and to-do lists for patrons to use and follow through (e.g., register for a library card, view borrowing privileges and circulation records, use a group study room, or explore the latest library exhibit)

➤ Adding a list of library-planned events and activities

➤ Adding status updates about current events, new acquisitions, workshops, and featured databases (these updates can be synced with the library's Twitter and Facebook accounts)

Fostering Community Engagement

Using Foursquare to foster social engagement with the wider campus community is a unique way to utilize the service. For example, libraries can exploit Harvard University's model of partnering with Foursquare (www.foursquare.com/harvard) to create a campus-based game that rewards students with badges and points for exploring the school and surrounding places of interest.[4]

F Y I

In September 2010, the World Economic
Forum selected Foursquare as one of 31
visionary companies given the award of
Technology Pioneer.[5] These technology

> start-up companies, selected from around the
> world, represent what is considered cutting-
> edge innovation, and are viewed as having a
> critical impact on the future of business,
> industry, and society.

Endnotes

1. "About Foursquare," Foursquare, www.foursquare.com/about (accessed August 10, 2011).

2. "Foursquare and Libraries—Anything There?" David Lee King Blog, January 25, 2010, www.davidleeking.com/2010/01/25/foursquare-and-libraries-anything-there (accessed August 10, 2011).

3. "Foursquare and Libraries—Definitely Something There!" David Lee King Blog, February 1, 2010, www.davidleeking.com/2010/02/01/foursquare-and-libraries-definitely-something-there (accessed August 10, 2011).

4. "Harvard on Foursquare: Harvard Uses Foursquare Mobile App," Harvard Gazette, December 10, 2010, news.harvard.edu/gazette/story/2010/01/harvard-and-foursquare (accessed August 10, 2011).

5. "Thirty-One Visionary Companies Selected as Technology Pioneers 2011," New Design World, www.newdesignworld.com/press/story/160980 (accessed August 10, 2011).

26

GIMP
productivity tool
www.gimp.org

Overview

GIMP (which stands for GNU Image Manipulation Program) was developed by Spencer Kimball and Peter Mattis as a response to what they perceived as the current lack of free (or at least reasonably priced) image manipulation software for GNU/Linux and UNIX platforms.

This freely distributed graphics editor can be used for tasks such as photo retouching and enhancing, image composition, and image authoring. As free software, GIMP is expandable and extensible, with the source code readily available for developers to augment with plug-ins and extensions to accommodate performing the simplest task to complex image manipulation.

Rival proprietary editors include the popular Adobe Photoshop, Jasc Paintshop Pro, and Microsoft Paint. The latest stable releases for operating systems Linux, Windows, and Mac OS X are available on the site's download page (www.gimp.org/downloads).

The official GIMP website (www.gimp.org) is a veritable resource-rich interface for the GIMP community, with links to information about downloading, installing, learning to use, and enhancing the software. The site also serves as a distribution point for the latest releases, news about related projects, and the voluntary donation program for future software development. The software was initially released in January 1996 and is currently available in multiple languages.

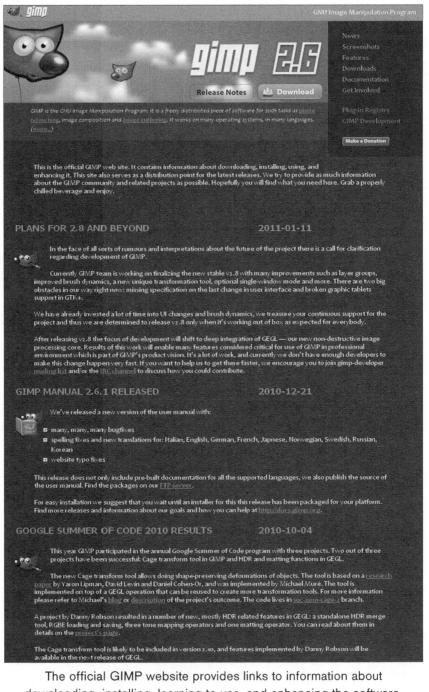

The official GIMP website provides links to information about downloading, installing, learning to use, and enhancing the software.

Features

The following is a truncated overview of some of the features available on the GIMP website (www.gimp.org/features):

➤   Fully customizable interface modulized into so-called docks, which allow users to select and view the behavior of their work environment by changing colors and icon size and accessing custom tool sets in a toolbox

➤   Access to a full suite of painting tools, including Brush, Pencil, Airbrush, and Clone

➤   Robust system support for tile-based memory management so that image size is limited only by available disk space; also allows unlimited number of images to be opened at one time

➤   Access to advanced manipulation tools, including transformation, selection, and foreground extraction tools

➤   Access to a suite of extensible software with more than 100 plug-ins already available, which allows for the easy addition of new file formats and new effect filters

➤   Support for multiple animation packages

➤   Support for a wide range of file formats including BMP, GIF, JPEG, PNG, and TIFF

➤   Support for various input devices, including pressure- and tilt-sensitive tablets and USB or MIDI controllers

➤   For new users, support by way of an updated FAQ page, access to online user manuals in several languages, a GIMP community-based wiki, and online tutorials for beginner, intermediate, and expert learners

How Cybrarians Can Use This Resource

Promoting Access to a Free Graphics Editor

For cybrarians wishing to use this software as a simple paint- or expert-quality graphics editor to perform tasks such as image retouching (in digitization projects), free-form drawing, resizing, editing, image format conversion, and creating photomontages and basic animated images (useful in designing library marketing materials), GIMP created a user-centered webpage (www.gimp.org/about/everywhere.html). This page is devoted to capturing testimonials and creative uses of the software. Illustrative examples are provided in the following categories:

➤ GIMP on the web

➤ GIMP in film

➤ GIMP in medicine and science

➤ GIMP in the computer world

➤ GIMP in commercial art

F Y I

Although GIMP is written and developed under a Linux platform, it can be installed and run on MS Windows and Mac OS X systems as well.

27

Google Analytics
productivity tool
www.google.com/analytics

Overview

In much the same way that Google developed a search engine, using powerful search engine technology to help web searchers find information they want quickly and efficiently, the company has created Google Analytics to generate traffic statistics on any given website. This resource is unquestionably one of the best free, next generation tools available for enterprise-class web analytics, giving statistics watchers (librarians, publishers, advertisers, and website owners), rich insights into website traffic and the effectiveness of their web-marketing strategies.

A dynamic array of flexible and easy-to-use features built into the Google Analytics' architecture allows users to analyze and track usage of web applications and social networking sites. These features include trend reporting, funnel navigation, content-by-titles listing of the most popular items on the website, site overlay, visitor segmentation, keyword comparison, visualized summaries, and data export. Specialists and nonspecialists alike, in all types of organizations, are using this popular resource to garner vital data to measure advertising return on investment and using their findings to strengthen marketing initiatives and create more user-friendly, navigable websites.

As is the case with similar web analytics services, Google Analytics can be enabled by adding hidden JavaScript code—referred to as the Google Analytics Tracking Code—into all pages of the website for which data is collected. This tracking code is essential for the success of the service, performing such functions as tracking and collecting visitor data and compiling this information into a format that can be easily read and interpreted by end users.

Google Analytics is just one of the many tools (see coverage of some of these tools in the preceding and following book chapters) in a continuous chain of products developed and offered freely for public consumption by technology giant Google, currently based in Mountain View, California. This service was released to the public in August 2006.

Features

➤ New members to the service can sign up for an account on the official website or use an existing Google account. All new account holders must complete an online account setup form providing information on the URL of the website they wish to track, an account name, and contact information, and

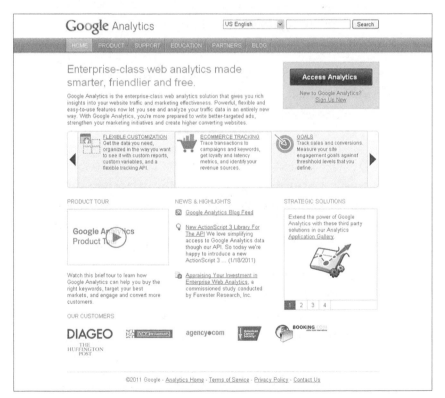

New users can sign up for an account on the Google Analytics website.

affirm acceptance of the user agreement. New subscribers are immediately assigned the JavaScript code to copy and paste into all the webpages they wish to collect data from and track. This code must be inserted right before the closing </head> tag in the HTML code of each page to be analyzed.

➤ Subscribers to the service have access to the following features:

- A tracking service is available for a wide range of platforms (mobile websites, mobile apps, web-enabled mobile devices) and applications (Ajax, Flash, and social networks).

- Access is available to a customizable collection of reports and summaries, which can be edited, saved, and organized on a dashboard with drag-and-drop functions. These customized reports can be automatically generated by scheduling and easily shared via email.

- Data can be exported using the Google Analytics Export API, by email, or by direct export from the service interface into one of several available formats including Excel, PDF, XML, CSV, and tab delimited files.

- An advanced segmentation feature is available for users to isolate and analyze subsets of traffic data. Users can select from predefined custom segments such as Paid Traffic and Visits with Conversions, or they can create new custom segments with an easy-to-use segment builder.

- The Visualized Summaries feature provides access to predefined visualized reports that summarize complex statistical data in a simple and easy-to-understand manner. Summarized data can be viewed using motion charts, spark lines, short narratives, and scorecards.

- Users can earn money by taking advantage of the built-in integration and access to Google-allied products such as

AdWords (application for creating ads, which appear under sponsored links in a Google search) and AdSense (a free program where online publishers can earn revenue by displaying relevant ads on their websites).

• Developers are encouraged to extend the functionality of this free web analytics service. To facilitate this process, the Google Analytics Team created an online gallery of applications (www.google.com/analytics/apps), which showcase how the service has been extended in innovative ways by other developers. Visitors to the gallery can view featured applications or browse subject categories such as business intelligence, content management, data collection, mobile solutions, and reporting tools.

• The Google Analytics Blog (analytics.blogspot.com) reports regularly on product enhancements, offers tips for using the service, and provides links to learning resources and training opportunities.

How Cybrarians Can Use This Resource

Utilizing a Statistics Service to Design User-Centered Websites

In the Wikipedia overview of the service, Google Analytics is cited as "the most widely used website statistics service, currently in use at around 57% of the 10,000 most popular websites."[1] This analysis should be of interest to cybrarians who are strong advocates for and support the implementation of efficient and cost-effective web applications in libraries. In this case, an application that can be used by libraries to generate detailed, visually appealing statistics on website traffic, yields data with rich insights into patrons' behavior—how they are finding and exploring libraries' websites and how they are interacting with website content—as well as information on patrons' geographic locations.

This data can be analyzed and put to use in improving website design and creating more user-centered websites, ultimately enhancing library patrons' web experience. This data can also be the source of information for developing more cost-effective marketing initiatives aimed at driving targeted traffic to libraries' web portals and reducing large budgets often spent on ongoing website management and maintenance.

F Y I

A current listing of high profile websites using Google Analytics is maintained in the Wikipedia entry on Google Analytics.[2]

Endnotes

1. "Google Analytics," Wikipedia, en.wikipedia.org/wiki/Google_Analytics (accessed August 10, 2011).

2. Ibid.

28

Google Books
digital library
www.books.google.com

Overview

Google Books is a resource developed by Google that searches the full text of books that have been scanned, converted to text using optical character recognition, and stored in a free digital database. This massive digitization, and somewhat controversial project, was made possible by Google's partnerships with several high-profile university and public libraries, including the University of Michigan, Harvard University, Stanford University, University of Oxford, and New York Public Library.

By its own admission, Google's mission is "to organize the world's information and make it universally accessible and useful."[1] By developing this digital library, Google seems well on its way to achieving its goal. Described as an "enhanced card catalog of the world's books," Google Books allows users to search for their favorite book title and immediately view basic bibliographic information about the book. If the book is out of copyright, users can view and download the entire book. In all cases, there are links on the page directing readers to online bookstores where they can purchase the book and to libraries where the book can be borrowed.

Although Google's scanning of millions of library volumes may bring untapped collections to new audiences, since the start of the project in 2004, Google has been mired in a legal battle following the filing of a class action lawsuit in 2007 by the Authors Guild, the Association of American Publishers, and a handful of authors and publishers over copyright and proprietary issues. At the core of the argument is concern that the search juggernaut's dominance of this market would threaten library values, privacy, access, cost (free service vs. fee-based), censorship, autonomy, and budgets.

Advocates for and against pending settlements have made successful arguments. Google responded by proposing what is now infamously known as the GBS (Google Book Settlement, www.googlebooksettlement. com). In November 2009, Google was granted preliminary approval of an Amended Settlement Agreement, and in February 2010 filed a brief (sites.google.com/a/pressatgoogle.com/googlebookssettlement/home) in support of a motion for final approval of the ASA. On March 22, 2011, the court denied the parties' request for final settlement approval, and all parties involved in the dispute are evaluating their next steps. So far, reaction has remained mixed, with many stakeholders in the publishing and library communities sharing the view that the new settlement has not gone far enough to settle the matter equitably for all concerned.

Features

➤ A user-friendly interface on the homepage (www.books.google. com) with a centralized search box for keyword searches of all the books in the database (approximately 15 million titles). An advanced search option is available for limiting searches to full or partial previews, books or magazines, language, title, author, publisher, publication date, subject, ISBN, and ISSN.

➤ Browse popular books by clicking on frontal views of colorful book jackets, or browse subject areas filed under categories such as business and economics, computers, family and relationship, health and fitness, literary criticism and collections, medical, philosophy, religion, social science, technology and engineering.

➤ Once a search is entered for a book, users are afforded a full view or limited view of the text depending on the copyright restrictions of the book. If the book is out of copyright, or the publisher has given Google permission to use the content, readers will be able to see a preview of the book and in some cases the entire text. If the book is in the public domain, you can download a PDF copy.

➤ Searchers have immediate access to Web 2.0 functionalities such as summaries, reader-supplied reviews, user-provided ratings and tags (viewable as a tag cloud), and links to related books. A Google Maps screenshot of places mentioned in the book is embedded for each book title.

➤ A feedback link allows users to report problems such as missing pages or unreadable text on specific pages.

➤ The About the Author section previews biographical information. Bibliographic information (title, author, edition, publisher, ISBN, book length, and subjects) is also provided for each title.

➤ Users with Google accounts can sign in to create and manage personal bookshelves (My Library), share books with friends, and view what their friends are reading.

➤ The Find in a Library link in Google Books points directly to OCLC's global catalog of library collections WorldCat.org (www.worldcat.org) and allows searchers to click through to their local library catalog and borrow any title found in Google Books, if the title is available.

➤ There are links to publishers' and book vendors' websites where the book can be purchased.

➤ Registered users can write book reviews, add tags, or rate the content using a five-star rating system.

➤ For authors, there are opportunities to promote books without spending money on marketing by using Google Books Partner Program (books.google.com/partner). Within this program, Google Books allows publishers and authors to submit their books for inclusion in Google's search results. Each Google Books result will display the book's author and title, a short excerpt containing the highlighted search terms, and other public data about the book.

How Cybrarians Can Use This Resource

Reference and Research

Reference librarians can direct students to Google Books as a valuable resource useful for completing class assignments, if the full text of the desired book is available.

Expanding Access to Eresources

Projects such as Google Books potentially offer significant new opportunities for libraries. The digitization of vast numbers of books, particularly those that are out-of-print, has enabled libraries to virtually expand physical collections and provide access to these digitized resources in innovative ways.

Expand the universe of information available to your users by integrating the Google Books search box into your library's main webpage or online catalog. This search box, which can be easily added by using three simple steps as described on the Google website (services.google.com/inquiry/books_email?hl=en), allows users to search for books of

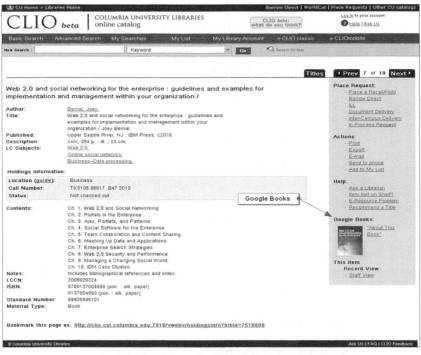

The Columbia University libraries have integrated
Google Books into their online catalog CLIO.

every topic and genre directly from your library's website. Columbia University Libraries (www.columbia.edu/cu/lweb) has successfully integrated Google Books into their online catalog CLIO.

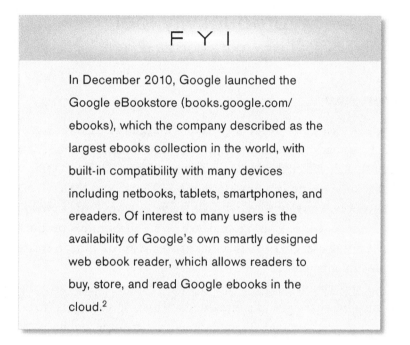

F Y I

In December 2010, Google launched the Google eBookstore (books.google.com/ebooks), which the company described as the largest ebooks collection in the world, with built-in compatibility with many devices including netbooks, tablets, smartphones, and ereaders. Of interest to many users is the availability of Google's own smartly designed web ebook reader, which allows readers to buy, store, and read Google ebooks in the cloud.[2]

Endnotes

1. "Google: Corporate Information," Google, www.google.com/corporate (accessed August 10, 2011).
2. "Discover More Than 3 million Google eBooks From Your Choice of Booksellers and Devices," Google Blog, googleblog.blogspot.com/2010/12/discover-more-than-3-million-google.html (accessed August 10, 2011).

29

Google Docs
productivity tool
www.docs.google.com

Overview

Google Docs is a web-based application that can be used to create documents, spreadsheets, drawings, flowcharts, forms, and presentations online. It is, in effect, the free online alternative to Microsoft Office proprietary suite of applications MS Word, MS Excel, and MS PowerPoint. It may not be power-packed with all the features and functionalities of MS Office, but it is gaining credence as a collaborative productivity tool, enabling users to work together as a team in real time to create and edit documents online.

Four applications comprise the Google Docs online suite: Documents (for creating, sharing, and editing documents), Spreadsheets (for creating spreadsheets online), Presentations (for creating online presentations), and Forms (for creating online surveys).

To start using Google documents, Google subscribers can simply sign in with existing Google Accounts. New users are required to create an account. Only one unique login and password is required to log in and use all the applications. For new users, help is offered in the form of articles, user guides, online video tours of each application, a Team Blog, and help forums to post questions and join ongoing discussions.

Features

Google Documents

➢ Upload MS Word, OpenOffice, RTF, HTML, or plain text documents. This includes drag-and-drop uploading.

Five applications comprise the Google Docs online suite:
Documents, Spreadsheets, Presentations, Drawings, and Forms.

➣   Create new documents or edit existing documents online
     simultaneously in a shared environment.

➣   Keep track of who made changes to a document and when,
     and revert to previous versions.

➣   Publish documents created online as webpages or post
     documents to a blog.

➣   Email created documents as attachments.

Google Spreadsheets

➣   Import and export these file types: .xls, .csv, .txt and .ods.
     Export data as a PDF or an HTML file.

➣   Format spreadsheet cells to customize data and edit
     formulas to calculate results.

➣   Chat in real time with others using an on-screen chat
     window.

➤   Embed a spreadsheet or a section of a spreadsheet in a blog or website.

Google Presentations

➤   Import presentations in .ppt and .pps file types and export new presentations created or modified.

➤   Insert images and videos into new presentations.

➤   Create and edit presentations online in a shared environment. Enable simultaneous real-time viewing of presentations from remote locations.

➤   Embed your presentations in a blog or website.

Google Drawings

➤   Create and edit drawings online in real time in a shared environment.

➤   Chat online with others who are editing or viewing the drawing.

➤   Download drawings using one of several supported formats (PNG, JPEG, SVG, PDF).

➤   Insert text, shapes, arrows, and images from your hard drive or from the web.

➤   Lay out drawings precisely with alignment guides, snap to grid, and auto distribution.

➤   Insert drawings into other Google documents, spreadsheets, or presentations using the web clipboard function.

Google Forms

Within Google Docs, users can create forms (surveys) to send to friends or colleagues, and keep track of the answers in one spreadsheet. Forms can be created from within Google Docs or from Google Spreadsheets. Here are the features common to both applications:

➤ To access forms in both applications, do the following: In Google Docs, click New > Form. In Google Spreadsheets, click the Form drop-down menu and select Create a Form.

➤ In both applications there are form templates that allow users to add questions and options for responses.

➤ The option is available to send the completed survey by email. Simply add the email addresses of the people to which you wish to send the survey and click the Email this Form button.

How Cybrarians Can Use This Resource

Promoting Access to a Web-Based Suite of Productivity Applications

There are immediate benefits to using this free, web-based application to create documents, spreadsheets, drawings, flowcharts, forms, and presentations online. Google created a webpage to illustrate real-life examples of how Google Docs users (teachers, businesses, personal users, and nonprofits) have found success using the application (www.google.com/google-d-s/tour5.html#). Some of the advantages include:

➤ Accessing your data from any computer with an internet connection and a standard browser, as all documents are stored online in a shared space

➤ Sharing and collaborating in real time on co-authored publications or committee work, as multiple users can view and make changes at the same time

➤ Setting limits on who can access documents to increase online security and privacy

➤ Using the availability of an on-screen chat window to discuss document revisions and new ideas

➤   Safely storing your work online with no fears of local hard
    drive failures or power outages

➤   Immediately publishing the finished work as a webpage, or
    posting the content to a blog

F Y I

The Google Docs Blog (googledocs.blog
spot.com) has regular postings to keep users
up-to-date on new features, tips and tricks, and
bugs and fixes.

30

Google Reader
news and feed aggregator
www.google.com/reader

Overview

The challenge for many web surfers is this: Where can I go to browse *all* my favorite websites (news feeds, blog articles, images, audio, and video news) in one place? Or to put it another way, is there a one-stop shop for all web content? Google Reader is an example of such a service, offering what all web surfers fervently wish for: a tool for gathering, reading, and sharing all the interesting blogs and websites you read on the web.

The concept behind the service is a web surfer's dream: Bring organization out of the chaos that the internet sometimes represents. How it actually works is relatively easy to understand. Many online information sources, such as websites, blogs, and news services, now broadcast their content to the web in so-called syndicated feeds or news feeds with new technologies like Really Simple Syndication (RSS) and ATOM.

A web-based aggregator service like Google Reader tracks and collects the syndicated feeds that a subscriber to the service identifies. Google Reader then posts these feeds on a personalized webpage, which can be viewed and read at the subscriber's convenience. The interface should be familiar to users with a Gmail account. In fact, using the service to keep up-to-date with your favorite websites is as easy as checking your email.

Google Reader is free and users can access the service using an existing Google account or by signing up for a new account. It can be accessed from any computer, and there is no need to install additional software.

Features

Add New Feeds

To subscribe to a new feed in Google Reader, click the Add a Subscription link in the left navigation bar and enter the URL of the blog or website you would like to subscribe to in the box provided. Google Reader will attempt to locate the appropriate feed. Feeds you subscribe to are listed in easy-to-navigate browse-and-view panes. Once you have subscribed to a feed, you can immediately view the number of new or unread items as noted next to the feed's title. Clicking on the feed's title will display the content of the feed in your primary viewing pane. At the top of the personalized page there are options to view all items or just new items. Individual items in a feed can be starred, tagged, shared, emailed, and liked (added as favorites).

Search and Discover Feeds

There are a number of options offered within Google Reader for searching and identifying the feeds you want to track and manage:

> ➤   Under the Browse for Stuff tab, help in identifying feeds is provided by the Google Team with a list of regularly updated, customized, or prepackaged feed bundles to get new users started quickly and easily. At the time of this writing, there were more than 400 bundles arranged under categories such as animation, blogging, genealogy, medicine, news, sports, staff picks, yoga, and XML.

> ➤   Clicking on the Browse for Stuff tab also leads to a single-search box for searching for feeds by typing in keywords.

> ➤   Google Reader automatically generates a list of recommended feeds, based on a user's existing feed subscriptions, feeds that are popular among people who share the user's interests, and information from personal web history. This list of recommended items can be found in the Explore section on the left navigation bar.

> ➤   If you are switching from another feed reader, you can import your existing subscriptions into Google Reader. To do this,

you first have to export your subscriptions in the OPML standard format.

➤ A new feature, the Google Reader Play (www.google.com/reader/play), has been described as "a fun, fast way to personalize and browse the most interesting stuff on the web." When you use Reader Play, Google tracks items you star, like, or share, and shows you similar items the next time you visit, utilizing the same technology used to generate your recommended items list. Feeds can be viewed in Reader Play as thumbnails, slideshows, or in the original layout.

➤ Google Reader can be added to iGoogle and can be accessed from any mobile phone browser.

How Cybrarians Can Use This Resource

Current Awareness Service

➤ Stay up-to-date in your field of interest as Google Reader constantly checks your favorite websites, news services, and blogs for new content.

➤ Share newsworthy items with your friends and colleagues.

The Google Reader personalized dashboard allows users to keep up-to-date with their favorite websites.

Workshops and Training Sessions

Although RSS feeds have steadily grown in popularity, the concept is not always easily grasped by library patrons. Librarians are using Google Reader to teach patrons how to read RSS feeds and how to use a feed aggregator to organize and manage their favorite resources. The University of Texas Libraries regularly offer classes and workshops on topics such as Google Reader and new tools on the web to assist patrons in staying up-to-date with their favorite Web 2.0 tools on the web.[1]

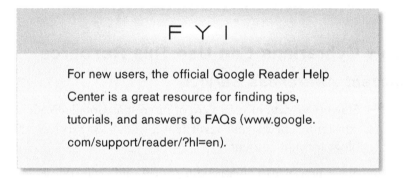

F Y I

For new users, the official Google Reader Help Center is a great resource for finding tips, tutorials, and answers to FAQs (www.google.com/support/reader/?hl=en).

Endnote

1. "Instruction Services," University of Texas Libraries, www.lib.utexas.edu/services/instruction (accessed August 10, 2011).

31

Google Sites
productivity tool
www.sites.google.com

Overview

Google Sites is a free wiki and webpage creation tool offered by Google as part of its expanded suite of productivity apps. Developed for corporate, professional, or personal use, Google Sites offers the immediate advantage of creating and publishing a new website in just a few clicks. New users have immediate access to advanced features including pre-built templates, customizable themes, a library of social gadgets, and a What You See Is What You Get (WYSIWYG) editor.

Additionally, new subscribers to the service who choose to embed web content in different formats (text, videos, images, presentations, and online forms) can feel secure that websites are created in a protected online environment and can make the decision to keep webpages public or private while maintaining full administrative control of who can access and edit the site.

Since the release of this product in 2008, Google has extended its role as a developer-friendly company by offering the Google Sites API to third-party developers, allowing this group open access to integrate new services and extend the platform.

Features

➢ Google users can sign in on the homepage (www.sites.google. com) using the login and password of an existing Google account, or create a new account; 100 MB of free storage is available to all new users.

➤ Single-click page creation is available with options to choose a prebuilt template, make selections from a library of themes, provide a site name, add a site URL (the option is available to change this URL to a custom domain name), enter a short description of the site, add permissions to control if the site is private or public, and note if the site contains mature content only suitable for adults.

➤ Subscribers can opt to register the site's URL with other Google services (Google Search, Google Places, Google Webmaster Tools) to optimize finding the newly created website when searching Google or other search engines.

➤ Users control customization of the website appearance by changing fonts, colors, layouts and themes, setting a fixed site width, and editing the sidebar and horizontal navigation bar.

➤ The tool contains a selection of prebuilt site templates arranged in the following categories: public, business collaboration, activities and events, schools and education, clubs and organizations, personal and family, and government and nonprofits.

➤ There are user-controlled settings for accessing and sharing information with other editors.

➤ Users can access revision history if there is a need to revert to previous versions of the website. There is also an option to compare revised versions.

➤ Users have the ability to add customized logos, images, and videos, and to embed documents, spreadsheets, forms, presentations, and slideshows.

➤ Other Google products can be integrated, including Google's Picasa Web Albums, YouTube, and Google Docs; there is easy installation of gadgets such as maps and online forms.

➤ Google Docs Blog (googledocs.blogspot.com) is a valuable resource for regular updates on product enhancements, tutorials, tips and tricks, and innovative applications of the service.

➤ The Google Sites help page (www.steegle.com/websites/
google-sites-help) provides links to all of the resources new
subscribers would require to set up and optimize their use of
this service, including links to FAQ and troubleshooting
pages.

How Cybrarians Can Use This Resource

Enhancing a Library's Web Presence and Workshop Offerings

New subscribers to Google Sites regularly post favorable reviews on the
product review page (www.google.com/sites/help/intl/en/overview.
html). These reviews are instructive; they plug the product's flexibility,
easy setup and use, low maintenance, and the effortless integration of
social gadgets and other Google products.

Google Sites is useful for cybrarians wishing to create rich webpages
to enhance their library's web presence. It can also be used as a tool to
distribute information via an intranet and for collaborating on team
projects. Cybrarians interested in conducting workshops to promote the
service to local patrons wishing to build personal- or business-oriented
websites can access a video recording of a webinar highlighting Google

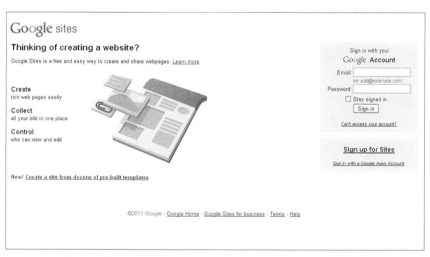

Google Sites offers access to advanced features for building websites.

Sites's main features and demonstrating how to perform basic tasks (www.steegle.com/websites/google-sites-howtos/basics-gbbo-webinar).

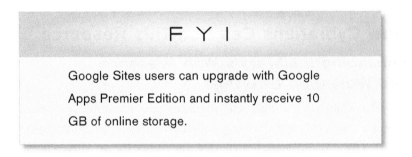

F Y I

Google Sites users can upgrade with Google Apps Premier Edition and instantly receive 10 GB of online storage.

32

HathiTrust
digital library
www.hathitrust.org

Overview

The HathiTrust Digital Library brings together the large-scale digitization efforts of more than 50 research institutions and libraries across the United States and Europe. As of August 2011, more than 9 million volumes have been digitized, and of this number, more than 2.5 million volumes are in the public domain. This project was initially conceived as a collaboration of the 13 universities of the Committee on Institutional Cooperation, the University of California system, and the University of Virginia to establish a repository for those universities to archive and share their digitized collections.[1]

Access to the digital library's public domain and in-copyright content is not restricted and is available to anyone with internet access. However, partnering institutions have access to more features and additional privileges such as the ability to download full PDFs of volumes that are in the public domain, and institutional access to the Collection Builder feature to create and share a personal collection of books.

HathiTrust complements similar efforts by Google and the Internet Archive to digitize the world's library collections. In fact, some HathiTrust partners are also depositing content digitized from their collections into Google Books (Chapter 28) and the Internet Archive (Chapter 34). With the goal of actively expanding its core collections, HathiTrust membership is open to any institution looking for an easy means to archive and provide access to their digital content.

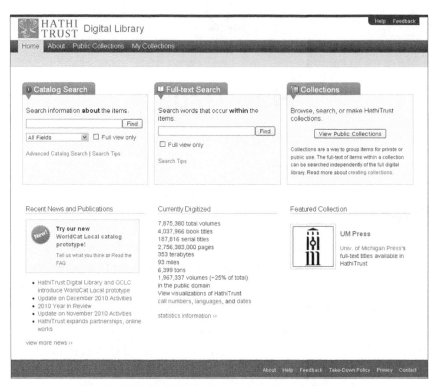

The HathiTrust Digital Library search and discovery
interface contains more than 9 million digitized volumes.

Features

➢ The HathiTrust Digital Library serves the dual functions of
digital preservation repository and a search, discovery, and
access platform. Discovery and access services include a
full-text search across the entire repository, a catalog search
(which searches fields such as title, author, and publication
date), a search of public collections created using the
Collection Builder feature, and an advanced search.

➢ Users can perform the following actions on successful
searches:

• Email the bibliographic record for a title.

• Generate citations in MLA and APA formats.

- Export the record to Endnote.

- Bookmark the item in their favorite browser.

- Download single-page PDFs (users affiliated with HathiTrust partner institutions can download full PDFs of volumes in the public domain).

- View a list of similar items.

- Obtain a persistent URL for the displayed title.

➤ Users wishing to obtain a physical copy of a book can click on the Find in a Library link in the bibliographic record to locate and borrow the title from the nearest library, or click on the Buy a Copy link to purchase the title from Amazon.com.

➤ In an effort to promote the availability of these digitized volumes, the HathiTrust Digital Library developed a Bib API (www.hathitrust.org/data), and other mechanisms using metadata, to allow libraries to create bibliographic records for the public domain materials in the digital collection and download these records to their online catalogs.

➤ OCLC and the HathiTrust have worked closely together to develop a unique WorldCat Local catalog prototype (hathitrust.worldcat.org) for discovery and access to all materials in the HathiTrust Digital Library.

How Cybrarians Can Use This Resource

Promoting Access to a Digital Repository of Research Materials

The University of Michigan (www.lib.umich.edu/michigan-digitization-project) is an example of an academic institution that has entered into groundbreaking agreements with partner institutions to digitize the entire print collection at the University of Michigan Library. Currently, this digitized collection is searchable within the library catalog Mirlyn, the HathiTrust Digital Library, and Google Books: a total of three online gateways available for the university community to access research materials in a shared environment.

HathiTrust can provide a similar platform for other libraries looking for a solution to archive and provide long-term access to digital content. Like the University of Michigan, these libraries can become partner institutions, taking advantage of an established infrastructure and the professional expertise required to archive and preserve vast amounts of digitized materials. Partners are charged a one-time start-up fee based on the number of volumes added to the repository and an annual fee for the curatorship of those volumes.

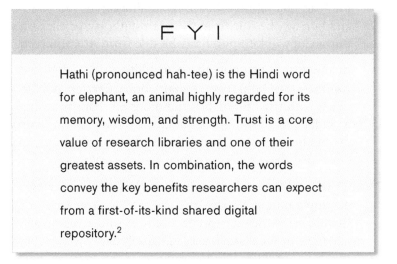

F Y I

Hathi (pronounced hah-tee) is the Hindi word for elephant, an animal highly regarded for its memory, wisdom, and strength. Trust is a core value of research libraries and one of their greatest assets. In combination, the words convey the key benefits researchers can expect from a first-of-its-kind shared digital repository.[2]

Endnotes

1. "HathiTrust Help-General," HathiTrust, www.hathitrust.org/help_general (accessed August 10, 2011).
2. Ibid.

33

Hulu
video hosting service
www.hulu.com

Overview

In recent times, the volume of TV shows and movies streamed over the internet has grown exponentially. The consumer base has also grown by leaps and bounds, with consumers snapping up streaming viewing devices such as Apple TV, and online providers of streaming content have become profitable enterprises.

Hulu is one of the earliest forerunners into this market, offering access to free online videos since 2007. Unlike YouTube, which allows users to post and view videos, Hulu is primarily a video hosting service partnering with some of the biggest names in the entertainment industry such as FOX, NBC Universal, MGM, Sony Pictures Television, and Warner Brothers to bring professional content to avid viewers.

Consumers who subscribe to the service (www.hulu.com) have the luxury of viewing full episodes of TV shows, both current and classic, and full-length movies, from their desktops. The company's stated mission is to help people find and enjoy the world's premium video content when, where, and how they want it.[1]

In 2010, in an effort to boost and maintain its viability as a business enterprise, Hulu incorporated a subscription model, Hulu Plus (www.hulu.com/plus), to complement its current freely available ad-supported model, Hulu.com. Hulu Plus streaming videos can be viewed from multiple devices including Blu-ray players, gaming consoles, set-top boxes, iPads, iPhones, and Android smartphones. Hulu has offices in Los Angeles, New York, Chicago, Seattle, and Beijing.

Features

Search Videos and Movies

On the main page (www.hulu.com), Hulu's search feature helps users find any premium video online even if it is not directly available on Hulu.com. Users can select specific categories to search, such as action and adventure, classics, news and information, reality and game shows, talk and interview, or the web. Within channels there are options to view clips, full-length episodes, and closed captioned content. Filtered searches are available for video content by clicking on tabs to view Most Popular, Recently Added, Recommendations, Favorites, or Spotlight Videos.

Customize Your Viewing Experience

Hulu gives users the ability to customize their viewing experience online. All videos are viewed within Hulu-branded, embeddable video players. Viewers are offered options in the player to dim the lights so they can focus on a show or movie, watch in full screen, pop out the video player and place it anywhere on the viewing screen, and resize the player. Hulu will also automatically adjust a video's stream to optimize any internet connection.

Share Videos and Movies

While viewing movies within the Hulu video player, viewers can email videos to a friend, embed a full movie or an episode of a hit show to blogs and personal websites, or post videos to social networking and bookmarking sites like Facebook, Myspace, Twitter, Delicious, and Reddit. With Hulu's editing tool, viewers are allowed to customize the start and end points of videos before sharing them within their personal network of friends.

Use Social Networking Functions

While viewing videos, users can choose to add reviews, rate videos, join a discussion about the video, and add tags (user-generated labels that assist like-minded viewers in finding related videos). There is also the availability of a video panel widget, which allows viewers to choose a screen design (vertical or horizontal) or thumbnails and copy the widget code to a personal website or blog.

Queue Favorite Videos

With Hulu's queuing feature, viewers can watch the videos at specific, designated times. There is also an option for adjusting the playback order.

Subscribe to Favorite Shows

Viewers can choose to subscribe to an episode or clip by clicking on the Subscribe button. Based on these subscription choices all new related videos are automatically dropped into a viewers' queue.

How Cybrarians Can Use This Resource

Augmenting Physical Library Collections With Streaming Content

Conventional wisdom dictates that in these tough economic times, libraries should consider streaming-content providers such as Netflix (www.netflix.com) and Hulu as credible options to augment physical video collections. There have been a number of arguments for and against this model, with most of the arguments against this option understandably being offered by the content providers.

Three noteworthy position pieces on this subject must be mentioned. The first is an article in *Library Trends*, "Netflix in an Academic Library: A Personal Case Study," in which author Ciara Healy admitted that "Netflix turned out to be an excellent, cost-effective solution" for her library.[2] The other is a guest blog post on the Tame the Web blog by Rebecca Fitzgerald, an acquisitions librarian at the Scheele Memorial Library, Concordia College, New York, who also commented on the fact that Netflix subscriptions "saved [her library] an enormous amount of money (around $3,000)."[3] And finally, Sarah

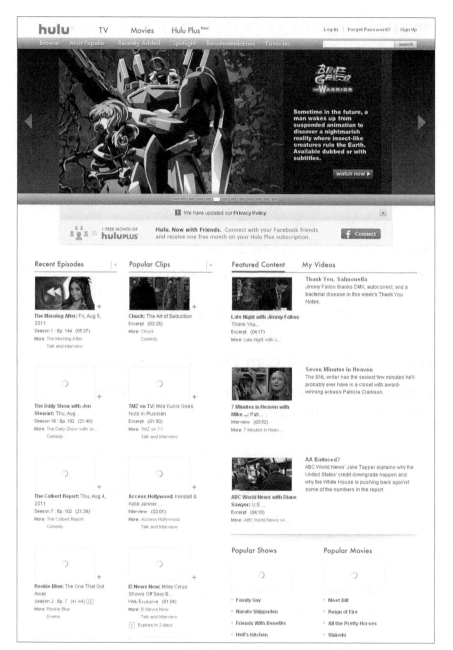

Hulu features recent episodes, popular clips, popular shows, popular movies, and other viewing categories.

Long's podcast Longshots featured a discussion titled "Is the Netflix Model the New Library Model?"[4] in which Sean Reinhart, director of the Hayward Public Library in California, talked about the launch of Hayward's Fines-Free Library Loan program. This program is based on the Netflix model where for a low monthly fee, library users have the benefit of unlimited loan periods and no fines.

Given these current trends in innovative, patron-driven services, Hulu, like Netflix, is a platform that can be used to support core curricula materials in many academic libraries. There are hundreds of documentaries and educational videos available on the free version of the service that can be promoted by libraries, and patrons could watch these live streams instantly from their computers, laptops, or mobile devices.

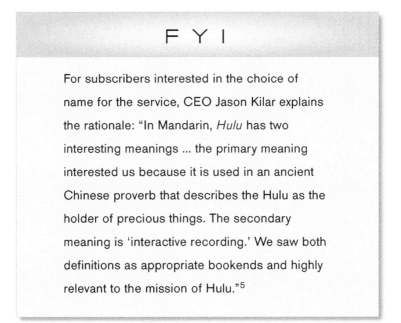

F Y I

For subscribers interested in the choice of name for the service, CEO Jason Kilar explains the rationale: "In Mandarin, *Hulu* has two interesting meanings ... the primary meaning interested us because it is used in an ancient Chinese proverb that describes the Hulu as the holder of precious things. The secondary meaning is 'interactive recording.' We saw both definitions as appropriate bookends and highly relevant to the mission of Hulu."[5]

Endnotes

1. "About," Hulu, www.hulu.com/about (accessed August 10, 2011).

2. Ciara Healy, "Netflix in an Academic Library: A Personal Case Study," *Library Trends* 58. 3 (2010): abstract.

3. Rebecca Fitzgerald, "Using Netflix at an Academic Library," Tame the Web, September 9, 2010, www.tametheweb.com/2010/09/09/using-netflix-at-an-academic-library-a-ttw-guest-post-by-rebecca-fitzgerald (accessed August 10, 2011).

4. "Is the Netflix Model the New Library Model?" Longshots Podcasts, April 28, 2010, www.librarybeat.org/longshots/play/230 (accessed August 10, 2011).

5. Jason Kilar, "What's in a Name?" Hulu Blog, May 13, 2008, blog.hulu.com/2008/05/13/meaning-of-hulu (accessed August 10, 2011).

34

Internet Archive
digital library
www.archive.org

Overview

Today, it is difficult to imagine a world without the internet. Since its adoption in the 1990s, the internet has been inextricably woven into every facet of our lives: influencing our communication patterns, the way we seek information, the way we think, and in some instances the way we act. Recognizing the intrinsic value of the internet, and the need to preserve it for present and future generations, the Internet Archive (IA) project was initiated to develop a nonprofit digital internet library.

The project goal, as stated on its About Us page, is to offer "permanent access for researchers, historians, scholars, people with disabilities, and the general public, to historical collections that exist in digital format."[1] This overarching mission of preserving, protecting, and providing access has its roots in an attempt to prevent a repeat of past failings to secure and save records of rich cultural and technological significance. This goal is reminiscent of the unfortunate demise of the Library of Alexandria, the ancient center of learning in Egypt that contained a copy of every book in the world, which was purportedly burned to the ground during the Roman conquest of Egypt in 48 B.C.E.[2]

Since its founding in 1996, IA has been able to archive complete snapshots of all webpages on every website created since that time. Users can search this database of 150 billion archived webpages using the Wayback Machine (www.archive.org/web/web.php), accessible from the homepage (www.archive.org). Access is also provided to collections in varying formats including ebooks, moving images, live music, audio recordings, and software. Much of the success of the project has been attributed to collaborations with institutions such as the

Library of Congress, the Smithsonian, and the web information company Alexa (www.alexa.com).

Features

➤ The IA Wayback Machine allows researchers to view archived versions of websites from as early as 1996. To view an archived page, access the Wayback machine (www.archive.org/web/web.php), type in a URL, select a date range, and then begin surfing an archived version of the website. To have a website archived, users can view instructions at the Open Directory Project (www.dmoz.org/docs/en/add.html) and at Alexa (www.alexa.com).

➤ From the main search page (www.archive.org), researchers can search all of the databases listed below by keywords, by browsing defined categories, or by advanced search:

  • Moving Image Archive: This library contains digital movies and videos uploaded by IA users, ranging from classic full-length films to daily alternative news broadcasts to cartoons and concerts. Many of these videos are available for free download.

  • IA Live Music Archive: The IA teamed up with etree.org (a community committed to providing the highest quality live concerts in a lossless, downloadable format) to preserve and archive the live concerts in this database. All music in this collection is from trade-friendly artists and should be used for noncommercial purposes only. There is the option to download a free music widget (www.widgetbox.com/ widget/internet-archive-free-music), which streams the RSS feed of new live music stored in the IA database on a blog or website.

  • Audio Archive: This library contains free digital recordings of alternative news programs, concerts, radio shows, book and poetry readings, and original music uploaded by IA users. Many of the audio recordings are available for free download.

- Ebook and Texts Archive: There are more than 2 million items here. The selections are varied and comprise fiction, popular books, children's books, historical texts, and academic books. These are available for download in the following formats: PDF, EPUB, Kindle, DAISY, and DjVu.

- Software Archive: This library was created to preserve and provide access to rare, legally downloadable software titles and background information on those titles. The collection includes a broad range of software-related materials such as shareware, freeware, video news releases about software titles, speed runs, previews, and skill replays of various software games.

How Cybrarians Can Use This Resource

Expanding Ebook Collections

In an era where libraries are actively expanding ebook offerings, the Internet Archive project offers a unique opportunity for libraries to augment print collections by providing access to this wide-ranging digital library.

Providing Access to Titles for the Print-Disabled

The IA also provides free access to more than 1 million books available in a specially designed format to support those who are blind, dyslexic, or otherwise visually impaired. These books have been scanned from hard copies and digitized into the DAISY (Digital Accessible Information System) format—a specialized format used by people with disabilities for easy navigation. DAISY files can then be downloaded to devices that translate the text and read the books aloud for the user to enjoy. These books can also be accessed from the Open Library webpage (www.openlibrary.org/subjects/accessible_book).

The Internet Archive provides access to digital collections
in varying formats including ebooks, moving images,
live music, audio recordings, and software.

Partnerships With Evendors

By visiting IA's sister project, the Open Library website (www.open library.org), patrons belonging to libraries with subscriptions to Overdrive's digital library collections can search for, find, and check out ebooks that are automatically returned after two weeks. Patrons will need to have a local library card to check out the book.

Volunteering to Contribute to the Open Library Project

The Open Library is a library project with the stated goal of providing a page on the web for every book published. The project began in November 2007 and now provides access to more than 20 million online records. This project is always seeking volunteers to edit existing records in the catalog by correcting errors, adding details (summaries, bibliographic information, book size, format, number of pages), as well as adding new book titles. Cybrarians wishing to volunteer and contribute to the project can sign up from the main page.

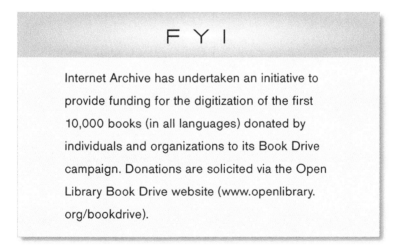

FYI

Internet Archive has undertaken an initiative to provide funding for the digitization of the first 10,000 books (in all languages) donated by individuals and organizations to its Book Drive campaign. Donations are solicited via the Open Library Book Drive website (www.openlibrary.org/bookdrive).

Endnotes

1. "About the Internet Archive," Internet Archive, www.archive.org/about/about.php (accessed August 10, 2011).

2. "Library of Alexandria," Wikipedia, en.wikipedia.org/wiki/Library_of_Alexandria (accessed August 10, 2011).

35

iTunes U
audio and video hosting service
www.apple.com/education/itunes-u

Overview

With a tagline reading "learn anything, anytime, anywhere," Apple's iTunes U is hoping to bring the power of the iTunes Store to education. Educational institutions such as Yale, Stanford, UC Berkeley, Oxford, Cambridge, and MIT are taking advantage of Apple's offer to distribute digital content from the iTunes U platform (www.apple.com/education/itunes-u) to faculty, students, and lifelong learners.

This platform contains educational content for everyone. Students can view lectures (video, audio, and screencast courses), laboratory demonstrations, and historical movie footage with no restrictions on time or place. Professors can use audio and video content from museums, universities, cultural institutions, and public television stations to supplement their lectures. ITunes U is also being used to distribute schedules, syllabi, notes, maps, and other information that is always invaluable to both students and faculty. For lifelong learners, there are public iTunes U sites with content such as foreign language lessons, audiobooks, oral history interviews, podcasts, and virtual tours created by notable institutions such as the Library of Congress, Smithsonian, Metropolitan Museum of Art, and U.S. Holocaust Memorial Museum.

The growing popularity of iTunes U sites and the increasing usage by faculty and students may be attributed to the simple fact that Apple leverages the familiar interface of the iTunes Store, which consumers of Apple's suite of products—laptops, iPods, iPads, iPhones—are accustomed to using. Add to this the low learning curve for persons wishing to immediately access digital content on the platform and the fact that not much technical expertise is required to add digital content, and one can immediately understand the lure of the service.

At the time of this writing, there were more than 350,000 free lectures, videos, films, and other resources worldwide housed on iTunes U, and more than 800 universities with active iTunes U sites. Enrollment to the program is available online (www.apple.com/education/itunes-u/apply.html).

Features

➤ Access to iTunes U content is available within the Apple iTunes Store interface and so may be familiar to users who regularly download content from this source. To access iTunes U sites, potential users must first download the latest version of iTunes from Apple's website (www.apple.com/itunes/download).

➤ The iTunes U interface is intuitive and easily navigable. The majority of the sites have been custom built by enrolled institutions and personalized with their branded logos, but the basic features are much the same.

➤ Users can access content (audio and video lectures, screencasts, podcasts, oral interviews, movies, audiobooks) by using the one of the following search options:

  • Browse subject areas in standard categories such as business, engineering, fine arts, health and medicine, history, humanities, language and literature, math, sciences, social sciences, society, technology, and education.

  • Browse a list of Staff Favorites and a list of Featured Providers (notable colleges and universities that have added content to the platform).

  • Browse a list of the top downloads.

➤ The iTunes U Quicklinks on the main page provides quick access to

- An A–Z directory of universities and colleges with hosted content

- Access to content from external organizations (Beyond the Campus link), such as the British Museum, Carnegie Institution for Science, Higher Education TV Channel, Poynter Institute, and Royal Opera House

- A K–12 list of resource organizations

- iTunes U power, or advanced search, with built-in filters for restricting searches by title, name of institution, or format (music, movies, TV shows, apps, books, podcasts)

➤ Enrolled institutions have full control over public or private access to data and can decide whether to make iTunes U content available only to members of their immediate community (internal access only via password protection) or to the community at large (public access).

➤ Users can download content on the go, directly to their iPhone, iPad, or iPod Touch devices. Media formats supported include MP3, MPEG-4, PDF, and EPUB.

How Cybrarians Can Use This Resource

Promoting Access to a Free Platform of Digital Resources

Cybrarians can promote the iTunes U program to educators at their institutions, advocating some of the immediate benefits:

➤ Placing your institution at the forefront of technology in education

➤ Giving faculty and students a chance to experiment with creating and posting digital online content in a shared virtual environment

➤ Sharing and distributing the digital content created with other peer institutions and lifelong learners, so that all can

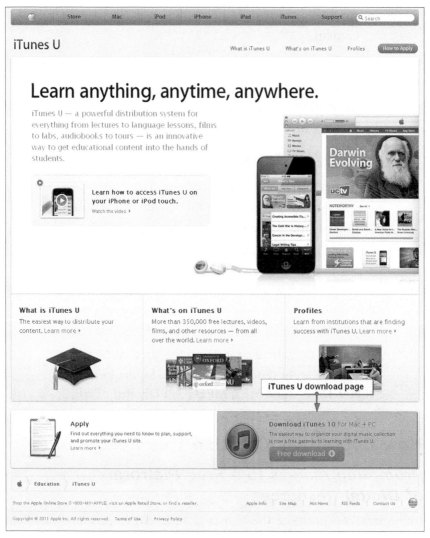

iTunes U can be downloaded from the Apple website.

benefit from your institution's virtual archive of knowledge and information

➤ Extending and enhancing students' learning by reaching students wherever they are in their social spaces

F Y I

Institutions interested in becoming iTunes U content providers must first complete an online application form (www.apple.com/education/itunes-u/apply.html). If the application is approved, the institution will have immediate access to the tools needed to create an iTunes U site.

36

Jing
productivity tool
www.techsmith.com/jing

Overview

Jing is a freely available, downloadable screencasting program that allows users to capture and share images or videos visible on their computer screens. Using Jing as a collaborative and visual tool, users have discovered that working together on projects, giving feedback, and sharing information are less painstaking tasks.

The program's appeal as on-the-go software lies in the fact that when downloaded, the Jing Sun Launcher icon is discreetly but strategically placed on the user's desktop and is always available for immediate capture of what is currently being viewed onscreen. Jing utilizes Screencast.com, its media-hosting service, to securely host all captured content. When content is captured, Screencast.com returns a URL link. This link is copied to a clipboard and can be retrieved later and shared with friends by pasting it into online conversations, email, chat, online forums, or social networks such as Facebook, Flickr, Myspace, and Twitter. Jing can also be configured to return HTML embed code for captured images and videos, and this code can be inserted directly into a blog, website, or wiki.

Jing is just one of the many screen capture and recording products offered by TechSmith (www.techsmith.com). Snagit and Camtasia Studios are other popular applications. The company was founded in 1987 by William Hamilton and is based in Michigan.

Jing advertises instant screenshots and screencasts that are
created using the Jing Sun Launcher icon on the user's desktop.

Features

➤   The software is available for download (Windows and Mac
    versions are supported) from Techsmith's website (www.tech
    smith.com/download/jing).

➤   The Jing Sun Launcher has two main functions: to initiate
     content Capture and to store copies of captured content as
     History. Users can also set and change preferences such as
     capture hotkey set up, hide the Jing Sun icon, customize
     sharing options, and choose the format of the video captured.

➤   Jing facilitates the creation of short videos or screencasts (up
     to 5 minutes of screen recording) with built-in narration for
     clarity. Images and text can be enhanced by annotating with
     arrows, notes, and comments.

➤   Jing's free version includes 2 GB of storage and bandwidth.
     Added functions of the Pro or Premium version include
     webcam video captures, high-quality video format, and direct
     upload to YouTube and other video sharing platforms.

➤   Jing integrates with TechSmith's other products Snagit and
     Camtasia. Within Jing, users can click on the Edit in Camtasia
     Studio or Edit in Snagit buttons, and captures are sent
     directly to these applications, allowing users to take advantage
     of the advanced editing and sharing capabilities of these two
     products to enhance content captured in Jing.

➤   Jing Learning Center (www.techsmith.com/learn/jing)
     provides support for first-time users by way of practical
     walkthrough tutorials, online manuals, video tutorials, and
     the Jing blog (blog.jingproject.com). A monthly online
     newsletter provides regular updates on new features, tips for
     using Jing, and user success stories.

How Cybrarians Can Use This Resource

Productivity Tool and Support for Library instruction

From the main webpage, hotlinks are provided to document Jing users'
success stories (www.techsmith.com/jing/uses). Innovative uses of the
software include:

➤   Collaborating on shared projects

➤   Sharing snapshots of documents

➤ Narrating online tutorials for library instruction

➤ Capturing a system-related problem on a computer and providing screenshots to a library system support team or vendor

➤ Demonstrating to users how to use a library resource or service using virtual reference chat

➤ Providing feedback on class assignments

➤ Posting images and videos on the library's Facebook page or Twitter account

F Y I

The name Jing was finally decided on by a core team of developers and designers after much discussion and suggested alternatives such as Kamikaze, Arcturus, and Orange Crush.[1]

Endnote

1. "How Did Jing Get Its Name?" Jing Blog, blog.jingproject.com/2010/02/how-did-jing-get-its-name.html (accessed August 10, 2011).

37

Justin.tv
live video broadcasting service
www.justin.tv

Overview

Justin.tv is a platform available for creating and broadcasting streaming live video to a global audience. All you need to create a channel and start a live broadcast on Justin.tv is a camcorder or webcam hooked up to any internet-connected computer (Windows, Mac, or Linux); an up-to-date browser such as Internet Explorer, Firefox, or Safari; and the latest version of Adobe Flash Player installed. With Justin.tv, you can share your broadcast and chat in real-time within seconds with a global audience.

Live video broadcasts have been shown to have proven success and are put to good use in both the corporate and political worlds to motivate a client base, promote new products and services, appeal for volunteer help, solicit donations to a charitable cause, or launch grassroots advocacy campaigns. A similar pattern of usage is evident with Justin.tv, as artists use the service to promote their work, comedians and entertainers use it to host interactive talk shows, musicians and DJs broadcast music and chat with their fans, and everyday folks use the medium to chat with friends and share their life stories.

Founded in 2006, the service is headquartered in San Francisco. Justin.tv viewers watch more than 300 million videos every month.[1] Justin.tv Android and iPhone apps were recently developed to empower users to easily create and share high-quality live video streams with their friends and social networks.

Features

➤ Sign up for an account to immediately start live broadcasting on the Justin.tv homepage (www.justin.tv) by following the steps outlined below:

1. Complete the online form with required information for username, password, date of birth, and email.

2. Click the Allow button to give Justin.tv access to your camera and microphone on your computer.

3. Add a title (140 characters or less) for the broadcast you would like to create.

4. A broadcast screen pops up to start the live broadcast. A URL link (for example, www.justin.tv/librarian#/w/ 416420624) is immediately available, and this can be shared with family, friends, or colleagues in an email, IM, blog, or personal website.

➤ For a live broadcast to be successful there must be a viewing audience. To garner a live audience, broadcasters can take advantage of the Justin.tv Facebook application to connect with and invite friends on their Facebook network to watch the live broadcast.

➤ The broadcast page can be customized and enhanced with the following features:

• Display a list of people whose broadcasts are similar to your interests and whom you wish to follow.

• Display a list of people who are following your live broadcast.

• Allow users to view your profile, which displays information about yourself and why you use Justin.tv.

• Click the Suggested User option, which allows you to follow videos recommended by Justin.tv.

- Access a chat room, which can be customized by changing chat color, adding time stamps, and choosing to hide chat or display as a pop-out window.

- Set a Twitter hashtag (for example, *#web 2.0*) that will be appended to all Tweets from your channel.

- Add tags or one-word descriptors to describe a broadcast and enable users to find the channel through keyword searches.

- Select language of choice for channels and set time zones.

- Indicate if the channel will stream mature content, or add an access code to make the channel private.

- Search by keywords in a central search box on the main page and get immediate access to live videos. Alternatively, there is the search option on the Live Channels tab to browse subject categories such as sports, social, news and events, entertainment, and science and technology.

Justin.tv homepage allows you to share your broadcasts and chat in real-time within seconds with a global audience.

How Cybrarians Can Use This Resource

Support for Library Programs and Professional Development

➤ Host live broadcasts of special library events such as Banned Books Week, National Library Week, Teen Read Week, National Library Workers Day, and in-house library programming activities.

➤ Host live interviews with local authors and community leaders.

➤ Host live panel discussions on current topics of interest.

➤ Host live broadcasts to promote and publicize new services to patrons.

➤ Search Justin.tv for live broadcasts of library conferences, workshops, and other continuing education opportunities.

F Y I

The Justin.tv community wiki (community. justin.tv/mediawiki/index.php/Settings) is an invaluable resource for new users, containing all of the information you need to get started on creating live broadcasts.

Endnote

1. "About Justin.Tv," Justin.tv, www.justin.tv/p/about_us (accessed August 10, 2011).

38

Khan Academy
video sharing service
www.khanacademy.org

Overview

Khan Academy is a nonprofit organization on a mission to provide a free world-class education to anyone. Students, teachers, homeschoolers, and adult learners have all been extended an open invitation to use the organization's vast vault of educational resources, available free of charge to "to help you learn whatever you want, whenever you want, at your own pace."[1] This resource can easily be described as a one-stop shop learner's guide to browsing and discovering educational videos and practice exercises on the web.

The video library provides instant access to more than 2,400 videos on science topics such as biology, chemistry and physics, humanities playlists on finance and history, and K–12 math. For instructors and learners alike, these course offerings are considered palatable as they are served up in digestible chunks of 10–20 minutes each, as opposed to longer conventional teaching videos. Key concepts are delivered in a conversational—not textbook—tone and all videos, practice exercises, and individual assessments are readily accessible from any computer.

Lead by founder and executive director Salman Khan, team Khan Academy is trying its best "to improve the way the world learns ... using the technology [that] exists today ... to build the tools and resources every student deserves."[2] The service's headquarters is in Mountain View, California.

Features

➣ New users to the Khan Academy can visit the homepage (www.khanacademy.org) and log in to the resource using an existing Google or Facebook account. Signing in to the site as a learner or coach is encouraged, as it gives users the ability to track their progress and earn rewards in the form of points and badges. Learners under the age of 13 must request parents, teachers, or coaches to create an account on their behalf.

➣ Once logged in, users have several options: They can browse or watch instructional videos, engage in practice exercises, coach, or contribute to an outreach or discussion group. Videos on the homepage are arranged in broad playlists or topical subject areas such as math (arithmetic, developmental math, algebra, geometry), science (biology, chemistry, physics, organic chemistry, cosmology and astronomy, computer science), humanities (history, finance), and test prep (SAT Math, GMAT, CAHSEE, California Standards Test).

➣ Access is provided to customizable self-paced learning tools, assessment or practice exercises, online help, personalized profiles, statistics for tracking progress, and rewards such as badges and points to encourage learning and measure progress.

➣ Once coaches, parents, or teachers have created individual profiles, they have immediate access to students' data, including a summary of class performance, and can view real-time class reports to assess students' progress and identify problematic areas.

➣ School administrators are encouraged to consider adopting this resource as a pilot in their school program and thus have the advantage of being selected for hands-on implementation, classroom visits, and direct collaboration with the Khan Academy Team (khanacademy.wufoo.com/forms/khan-academy-school-implementation-application).

➣ Access is also provided to a collection of interviews and

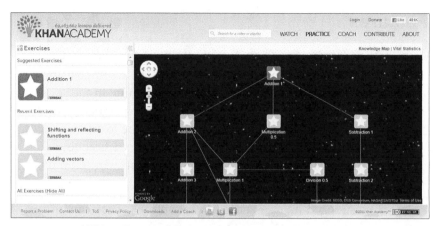

With a library of more than 2,400 videos covering
everything from arithmetic to physics, finance, and history,
Khan Academy is on a mission to help users learn whatever
they want, whenever they want, at their own pace.

presentations by the site's founder Salman Khan on forums
such as PBS NewsHour, CNN, Gates Notes, and TED 2011.

How Cybrarians Can Use This Resource

Reference and Research

Given the explosive growth in online content with millions of self-
guided instructional webpages to scour when searching for educational
resources, it makes sense that learners (all age groups, preschool to
adults) would find this resource an attractive alternative to conventional teaching videos and one that can provide a richer learning experience. School librarians may find this a useful resource to share with
K–12 teachers to reinforce instruction in math, science, and the
humanities. One possible assignment can be to ask students to create a
profile on the Khan Academy website and complete the practice test
relevant to the current teaching curriculum. Teachers can sign up and
monitor students' progress by viewing the online class reports. Use of
virtual and user friendly learning tools such as the knowledge map may
be a crafty way of driving students to collaborate with other students
and utilizing parents and teachers in the lifelong learning process.

F Y I

As a 501c3 not-for-profit organization, Khan Academy has received generous donations from the Bill and Melinda Gates Foundation (www.youtube.com/watch?v=UuMTSU9DcqQ) and won Google's Project 10^{100}, which was a call for ideas to change the world.[3]

Endnotes

1. Khan Academy homepage, www.khanacademy.org (accessed August 10, 2011).

2. "The Team," Khan Academy, www.khanacademy.org/about/the-team (accessed August 10, 2011).

3. "Project 10^{100} Winners," Google, www.project10tothe100.com (accessed August 10, 2011).

39

LibGuides
content management system
www.springshare.com/libguides

Overview

In a Web 2.0 world, where librarians are competing with the public perception that Google and Wikipedia are primary research tools, LibGuides is being promoted as libraries' "ace in the hole" content management tool, which has *finally* been developed to assist librarians in redefining and redeeming their roles as information superheroes, knowledge professionals, and info sages.

LibGuides's user base is expanding rapidly, and all library types (academic, public, special, and school libraries) are currently using this tool to create subject, course, and community guides. Libraries are also creating information portals to provide research assistance to clients, to promote information literacy, and to develop and maintain websites and intranets.

Librarians with minimal technical skills have the ability to integrate Web 2.0 functionalities such as web chat within subject guides, thus enabling patrons to ask for help in real time while doing research. Additionally, they can post updates on Twitter and embed LibGuides content in Facebook. Patrons can share their favorite LibGuides on any social networking site, including Facebook, Twitter, Digg, and Delicious. LibGuides-supplied widgets and APIs can be easily adapted by web developers and used to distribute content to websites, blogs, and courseware systems.

The LibGuides website has a free, fully functional LibGuides demo (demo.libguides.com) available for anyone to view the system in action. There is a subscription fee for full access to the resource. Prospective buyers can complete an online form (www.springshare.com/libguides/trial.html) to receive a quote for the service.

LibGuides offers a free, fully functional LibGuides demo site for prospective subscribers.

Features

The following is a list of LibGuides features, adapted from the LibGuides features page (www.springshare.com/libguides/features.html):

➤ The Post to LibGuides browser button allows librarians to add content to guides from anywhere on the web.

➤ Users can receive email alerts whenever new content is published in guides. These alerts are useful for patrons who wish to stay current in their specific field of interest.

➤ Customizable templates and style sheets are available, and these can be reused and shared with others in the LibGuides community.

➤ The availability and support for LibGuides widgets and APIs enable librarians and systems developers to promote the resource by embedding LibGuides content into webpages, blogs, and courseware pages.

> Integrated social networking and bookmarking functions are available for applications such as Twitter, Facebook, web chat, IM, Digg, and Delicious.

> LibGuides supports the creation of tags (keywords or descriptors), enabling patrons to search for and easily find information. Additionally, guides can be associated with any number of librarian-defined subject categories.

> The system allows the embedding of multimedia objects such as videos, RSS feeds, podcasts, and screencasts when guides are created.

> LibGuides provides full usage statistics, which are important to justify continued subscription to the service.

> To ensure that URL links are up-to-date, the system has a link checker, which automatically checks for broken links and creates a broken links report.

How Cybrarians Can Use This Resource

Promotion of Library Resources and Services

There are testimonies, reviews, and examples from libraries that have successfully implemented the service (www.springshare.com/libguides/reviews.html) on the LibGuides website. The immediate benefits for cybrarians wishing to implement LibGuides are:

> Distribution of library content and services outside of the library website to social networks and other platforms (Facebook, Twitter, blogs, courseware systems).

> Increased exposure and promotion of library resources and services. For example, Nova Southeastern University Libraries (Fort Lauderdale, Florida) participated in the university's 12th Annual Technology Fair and won first place in the professional category for their creative adaptations of CampusGuides for educational technology (support.springshare.com/2010/10/26/campusguides-transform-librarians-into-tech-innovators).

➤ Bringing the Library 2.0 experience to patrons.

➤ Web 2.0 technologies immediately accessible and usable for cybrarians, even those with minimal technical training.

F Y I

It is worth noting the availability of the free alternative open source Content Management System Library à la Carte (alacarte.library. oregonstate. edu), developed by the Oregon State University. This system enables librarians to easily and quickly create dynamic webpages that integrate Web 2.0 features such as chat and RSS feeds with traditional library content, such as catalogs and article databases.

40

Library Success
wiki
www.libsuccess.org

Overview

Meredith Farkas, author of *Social Software in Libraries* (Medford, NJ: Information Today, Inc., 2007), which is now considered a seminal work on Web 2.0 in libraries, and an honoree of *Library Journal*'s Movers and Shakers, created Library Success: A Best Practices Wiki as a one-stop shop for great ideas and information for all types of librarians. She explains the reasoning behind creating this wiki in the opening paragraph of the wiki's introduction: "All over the world, librarians are developing successful programs and doing innovative things with technology that no one outside of their library knows about. There are lots of great blogs out there sharing information about the profession, but there is no one place where all of this information is collected and organized. That's what we're trying to do."[1]

Editors are encouraged to write about innovations at their library or about other libraries that they consider a success. As a shared resource, this wiki not only provides a platform for sharing and contributing ideas; more importantly, it encourages librarians to replicate the successes of others.

As an open wiki, anyone can create an account to start adding or editing content. Topics are displayed in an alphabetized list of categories and include areas such as management and leadership, materials selection and collection maintenance, professional, programming, readers' advisory, reference services and information literacy, resource sharing, selling your library, and technology.

Features

➤ Users can create an account from the homepage (www.lib success.org) by adding a username, password, and email address. Newly registered members are encouraged to add information to their own user profile page and add it to the Wiki User List (www.libsuccess.org/index.php?title=Wiki_User_List).

➤ Recent changes made to the wiki can be viewed in one of two ways: by visiting the Recent Changes (www.libsuccess.org/index.php?title=Special:RecentChanges) page or subscribing to an RSS Feed for recent changes.

➤ As a collaborative project, there are guidelines for Wiki Use, with dire warnings against copyright infringement, vandalism, personal attacks, and product promotions (www.libsuccess.org/index.php?title=Guidelines).

➤ Users can add content to the alphabetized list of topics or choose to create a new category. Content within each category is arranged (with slight variations) in the following format:

• Success Stories

• Best Practice Guides

• Great Ideas

• Blogs/Websites to Watch

• Specific Blog Posts/Articles to Check Out

How Cybrarians Can Use This Resource

Collaborative Space for Promoting Library Innovations

For cybrarians, this resource is a unique one-stop shop and collaborative space to write about and promote recent innovations in your library. For example, in the Technology section there are links to libraries that have successfully implemented Web 2.0 technologies.

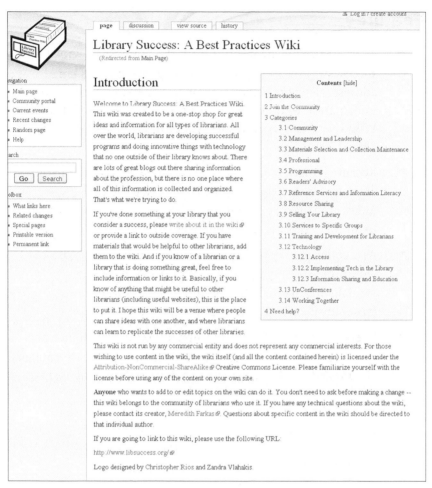

On the Library Success: A Best Practices Wiki introductory page, Meredith Farkas explains the reasoning behind its creation.

Under the section Materials Selection and Management, users can find guidelines for selecting materials and organizing and weeding library collections. Under Readers' Advisory, tips and tricks are offered for leading book groups, recommending books, and writing reviews. Advice offered for professional growth and development includes keeping up with the profession, looking for jobs, taking advantage of publishing and speaking opportunities, finding continuing education resources, and reading self-promotion tips for new librarians.

FYI

Library Success: A Best Practices Wiki is powered by MediaWiki, the same free software open source wiki package used to create Wikipedia.

Endnote

1. "Introduction," Library Success: A Best Practices Wiki, www.libsuccess.org/index. php?title=Library_Success:_A_Best_Practices_Wiki (accessed August 10, 2011).

41

LibraryThing
social cataloging service
www.librarything.com

Overview

A sneak peek at most cybrarians' wish lists would most likely reveal an entry for a personalized library, a place (virtual or brick and mortar) to catalog books they are currently reading, which are stored at home on bookshelves or at work. An added bonus would be to connect to a community of like-minded book lovers who are currently reading or have read books stored in this library.

LibraryThing, a social cataloging web application, brings this personalized online library to life. Using this application, you can enter what you are currently reading—or your whole library—and create a personalized online catalog. To add new books to your online catalog, simply enter titles, authors, or ISBN numbers in the search box on the LibraryThing homepage. LibraryThing then searches the "Library of Congress, all five national Amazon sites, and over 690 world libraries, and returns with precise book data."[1] For each title added to your catalog, you can add and edit bibliographic data, tag books with your own subjects, and use the Library of Congress and Dewey classification systems to organize your collection. This catalog is portable and can be accessed from any computer or mobile phone.

LibraryThing is much more than an online service for cataloging books; it is also a shared community of book lovers and a social space, sometimes described as "Myspace for books" or "Facebook for books." As a shared community, LibraryThing members can check out other user's libraries, see who has the books similar to what is held in their library, swap reading suggestions, discuss chapters, dissect plots, and make recommendations for the next best read. Since its creation in

August 2005, this shared community has cataloged more than 65 million books.[2]

Members who sign up for free accounts can catalog up to 200 books. A paid account ($10 for a year or $25 for a lifetime) allows you to catalog any number of books. Organizational accounts cost the same as personal accounts. LibraryThing creator Tim Spalding, a web developer and web publisher, is based in Portland, Maine.

Features

➤ Signing up for LibraryThing from the homepage (www.librarything.com) is relatively fast. All you need to do is create a member name and password, and choose your account type (personal or organizational). After signing up, new members can enter information (books in collections, reviews written, groups you have joined, favorite author, books currently reading, and membership information) in a profile page that will be shared with other members of the LibraryThing community.

➤ Once signed in, all members have access to a customizable personal homepage composed of modules. The modules are not static features of your homepage, as each can be reordered or removed by using LibraryThing's drag-and-drop functionality:

- Recently Added: Shows a list of recently added books in list or cover view

- Recent Recommendations: Shows new title recommendations based on your catalog of books, automatically generated or recommended by another LibraryThing member

- Connection News: Connects users with their network of friends and other LibraryThing members and notifies them when someone in their network makes changes to their catalog or adds, rates, or reviews books

- Local Events: Assigns users a local page (LibraryThing Local) that lists events in your area based on your current geographic location and includes events such as book launches and signings, book discussions, book fairs, and author visits to libraries and bookstores

- Talk (Forums): Allows LibraryThing members to voice their opinions and share ideas, and either join existing groups, which are aligned to talk forums, or create new groups to connect with other readers who share similar interests

- Your Zeitgeist: Provides statistics about your library and your activities on LibraryThing, including statistics on the number of books in your collection, the total number of tags used, the number of book covers available, and talk and group statistics

- Your Top Tags: Lists frequently used tags in your library using hyperlinks

- Members With Your Books: Lists LibraryThing members who own titles in your collection

- Tag Watch: Updates on tags applied by LibraryThing members

- LibraryThing News: Provides updated news from LibraryThing staff on new features, new projects, scheduled author interviews, and free advance copies of books

- From the Blogs: Links to the recent postings in the LibraryThing Blog and the Thing-ology blog

- Featured Authors: Promotes authors who are LibraryThing members

- Early Reviewers: Provides advance readers editions of upcoming books from select publishers in exchange for member reviews (LibraryThing Early Reviewers program)

- Member Giveaway: Lists the book titles LibraryThing members are giving away for free to members who are willing to review these books

- Author Chats: Allows users to pose questions to authors who appear live in the talk forums

- Recently Added by Other Members: Lists new books added to LibraryThing

- Popular This Month: Displays the current month's most popular books, based on the number of users adding the book to their catalog

- Hot Reviews: Displays reviews that are well-written and have received favorable comments by other LibraryThing members

- On This Day: Lists notable events that happened on this day in history, obtained from the LibraryThing Common Knowledge database where members contribute interesting data and facts about books in their catalogs

A comprehensive list of the features described above can be viewed at the LibraryThing wiki (www.librarything.com/wiki/index.php/HelpThing:Home).

How Cybrarians Can Use This Resource

➤ Register to become a member of the LibraryThing Early Reviewers program (www.librarything.com/wiki/index.php/Early_Reviewers), and review advance copies of new titles. As a bonus, reviewers receive a free copy of the book reviewed.

➤ Consider purchasing the LibraryThing for Libraries (LTFL) subsystem to integrate LibraryThing's social data into your catalog. LTFL will immediately enhance your OPAC with new content and functionalities such as tag-based browsing, viewable and clickable tag clouds, book recommendations, ratings, reviews, and access to a virtual bookshelf. A list of

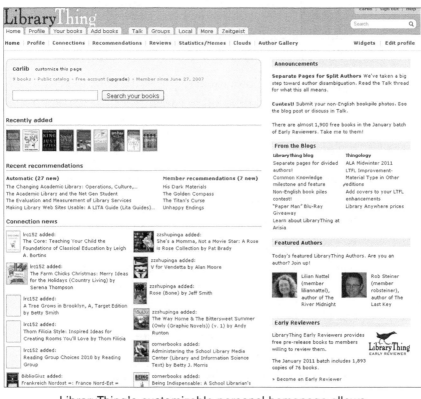

LibraryThing's customizable personal homepage allows
users to interact with modules that can be reordered or removed
by using LibraryThing's drag-and-drop functionality.

libraries that have implemented this service is maintained on
the LibraryThing website (www.librarything.com/wiki/index.
php/LTFL:Libraries_using_LibraryThing_for_Libraries).

➤ Use a LibraryThing widget (www.librarything.com/widget) to
display new books or featured books on your library's website
or blog.

➤ Add your library to LibraryThing Local (www.librarything.
com/local), where you can add your library as a venue,
including information such as library name, address,
telephone number, hours of operation, website, and a photo.
Also add information about upcoming events (book launches

and signings, book discussions, book fairs, and author visits to libraries and bookstores).

➤ Libraries with small collections can use LibraryThing as an online catalog for their collection.

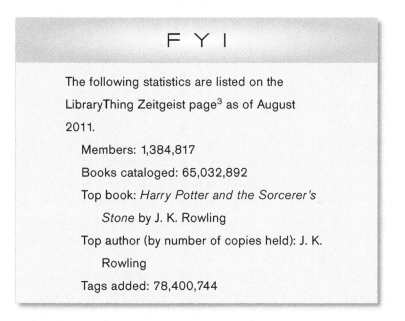

F Y I

The following statistics are listed on the LibraryThing Zeitgeist page[3] as of August 2011.

Members: 1,384,817

Books cataloged: 65,032,892

Top book: *Harry Potter and the Sorcerer's Stone* by J. K. Rowling

Top author (by number of copies held): J. K. Rowling

Tags added: 78,400,744

Endnotes

1. "LibraryThing Press Information," LibraryThing, www.librarything.com/press (accessed August 10, 2011).
2. "Zeitgeist Overview," LibraryThing, www.librarything.com/zeitgeist (accessed August 10, 2011).
3. Ibid.

42

Library 2.0
social network
www.library20.org

Overview

The concept of Library 2.0 is a direct spin-off of the term *Web 2.0*, and follows some of the same underlying principles. The term was first coined by Michael Casey, on his blog LibraryCrunch,[1] and has been given much mileage and discussion by Michael Stephens in the library literature, conferences, and his blog Tame the Web.[2] At the most basic level, a definition of *Library 2.0* would read something like this: a library modeled on Web 2.0 technologies where emphasis is placed on user-centered change and participation in the creation of content and community-based services.

The social network Library 2.0 was developed in response to the desire to continue this discussion on Library 2.0 outside the professional literature, specifically for librarians and other information professionals interested in being part of a forum with continuous conversations about the need for and relevance of Library 2.0. Powered by Ning (www.ning.com; see Chapter 55)—a platform for creating social networks—this network was initiated by Bill Drew in early 2007 and is currently maintained by Steve Hargadon.

Librarians and others with an interest in Library 2.0 are encouraged to join the network by signing up from the homepage (www.library20. org) and writing a short blurb about themselves on the Introductions page. The network is moderated and all members must be approved.

Features

The following features are all accessible from the Library 2.0 homepage:

➤ Links to other valuable networks such as Teacher Librarian Ning, Library 2.0 in other languages, and Classroom 2.0 are available.

➤ Members can view and add events (library conferences, fundraisers, book discussions, exhibitions) into an online form, and upload photos that display on the homepage.

➤ Network members create daily postings on a variety of topics.

➤ There is a photostream of current members in the network. Clicking on these photos provides access to a full member profile.

➤ All network members can create a personalized My Page.

➤ There is a link on the homepage to more than 900 forum discussions, arranged in categories covering subject areas such as academic libraries, content management systems, Google, Facebook, and online identity.

➤ Users can link from the homepage to blog postings.

Library 2.0 allows new users to join the network
by signing up and then writing a short blurb about themselves.

➤   Users can use a widget to create a Library 2.0 badge and embed the code in a blog or webpage.

How Cybrarians Can Use This Resource

Current Awareness Service

For cybrarians who maintain a professional interest in the topics Web 2.0 and Library 2.0, this is a great network to join in order to keep updated with new concepts, innovative services, new publications, and training opportunities. There are opportunities to join the ongoing conversations in the forums and blogs and to add your voice and record your thoughts on relevant issues.

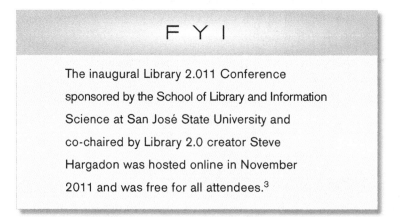

F Y I

The inaugural Library 2.011 Conference sponsored by the School of Library and Information Science at San José State University and co-chaired by Library 2.0 creator Steve Hargadon was hosted online in November 2011 and was free for all attendees.[3]

Endnotes

1. Michael Casey, "Working Towards a Definition of Library 2.0," LibraryCrunch, October 21, 2005, www.librarycrunch.com/2005/10/working_towards_a_definition_o.html (accessed August 10, 2011).

2. Tame the Web blog, www.tametheweb.com (accessed August 10, 2011).

3. "2.011 Conference," Library 2.0, www.library20.com/page/2011-conference (accessed August 10, 2011).

43

LinkedIn
social network
www.linkedin.com

Overview

It is often said that your professional network of trusted contacts gives you an added advantage in your career path and should be considered one of your more valuable assets. In a global village with increasing connectivity, LinkedIn, a professional network with a stated mission of connecting the world's professionals to make them more productive and successful, has already connected more than 100 million professionals in more than 200 countries to their trusted contacts.[1]

Professionals joining the network create a profile that summarizes their professional expertise and accomplishments. They then attempt to build their personal network connections by inviting trusted contacts to join LinkedIn. Given time, this network expands exponentially, linking you to past and present colleagues, friends, classmates, qualified professionals, and experts in your field of endeavor. Eventually, your network becomes a valuable asset as it publicizes information about you as a professional, putting you in contact with potential employers and clients and giving you a forum to exchange knowledge, ideas, and opportunities.

The LinkedIn basic service is free. There is the option to purchase an upgraded or premium account with more tools for making connections to a wider network of professionals. The service, currently headquartered in Mountain View, California, was officially launched on May 5, 2003, hence the affectionate referral by employees to Cinco de LinkedIn. It is currently available in English, French, German, Italian, Portuguese, Spanish, Russian, Turkish, and Romanian.

Features

➤ Once signed up for a LinkedIn account from the homepage (www.linkedin.com), LinkedIn members set up a profile, which helps establish their professional identity online. In the online profile form provided, members can add information such as current and past positions, schools and colleges attended, telephone number, address, birth date, and marital status. Additionally, users can add personal websites, Twitter account information, a personal summary, specialties in their field of interest, groups and associations involved in, and honors and awards received, as well as solicit recommendations from their network.

➤ New members have immediate access to a personalized LinkedIn homepage or professional dashboard that provides an overview (network update) of what is going on in their network and allows members to view their latest messages, read current company news, and browse the job offerings that match their interests.

➤ There are search boxes on all LinkedIn pages with pull-down menus to enter keyword searches filtered by broad categories (people, jobs, answers, groups, or postings in your inbox).

➤ The following LinkedIn Applications from third-party clients can be added to enrich profiles and homepages:

- LinkedIn polls (to collect survey data)

- SlideShare presentations (to upload and share presentations)

- My Travel, by TripIt, Inc. (to view where your LinkedIn network is traveling and share your upcoming trips)

- Events by LinkedIn (to search and find professional events)

- Blog Link by SixApart (to connect your blog to your LinkedIn profile)

- Reading List by Amazon (to share books you are currently reading with other LinkedIn members)

- LinkedIn Groups Directory (to stay informed and keep in touch with people who share your interests by creating a group or joining an existing group at www.linkedin. com/groups)

- Google Presentation (to upload a PowerPoint presentation to your LinkedIn profile)

➤ Members have the option of quickly accessing LinkedIn from anywhere on the web by installing a browser toolbar available for Internet Explorer and Firefox.

➤ Technical support is provided by way of videos, screenshots, and FAQs for members wishing to learn more about LinkedIn features.

➤ Members can access network updates, view profiles, and search the service by using LinkedIn's mobile applications. Free apps are currently available for the BlackBerry, iPhone, and Palm Pre. A mobile website (m.linkedin.com) is easily accessible from any mobile browser.

➤ LinkedIn works with Twitter, and members can tweet LinkedIn statuses to Twitter followers or automatically post tweets as their LinkedIn status.

How Cybrarians Can Use This Resource

Developing a Professional Network

Personal networks created in LinkedIn profiles are discoverable by most search engines, and many professionals have used the network to their advantage to leverage career success by showcasing and sharing their skills and talents with a global audience. LinkedIn members have posted success stories about their experiences on the website (press.linkedin.com/success-stories). Here are some of the advantages of creating a personal network on LinkedIn:

LinkedIn connects more than 100 million professionals
in more than 200 countries to trusted contacts.

➤ Control your professional identity online.

➤ Publicize information about yourself as a professional such as current place of employment, educational background, recommendations from colleagues, publications, and research interests.

➤ Access a virtual meeting place where you will meet potential clients, service providers, and subject experts in your field of interest.

➤ Facilitate collaboration on projects (data gathering, sharing files, and solving problems) with colleagues.

➤ Host discussions to gain insights and share ideas with like-minded professionals in a private group setting.

➤ Discover network connections that can help you in your career path.

➤ Post and distribute job listings to find the best talent for your organization (administrators only).

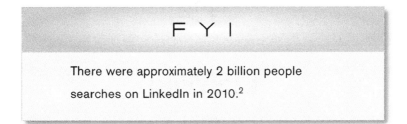

F Y I

There were approximately 2 billion people searches on LinkedIn in 2010.[2]

Endnotes

1. "About Us," LinkedIn, press.linkedin.com/about (accessed August 10, 2011).
2. Ibid.

44

LISWiki
wiki
www.liswiki.org

Overview

Wikis, when first developed, were somewhat of a novelty. The word itself (*wiki* is the Hawaiian word for *fast*) was alien to many, having never been encountered in the library lingua franca. Unfolding the mystery of a new and unfamiliar tool to librarians, the LISWiki project was launched on June 30, 2005, "to give the library community a chance to explore the usefulness of Wikis."[1]

The developers of LISWiki are quick to note that LISWiki was not intended to replace or detract from Wikipedia (an online free encyclopedia that anyone can edit, covered in Chapter 89), or house an authoritative library and information science compendium of articles. Instead it should be viewed as a "niche encyclopedia covering library-related issues."[2] LISWiki uses the same MediaWiki software used by Wikipedia as its foundation.

All library and information professionals are encouraged to open an account and create or edit articles in their areas of expertise. At the time of this writing, there were 1,386 articles and calls for new contributions. There are warnings, however, that although this is a free, editable resource, contributions considered inaccurate, off-topic, or spam will not be accepted.

Features

➤ Contributors are encouraged to create an account to keep track of their edits by clicking the Create Account link on the homepage (www.liswiki.org) and completing the online form

LISWiki encourages all library and information
professionals to open an account and create
or edit articles in their areas of expertise.

with username, password, email, and real name (the latter
two are optional).

➤   On the homepage there are links to the following features:

- Hypertext links to View All Articles or Browse Articles are arranged alphabetically. Articles that have not been fully developed, or contain simple dictionary-type definitions, are referred to as stubs, or placeholder articles. Enhancing a stub article is a good place for new contributors to start working with LISWiki.

- On the left navigation menu, there are links to view Recent Changes or Random Pages.

- A search box allows users to perform keyword searches.

- A community news page provides regular updates for LISWiki contributors.

- The Articles of Interest section spotlights trending topics in libraries. The Areas for Development page lists articles targeted for enhancement.

How Cybrarians Can Use This Resource

Publishing Platform

Although still in the early stages of development, this subject-themed encyclopedia, when fully developed and established as an authoritative resource, can be used as a reference tool for knowledge and information about libraries, librarianship, and the field of library science. This is a resource that cybrarians can use to publish works of interest and relevance to the library community.

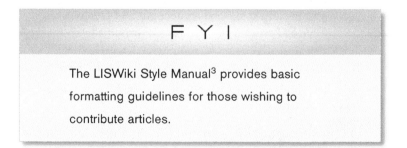

F Y I

The LISWiki Style Manual[3] provides basic formatting guidelines for those wishing to contribute articles.

Endnotes

1. "LISWiki: About," www.liswiki/wiki/LISWiki:About (accessed August 10, 2011).
2. Ibid.
3. "LISWiki Style Manual," www.liswiki.org/wiki/LISWiki:Style_Manual (accessed August 10, 2011).

45

LISZEN
search engine
www.liszen.com

Overview

LISZEN is a search engine devoted to library blogs that was launched on October 27, 2006, by its creator Garrett Hungerford. Initially, the service was launched with 530 searchable library blogs. Since then this figure has increased to more than 700 library blogs. A list of blogs searched by LISZEN can be found on the Library Zen & LISZEN wiki (www.libraryzen.com/wiki/index.php?title=LISZEN). This wiki is modeled on the MediaWiki software used by Wikipedia.

This list is regularly updated with library-related blogs and includes popular entries by renowned blogs and bloggers in the library world such as the ALA TechSource Blog, BlogJunction, Catalogablog, David Lee King, FRBR Blog, Information Wants to Be Free, Librarian in Black, Library 2.0, Stephen's Lighthouse, The Shifted Librarian, and Thingology. Any blogger can add a blog to LISZEN, but there is a caveat that it must be related to library and information science.

Features

> The LISZEN search box, the main feature on the search-engine's homepage (www.liszen.com), was designed using a very minimalist approach. It is powered by Google's Custom Search and is the front end for searching all the library-related blogs listed on the Library Zen Network wiki. Users can enter any search query, on any topic, and immediately receive a results page with blogs relevant to the topic searched. Searches can be further refined by limiting to

the following categories: individual blogs, special libraries, academic libraries, and school libraries.

➤ An online form for submitting a blog to LISZEN is available on the LISZEN homepage. Bloggers are required to input the following information: name, email, blog name, blog URL, blog language, and blog type (personal, academic, public, school, organization). After the form is completed, bloggers can visit the Library Zen Network wiki (www.libraryzen.com/wiki/index.php?title=LISZEN), create an account, and manually add their blogs to the existing list.

➤ There are LISZEN Browser plug-ins for users wishing to install this tool to Internet Explorer and Firefox.

➤ Users are encouraged to promote the library search engine by adding a LISZEN logo to their blogs or personal websites.

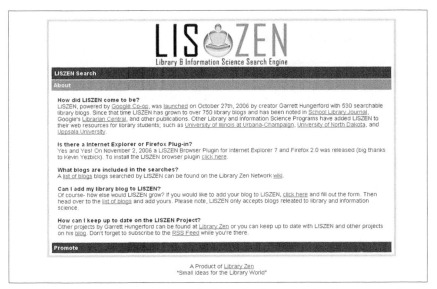

The LISZEN search box was designed using a minimalist approach and is the main feature on the search engine's homepage.

How Cybrarians Can Use This Resource

➤   Library and Information Science programs at the University of Illinois at Urbana–Champaign, the University of North Dakota, and Uppsala University have added LISZEN to their web resources for library students.

➤   Cybrarians interested in following trends on topics such as Library 2.0, ereaders, digital libraries, information literacy, and mobile OPACs can plug in their search query and LISZEN will return a list of blogs with relevant results.

F Y I

Other projects by LISZEN creator Garrett Hungerford can be found on his Library Zen page (www.libraryzen.com).

46

Livemocha
social network
www.livemocha.com

Overview

Livemocha is publicized as the world's largest online language-learning community. This award-winning web-based service seeks to upend rival language-learning software company Rosetta Stone by offering basic instructional tutorials and exercises in 35 different languages to more than 9 million members, from more than 195 countries around the world.[1]

The service's mass appeal can be attributed to its social approach to learning a language—entwining language course curricula with community interaction. A series of free and paid lessons online connect language learners with native speakers around the world in real time. This close-knit network of users generates an average of 35,000 speaking and writing exercises on a daily basis, with members actively engaged in reviewing and grading each other's work while practicing real-time conversation skills.

Livemocha's free basic series courses 101, 102, 201, and 202 are offered at beginner through intermediate levels, and include learn-and-review exercises as well as features such as chat, flashcards, and messaging. The premium course offerings, available with payment of a subscription fee, are also offered at beginner through intermediate levels, but these have additional, enhanced services such as grammar help, pronunciation tips, and sentence construction exercises. The travel crash course (free for members who invite three friends through referral) is ideal for travelers wishing to memorize and master useful words and phrases for an upcoming trip.

New members have access to universally known language offerings such as English, French, German, Italian, and Spanish. The service was established in 2007 and is based in Bellevue, Washington.

Features

➤   Membership is completely free to language learners who complete the online registration form on the service's homepage (www.livemocha.com). All members must provide the following information on the form: native language, language of choice to learn, language skill level, email address, and password.

➤   Livemocha members have access to a simple but effective approach to language learning, which combines online lessons (flash cards, videos, multiple-choice questions);

Livemocha offers a series of free and paid
lessons online to connect language learners with
native speakers around the world in real time.

writing, speaking, and listening exercises; and live online conversations with native speakers.

➤ Listening comprehension modules are enhanced with the use of audio, images, video, text, and speaking exercises purposely designed to improve pronunciation and allow practice in sentence construction. Native speakers can offer feedback on speaking and writing exercises for other language learners in the community. Reviewers can rate the submissions (1–5 rating scale) and leave comments on areas including grammar, word choice, spelling, and pronunciation.

➤ Learners are offered the option of a live recording of words and phrases learned in a lesson, and can submit this as an exercise for review to the Livemocha community.

➤ The Livemocha homepage was developed as a dashboard, enabling community users to create and view profiles, note courses taken, monitor their progress as students or contributions as teachers, access chat, and send messages via email. The service also has a Suggested Language Partners feature, which matches users who are learning a new language with a native speaker of that language.

How Cybrarians Can Use This Resource

Promoting Access to a Free Online Language-Learning Service

In a global community where there is growing interest in learning new language skills to facilitate commerce, open communication, an understanding of different cultures, and the availability of new technologies to provide quick online access to language-learning services such as Livemocha, it seems only natural for cybrarians to harness the benefits of this service.

Live links on the library's webpages (subject guides, continuing education, or new resources pages) can promote Livemocha as an easily accessible, affordable service, useful for patrons willing to teach their native language or learn and practice speaking a new language. Real-time testimonials about the benefits and usefulness of the service are posted and updated regularly on the Livemocha homepage (www.live mocha.com).

F Y I

Livemocha was named by Time.com as one of the 50 Best Websites of 2010.[2]

Endnotes

1. "About Us," Livemocha, www.livemocha.com/pages/about (accessed August 10, 2011).

2. "50 Best Websites 2010," Time.com, August 25, 2010, www.time.com/time/ specials/packages/article/0,28804,2012721_2012929_2012923,00.html (accessed August 10, 2011).

47

LucidChart
productivity tool
www.lucidchart.com

Overview

LucidChart is an online diagramming tool developed to create and publish customized flowcharts and other diagrams. Promoted as a tool using the HTML5 web standard and JavaScript, the developers maintain that LucidChart can work on any operating platform (Windows, Mac, and Linux); work from within most web browsers including Microsoft's Internet Explorer, Mozilla's Firefox, and Google's Chrome; and is accessible from any device with a browser (including the iPad). This flexibility between the different systems and programs gives LucidChart the distinction of having a broader reach and more advanced real-time collaboration capabilities than any other diagramming application on the market.

LucidChart subscribers have access to an intuitive interface for creating, printing, and publishing flowcharts, network diagrams, sitemaps, mind maps, wireframes, iPhone app mock-ups, and many other types of diagrams online. The application was built to be collaborative from the ground up, and it drives collaboration among team members on any shared project by enabling sharing of webpages, PDF documents, and images, and the ability to view changes being applied by others almost instantaneously.

In providing the diagramming tools to communicate ideas visually and more effectively, developers of this self-professed "canvas for the world's ideas" are strong in their conviction that drawing diagrams is a unique way to augment the learning process and an effective way of representing items and their relationships in a holistic, visual fashion. This vision has led to the offer of a free version of LucidChart (www.lucidchart.com/pages/education) to K–12 educators and students, and group rates and discounts to higher education institutions. The service was launched in December 2008 and is based in Provo, Utah.

Features

➣   New users can access the free version of the application on the website's homepage (www.lucidchart.com/users/register Level). This free option includes 25 MB storage for online documents, provisions for two additional collaborators, and a limit of 60 objects per document.

➣   Access is provided to an extensive library of objects and shapes for creating visuals. Users can also upload and add personal images and company logos to documents.

➣   Real-time collaboration is offered by way of shared mock-ups with project team members and the option to review, edit, and comment on work created online.

➣   An intuitive interface is available with preferences to draw on a blank canvas or use the sample templates provided, as well as the option to connect and disconnect objects easily by moving lines between the shapes. Drag-and-drop functionality is available if using shapes and figures from the program's toolbox, or if downloading images or documents directly from a computer.

➣   The built-in rich text editor allows for a dynamic color palette to restyle text and change colors and styles on objects drawn.

➣   Users can publish diagrams created to a wiki, corporate website, or personal blog. When changes are made to the diagram, the image is automatically updated on the published copy.

➣   LucidChart automatically saves and stores all versions of diagrams created with hourly backups to multiple data centers. Users can also easily save a personal copy of any diagram created as a print-quality PDF.

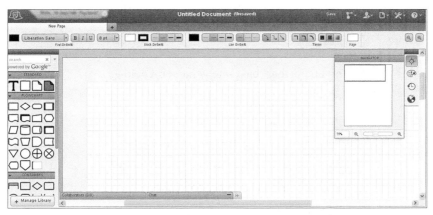

LucidChart has an intuitive interface for creating diagrams.

➤ The LucidChart community page provides access to featured examples from its community of users, access to discussion forums, Twitter feeds, and updated blog posts, as well as case studies from organizations using the product in the field.

How Cybrarians Can Use This Resource

Collaborative Online Diagramming Tool

LucidChart's community of users created a shared library of flowcharts and other diagrams, and this is regularly updated on the software website (www.lucidchart.com/community/examples/1/flowcharts). The categories and subject areas covered are exhaustive and detailed enough to assist cybrarians in their creation of flowcharts, mind maps, network diagrams, drawings, floor plans and room layouts, SWOT Analysis, and organizational charts as required within their libraries.

A regularly updated product review page (www.lucidchart.com/pages/reviews), written in multiple languages, provides analysis by the Web 2.0 community about the ease of use and collaborative nature of LucidChart. Featured case studies (www.lucidchart.com/pages/case) profile innovative ways companies and nonprofit organizations are using the software.

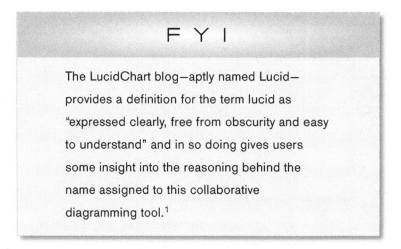

F Y I

The LucidChart blog—aptly named Lucid—
provides a definition for the term lucid as
"expressed clearly, free from obscurity and easy
to understand" and in so doing gives users
some insight into the reasoning behind the
name assigned to this collaborative
diagramming tool.[1]

Endnote

1. Lucid Blog, www.lucidchart.com/blog (accessed August 10, 2011).

48

Lulu
online publishing service
www.lulu.com

Overview

Described as a digital marketplace that eliminates traditional entry barriers to publishing, Lulu (an online self-publishing service) is a boon for modern day online content creators such as authors, educators, videographers, and musicians. Lulu provides this disparate group with the tools to format their digital content (choice of book covers, binding, size, print quality), publish, promote, and sell their intellectual end products—print books, ebooks, videos, CDs, DVDs—to an online global marketplace.

The rapid growth of Lulu, driven by more than "1.1 million registered creators and approximately 20,000 titles published every month"[1] since it was launched, is yet again mounting evidence of the phenomenal growth in epublishing and an increasing need for nontraditional publishing outlets for user-generated econtent. Creators earn 80 percent of all generated revenue (the 80/20 revenue split model) and are encouraged to take advantage of Lulu's dedicated marketplace, equipped with custom storefronts, a real-time calculator to help users work through the retail price and royalty combinations, and advanced listing and distribution services to make their products readily accessible to all.

Guided by founder and CEO Bob Young, a technology entrepreneur who was nominated as one of *BusinessWeek*'s Top Entrepreneurs in 1999, Lulu has corporate offices in the U.S., U.K., and Canada.

Features

➤ My Lulu: New members to the service can click on the My Lulu tab on the homepage (www.lulu.com) to register and create an account. This requires completing an online form and supplying the following information: full name, email address, username, password, country, and language (the latter two are optional). Once registered, members can visit the My Lulu personalized page for updated information on order history, downloads, and book publishing projects.

➤ Publish: This tab provides tools and guidelines for publishing books (print books, ebooks, photo books, yearbooks), calendars, portfolios, CDs, and DVDs. Publishing services include adding a free ISBN, access to Lulu's tools to format digital content, and marketing and distribution assistance. A detailed step-by-step guide for first-time book publishers is also provided.

➤ Buy: Clicking on this tab provides immediate access to Lulu's dedicated marketplace. This includes a central search box for keyword searching of all products and the ability to limit searches by format (print books, ebooks, calendars, CDs, DVDs, and digital files). Prospective buyers can browse titles in the Spotlight on Books, New on Lulu, and Staff Picks sections or browse books and other products arranged in categories such as arts and photography, biographies and memoirs, business and economics, children, comics and graphic novels, cooking, home and garden, mystery and crime, parenting and families, reference, sports and adventure, and teens.

➤ Services: Listed here are the publishing services provided by Lulu's professional team of editors, designers, writers, and marketers who assist new authors with services such as prepublishing (editing, formatting, cover design, indexing, and ghostwriting), marketing, and distribution.

➤ Community: Links are provided here to Lulu's discussion forums, Lulu groups, and the Lulu blog.

➤ Connect: New members can click on this tab to search Lulu's knowledge base, discuss tips and tricks with Lulu users in active forums, suggest enhancements to improve service, and find technical support.

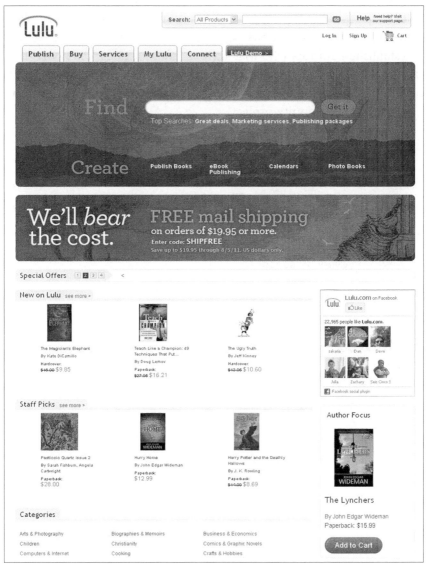

Lulu provides users with the tools to publish,
promote, and sell products to an online global marketplace.

How Cybrarians Can Use This Resource

Promoting Access to a Self-Publishing Platform

Libraries at the Rochester Institute of Technology have found a novel way of using Lulu to encourage users to self-publish their works and promote these works within a Lulu community by creating a forum called OpenBook@RIT. There is a promotional ad on the libraries' website (library.rit.edu/publishing/self-publish.html) encouraging new or established authors who may have a "book of poetry, art portfolio, music composition or other creative endeavor" to publish this work by becoming part of the OpenBook@RIT (connect.lulu.com/t5/Connect/ct-p/en_US) community project.

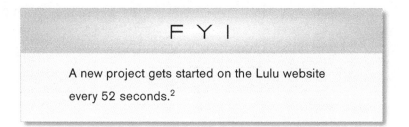

F Y I

A new project gets started on the Lulu website every 52 seconds.[2]

Endnotes

1. "About Lulu.com," www.lulupresscenter.com/page/view/p/lulu_com (accessed August 10, 2011).
2. Ibid.

49

MARC21 in Your Library
online cataloging webinar
www.marcofquality.com/webinars/webm21.html

Overview

Deborah Fritz has been doing yeoman service for the cataloging community since 1992 through her company The MARC of Quality (TMQ), which provides quality training, software, and database services to help catalogers and other metadata specialists "create better MARC records."[1] It is unlikely that there is an original or copy cataloger (author included) in the U.S. or other part of the world who has not completed her trademark intensive and in-depth courses such as MARC21 in Your Library, Book Blitz, Just for Copy Cats , Dewey Daze, and LCSH for Beginners, or read her well-researched and expansive work *Cataloging with AACR2 & MARC21: For Books, Electronic Resources, Sound Recordings, Videorecordings, and Serials.*[2] As she reiterates on her website, she is on a "mission to help catalogers organize all the information in the world."[3]

Recognizing that libraries are in tough economic times and may not have the budget allocations to pay for travel to attend TMQ courses, and, perhaps, more importantly, recognizing the value of online teaching in reaching an extensive global audience, TMQ recently rolled out MARC21 in Your Library as a series of web-based (webcast and self-paced) mini-courses, available anytime on the TMQ website (www.marcofquality.com). This course is an introduction to MARC21 and how it is meant to work in a library automation system. It explains what the MARC standards are and how those standards tie in with cataloging rules to help catalogers create data that will function effectively in a library catalog.

The courses are offered in a blended format, with free, introductory self-paced (Part One) sessions offered online. The follow-up (Part Two) sessions provide more in-depth instruction and are offered to participants as either subscription paid online webinars or face-to-face (on-site) sessions at a host site. Attendees can register for the online webinars on the OCLC website, as OCLC has partnered with TMQ to offer this course (training.oclc.org/home/-/courses/details/93221001). There are plans to offer similar courses in the future.

Features

At the time of this writing, Part One of the free webinars, titled MARC and Bibliographic Information: The Underlying Fundamentals, was available on the TMQ website (www.marcofquality.com/webinars/webm21.html). This webinar consists of nine self-paced mini-courses described as follows:

1.1 Bibliographic Information—What Is It? (Self-paced, approximately 25 minutes)

1.2 Bibliographic Information—Why Do We Need It? (Self-paced, approximately 20 minutes)

1.3 Bibliographic Information—How Do We Know What To Provide? (Webcast, approximately 30 minutes)

1.4 Bibliographic Information and MARC (Webcast, approximately 20 minutes)

1.5 MARC Records—What Are They? (Webcast, approximately 20 minutes)

1.6 MARC Records—Why Do We Need Them? (Webcast, approximately 15 minutes)

1.7 MARC Records—Where Do We Get Them? (Self-paced, approximately 30 minutes)

1.8 MARC Records, Bibliographic Information, and Library Catalogs (Self-paced, approximately 65 minutes)

1.9 MARC and Bibliographic Information—How Do I Speak It? (Webcast, approximately 35 minutes)

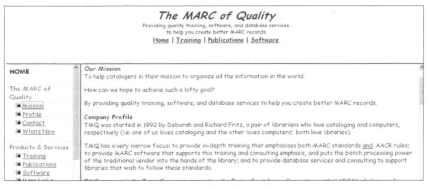

The MARC of Quality (TMQ) recently rolled out
MARC 21 In Your Library as a series of web-based mini-courses
for catalogers and other metadata specialists.

The following features guarantee that this mode of learning is participatory and fun:

➤ No registration or login is required to view the free webinars.

➤ Content covered in previous modules is summarized at the start of each new module, and often a URL link to the previous module is embedded, so that participants can click through, complete the review, and then return to the module they are currently viewing.

➤ Participants can return to each module at the point where they left off.

➤ Modules are interactive with quizzes included at the end to allow for reinforcement of key concepts.

➤ Embedded live URL links allow click-throughs to online resources referred to in each module.

➤ Participants are encouraged to give feedback for each module via email.

How Cybrarians Can Use This Resource

Professional Development

This series of courses has been targeted to a varied audience, including directors, reference and acquisitions staff, copy catalogers, beginning catalogers, and experienced but untrained catalogers. The obvious advantage of completing the training online is that it eliminates the cost of traveling and can be completed at your computer without leaving your workplace. This mode of training also facilitates group viewing and interactive learning. Cybrarians attending these workshops are certain to gain a working knowledge of the MARC format, understand the importance of coding in a MARC record, and see how this coding affects the proper functioning of the library catalog.

F Y I

The MARC of Quality homepage (www.marcof quality.com) is a source of information for other products and services offered by the company.

Endnotes

1. "The MARC of Quality: Our Mission," The MARC of Quality, www.marcofquality. com (accessed August 10, 2011).

2. Deborah Fritz, *Cataloging With AACR2 & MARC21: For Books, Electronic Resources, Sound Recordings, Videorecordings, and Serials* (Chicago: American Library Association, 2004).

3. "The MARC of Quality: Our Mission."

50

Meebo
instant messaging service
www.meebo.com

Overview

Meebo, a company founded in September 2005 and based in Mountain View, California, offers two IM (instant messaging) products of use to cybrarians: Meebo Messenger and Meebo Me. Meebo Messenger is a useful tool for connecting with all of your friends who may be scattered across multiple IM platforms. Using Meebo Messenger, users create one login and can immediately access and chat with friends on all the major IM networks (AIM, Yahoo!, Facebook, Windows Live, Messenger, Google Talk, ICQ, Jabber) in a single buddy list, from any browser.

Use Meebo Me to download a chat window widget to facilitate IM integration into your library webpage or blog. Having a chat window allows you to instantly strike up a conversation or answer questions with visitors to your webpage or blog. Meebo Me automatically publishes your online status so friends or visitors can see if you are online and available when they visit your site.

Meebo Messenger apps are currently available for the iPhone, iPod Touch, Android, and BlackBerry. For other mobile devices, Meebo for Mobile (www.meebo.com/mobile/#FrontPage) allows any smartphone with a JavaScript-enabled web browser to connect to Meebo Messenger using an interface designed for mobile devices. Meebo Me and Meebo Messenger are available on the Meebo products page (www.meebo.com/products).

The Meebo products page offers cybrarian-friendly
Meebo Me and Meebo Messenger.

Features

Meebo Messenger

To get started with Meebo Messenger (www.meebo.com/messenger), create a Meebo ID by registering your full name, email address, and password. All registered Meebo members have access to the following features on the Meebo Messenger interface:

➤ Sign in with a single Meebo ID and have immediate access to IM and multiple social platforms to communicate and share with friends. Most of the major IM networks are supported.

➤ Customize appearance and preferences by setting custom backgrounds and buddy icons.

➤ Access applications such as games, video chat, and file transfer.

➤ Save conversation history and search chat history.

➤ Preview messages on the chat list and sort chat.

➤ Take advantage of the full support for emoticons.

➤ Manage your conversations in a desktop-like environment by opening, closing, minimizing, and resizing chat windows.

Meebo Me

Meebo Me is a widget that can be embedded in a blog or website to allow visitors to chat with you in an IM chat window in real time. The Meebo Me widget will also reflect your current status, allowing visitors to view whether you are available or offline. The Meebo chat widget can be easily added to any interface using the following steps:

1. Go to the Meebo Me widget homepage (www.meebome.com).

2. Follow the instructions to add customization to the Meebo Me widget such as title, display name, size, and color theme.

3. Wait for the code to be automatically generated at the end of the process. Embed this code into a webpage or blog and have instant access to the Meebo Me widget.

How Cybrarians Can Use This Resource

Integrating Meebo Chat Widgets Into Library Webpages, Blogs, and Online Catalogs

A list of libraries using Meebo Me for embedded chat on webpages, blogs, and online catalogs can be found at the Library Success Wiki (www.tinyurl.com/3tlww9n).

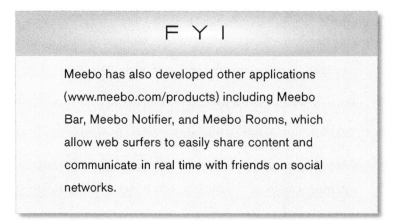

FYI

Meebo has also developed other applications (www.meebo.com/products) including Meebo Bar, Meebo Notifier, and Meebo Rooms, which allow web surfers to easily share content and communicate in real time with friends on social networks.

51

Mikogo
web conferencing service
www.mikogo.com

Overview

According to the 2010 *Library Journal* annual budget survey, libraries have reported that they are still feeling the effects of the most recent economic crisis. Many of the libraries surveyed indicated that they have been particularly vulnerable to budget cutbacks, with declines of 2.6 percent in total budgets and 3.5 percent in materials budgets.[1] Forced to realign goals regarding overall library spending, more than half of the libraries stated that they cut or eliminated budgets for conferences, travel, and education. Library administrators are encouraging, and, in some instances, demanding that staff rely on virtual conferences and meetings, offered by using web conferencing software, to fulfill their continuing education needs and obligations to professional associations.

There is a host of competing web conferencing software (notably Adobe Connect, WebEx, and GoToMeeting) on the market. One of the newer products, Mikogo, was developed as an easy-to-use, cross-platform, desktop-sharing tool ideal for web conferencing. Mikogo may be attractive to some because there is no need for participants to register or download and install software to their computer.

To initiate the service, conference participants must first visit the native website (www.mikogo.com), click on the option Join Session, run the software, and then enter a unique nine-digit session ID supplied by the organizer. A connection is instantly established, and the participants can view the organizer's screen in real time via the Mikogo viewer window. In addition to hosting web conferences, Mikogo users can use the software to host online meetings, webinars, and product demonstrations, and provide remote support for technical problems.

As a cross-platform application, Mikogo can be downloaded and installed on both Windows and Macintosh computers. The downside is that the product is only free for hosting small meetings (a maximum of 10 attendees), and this free version includes only basic or standard features. Enhanced functionality can be obtained by paying moderate subscription prices for an upgraded version offered by the Germany-based company BeamYourScreen GmbH (www.beamyourscreen.com/EN/welcome.aspx).

Features

➤   New users interested in downloading this desktop-sharing tool to host mini web conferences, online meetings, and product demonstrations or to offer remote support can register and download the free version of Mikogo on the company's website (www.mikogo.com).

➤   The following features are integrated into the free version of the software and highlighted on the product page (www.mikogo.com/product/features):

• Desktop sharing

• Multiple meeting participants (maximum of 10 persons per session)

• Switch presenter

• Remote keyboard and mouse control

• Initial viewing direction and remote control settings

• Session scheduler

• Session recording and playback

• Whiteboard

• Transfer files

• Application selection

• Back monitor

- Participant pointer

- Copying and pasting email meeting information

- Pausing transmission

- Speed and quality settings

➤ A portable version of the software is available (www.mikogo.com/download/windows-download). This allows the meeting host to start a Mikogo session from a USB drive, without having to install the software.

➤ The Mikogo blog (www.mikogo.com/blog) provides regular postings on product enhancements, online tutorials, and company news.

➤ Updates on innovative uses and benefits of the software are provided on the product's case studies (www.mikogo.com/testimonials/case-studies/case-study-bolero-innovations) and testimonials (www.mikogo.com/testimonials/testimonials) webpages.

How Cybrarians Can Use This Resource

Support for Elearning

For cybrarians who have hosted webinars and live online meetings, or taught distant students in a virtual classroom, the difficulties sometimes encountered by presenters and attendees can be easily identified. For presenters, the software may be expensive to purchase, and there is a steep learning curve. For the attendees, it may be difficult to download and install the software without technical expertise, and they may also encounter problems during the live presentation in maintaining an active telephone or Voice over Internet Protocol (VoIP) connection. These difficulties should be eliminated by using Mikogo.

The main benefit of using this multiplatform application is savings in start-up time and cost (the basic service is free). If there is need to host meetings with a group of more than 10 persons, consideration can be given to upgrading to the subscription product BeamYourScreen

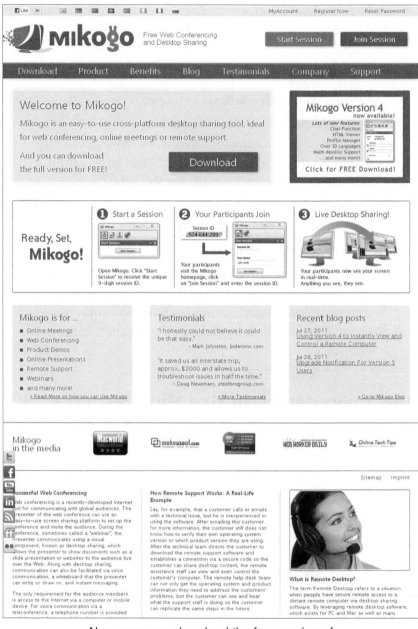

New users can download the free version of
Mikogo from the company's website.

(www.beamyourscreen.com/EN/we/wme.aspx) offered by the developers of Mikogo that can be downloaded for a free seven-day trial.

F Y I

Mikogo can be considered a viable alternative to the more popular open source web conferencing application Dimdim (www.dimdim.com), which was acquired by Salesforce.com and ended all active customer registrations in March 2011.

Endnote

1. Norman Oder, "Permanent Shift?: Library Budgets 2010," *Library Journal* (2010), www.libraryjournal.com/lj/community/managinglibraries/849932-273/permanent_shift_library_budgets_2010.html.csp (accessed August 10, 2011).

52

Moodle
course management system
www.moodle.org

Overview

Moodle is a free, open source, web-based course management system, currently being employed to develop online learning sites. This popular web application is used mainly by educators as a tool in the creation of more than 1 million active online learning communities for their students. These sites have been registered in 210 countries.[1]

The application's popularity stems from built-in extensible and scalable features, which facilitate large-scale deployments and multiple uses. Many institutions use Moodle as their platform to conduct fully online courses; some use it to augment face-to-face courses (blended learning) or as a way to deliver content to students and assess learning using assignments or quizzes. A proactive group of followers have used the activity modules (forums, databases, and wikis) to build collaborative communities of learning around their subject interest.

Licensed under the GNU General Public License, developers are allowed to copy, use, and modify Moodle with the proviso that they agree to provide the source to others, not modify or remove the original license and copyrights, and apply the same license to any derivative work. Moodle is maintained by a core group of developers based in Australia and an extensive network of volunteers.

Features

➢ Registration to use the web-based application is voluntary. Moodle can be downloaded from the main website (www.moodle.org/downloads) and installed on Windows,

Mac, and Linux servers that can run PHP (scripting language), and support an SQL (Structured Query Language) database (for example, MySQL).

➤ Registered Moodle sites (www.moodle.org/sites) are visible on an updated, interactive map and are also viewable as a tag cloud list of countries. Each country profile shows a comprehensive listing of organizations and the community of users in that specific country.

➤ The Moodle demonstration site (demo.moodle.net) is a sandbox with some sample demo accounts that teachers, students, managers, and administrators can log in to and explore the features of using the most recent stable release. The database and files in this demo site are erased and restored to a clean state every hour, so that changes made are not saved permanently. Users who access this demo site can view Moodle's applicability in supporting the following:

- Creation of small and large learning communities

- Support for elearning activities and different learning and teaching styles

- Delivery of learning activities and publishing of online resources

- Support of online collaboration and communication

- Compatibility with different learning standards and tools (Sharable Content Object Reference Model SCORM, Learning Activity Management System LAMS, ELGG social networking software, OpenID, and Second Life)

- Easy customization to support users with different needs

- Multiple-language support

➤ The Moodle support page (www.moodle.org/support) is a regularly updated resource for online manuals and other documentation, introductory video tutorials, FAQs, and online forums for newly registered members requiring technical and other types of support.

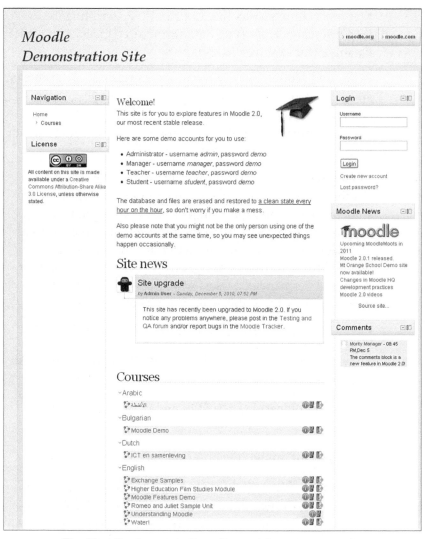

The Moodle demonstration site contains some sample
demo accounts where users can log in and explore features.

How Cybrarians Can Use This Resource

Promoting Access to a Virtual Learning Environment

Designed *by* teachers *for* teachers, the focus of the Moodle project is
always on giving educators the best tools to manage and promote

learning. Cybrarians can adopt this approach when promoting the resource to teachers, lecturers, and students in their library communities. The Moodle demonstration site is the obvious starting point, as it can be easily accessed to learn about the application and experiment with the features and functionalities, and as a showcase to demonstrate how Moodle can be configured for use at any institution by substituting realistic courses, users, and data.

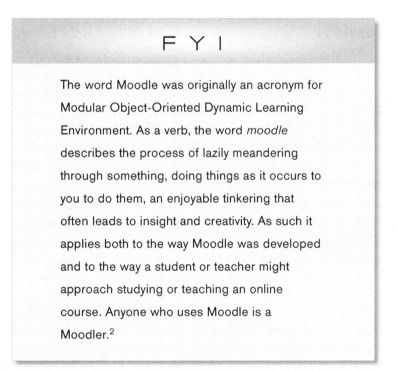

F Y I

The word Moodle was originally an acronym for Modular Object-Oriented Dynamic Learning Environment. As a verb, the word *moodle* describes the process of lazily meandering through something, doing things as it occurs to you to do them, an enjoyable tinkering that often leads to insight and creativity. As such it applies both to the way Moodle was developed and to the way a student or teacher might approach studying or teaching an online course. Anyone who uses Moodle is a Moodler.[2]

Endnotes

1. "Moodle Community," Moodle, www.moodle.org/community (accessed August 10, 2011).
2. "About Moodle," Moodle, docs.moodle.org/en/About_Moodle (accessed August 10, 2011).

53

Movable Type
content management system
www.movabletype.com

Overview

Developed by the company Six Apart Limited in 2001, Movable Type is one of the more advanced social publishing platforms freely available on the web to create websites and blogs, and build social networks. On the company's website, the software is touted as a "robust social publishing platform which powers some of the websites and blogs of the world's largest media companies and Fortune 100 businesses, small and medium sized businesses, and power bloggers."[1]

Unlike other freely available blogging software like Blogger (Chapter 10) and WordPress.com (Chapter 93), the software must be downloaded and installed on a computer, and users access the application through a web browser to perform tasks like publishing content or managing blogs.

Potential users can download one of three packages currently available on the website (www.movabletype.com/download). The two free versions of the software are marketed for different audiences. Movable Type 5 is marketed to developers who want an advanced open source platform to build, extend, and customize. Movable Type 5 Pro is for individual bloggers and Pre-K–12 educational institutions wishing for a powerful set of tools to build blogs, websites, and communities. Movable Type 4 Enterprise and the business version of Movable Type 5 Pro are both marketed as paid-for subscription packages for corporations.

On the Movable Type download page, users can download
and install the software onto their computers.

Features

➤   Blogs and websites can be created with a WYSIWYG (What You See Is What You Get) editor, which makes it easy to create and edit webpages and posts.

➤   There is a wide availability of templates with themes to customize the design of blogs or websites. The software also supports uploading files of all types—images, video, and audio.

➤   Administrators of the software can view revision history for entries, pages, and templates; manage trackbacks; set authorizations for members to create profiles and add or delete content; add permissions for visitors to recommend content; and add comments.

➤   Built-in RSS feeds enable visitors to subscribe to content feeds.

➤   Movable Type supports tags, tag search, and tag clouds.

➤   There is technical support for new users as well as access to an updated online user manual.

How Cybrarians Can Use This Resource

Promoting the Value of Blogs to the Academic Community

Blogs are currently being used in myriad ways by individuals, corporations, and nonprofit organizations, but an academic setting provides some unique uses of blogs. Librarians at the University of Minnesota Libraries use Movable Type to host blogs created by faculty, staff, and students at the university. The UThink blog hosting service (blog.lib. umn.edu) is home for over 9,000 blogs, a remarkable feat by any institution.

On the UThink FAQ page (blog.lib.umn.edu/uthink/about.phtml) librarians offer the following advantages for faculty, staff, and students using the service to create their own blogs:

➤   Blogs are excellent tools for students, faculty, and staff at the university to voice their opinions.

➤ Blogs offer a way to discuss issues, voice new ideas, and immediately receive input from others in the campus community.

➤ Blogs provide the framework for students, faculty, and staff of the university to network and build communities of interest.

➤ Blogs are excellent online collaborative tools providing the means to write about research interests and solicit comments about these writings.

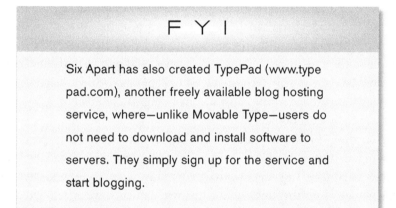

F Y I

Six Apart has also created TypePad (www.type pad.com), another freely available blog hosting service, where—unlike Movable Type—users do not need to download and install software to servers. They simply sign up for the service and start blogging.

Endnote

1. "About," Movable Type, www.movabletype.com/info (accessed August 10, 2011).

54

Myspace
social network
www.myspace.com

Overview

Myspace first launched in January 2004 and was considered the proto-type of the modern-day social network, empowering its community of users to interact around entertainment and pop culture, "connecting people to the music, celebrities, TV, movies, and games that they love."[1] Today, Myspace is still recognized as one of the world's largest social networks, but the enviable position of being ranked as No. 1 has been taken over by Facebook.

According to the website CrunchBase, since 2008 Myspace user growth has stagnated and page views and other metrics have fallen. The article attributes this decline to two main factors: 1) poor website design, because "throughout its history, critics have often cited the chaotic and disorganized interface as a severe drawback to usability of the site,"[2] and 2) unfavorable publicity and controversy due to child predators, cyberbullying, insufficient restrictions enforced to ban underage members, phishing, and other privacy and security issues— common ailments of all social networks. Despite this downward turn, Myspace still boasts staggering statistics and claims to have more than 50 million users worldwide, half of which reside in the U.S.[3]

The Myspace community has extended beyond the U.S. and is local-ized in 30 countries and translated into 16 languages.[4] In a bid to match up to the more popular Facebook, in October 2010 Myspace debuted a new web portal and accompanying suite of products branded as a social entertainment destination for Gen Y users (Millennials), who visit the network to read about their favorite celebrities, play games, listen to and discover new music, create their own playlists, watch videos, comment on content, and generally connect with other like-minded fans.

In October 2010, Myspace debuted a new web portal branded
as a social entertainment destination for Millennials.

Headquartered in Beverly Hills, California, Myspace was acquired by News Corporation in 2005 and became a subsidiary of Specific Media in June 2011.

Features

New and established users witnessed the global rollout of the new Myspace, which was vastly different in layout, design, color scheme, and logo (new logo includes an open bracket that can be personalized) from the previous version. The network's new visual and somewhat more aesthetically pleasing identity was created to improve navigation, put content center stage, deliver the best social entertainment experiences, and help fans easily find relevant content. New features include:

> A new-look Myspace welcome page showcasing new content as it is added in real time. Additionally, once a user logs in to Myspace, their personalized page will be populated with content (music, movies, photos, videos, games, events, and groups) tailored to their subject interests.

> Registered users can toggle among three different views of the homepage, each specifically designed to display their content stream in a different way: list or traditional view, grid or magazine-like view, and play or video format view.

> A mobile version (m.myspace.com) of the redesigned site is accessible on any mobile browser. Customized Myspace apps are available for the iPhone and Android devices.

> Topics pages provide a centralized location to view aggregated entertainment information about specific topics from a variety of news sites and blogs.

> Content hubs are specifically dedicated to movies, television, and celebrities, combining editorial content with trending articles from various third-party partners.

> Personalized streams automatically recommend content based on users' preferences and habits.

➤ The recommendations feature suggests relevant topics based on the user's viewing and listening history and also provides a listing of fans with similar interests.

➤ Right Now on Myspace spotlights trending content in real time, assisting fans in finding music and videos recently added to the network.

➤ The Discovery tab combines videos currently being viewed by friends with popular videos trending in real time on Myspace.

➤ The My Stuff tab guides fans to immediately view all content on Myspace such as profiles, photos, videos, music, games, movies, and uploaded content.

➤ Badges (graphic icons that appear in a user's stream) are given as rewards to curators and fans for their continued social engagement on the network.

How Cybrarians Can Use This Resource

Invading Library Patrons' Social Spaces

Libraries have discovered that Myspace, like other social networks Ecademy (Chapter 21), Facebook (Chapter 22), LinkedIn (Chapter 43), Orkut (Chapter 58), and XING (Chapter 95), is a social platform to connect to and engage users. With more than 50 million Myspace users worldwide, one can readily surmise that statistically a large segment of these fans will be the same patrons who use the library on a daily basis. Myspace as a web portal with a broad array of content seems as good a social space as any to meet these patrons, engage in conversations, and discover content while promoting libraries. In fact, many libraries have already done so and set up profile pages in Myspace. Library Success: A Best Practices Wiki features an index of libraries (www.libsuccess.org/index.php?title=MySpace_%26_Teens) with high-profile Myspace pages oriented to promoting library services and collections to teens:

➤ Arapahoe Library District, Englewood, Colorado (www.myspace.com/arapahoelibrary)

➤ Brooklyn College Library (www.myspace.com/brooklyn collegelibrary)

➤ Denver Public Library (www.myspace.com/denver_evolver)

➤ Lancaster Library, U.K. (www.myspace.com/getitloudin libraries)

➤ Steele Creek Library, Charlotte, North Carolina (www.myspace.com/steelecreeklibrary)

➤ Stoneham Public Library, Stoneham, Massachusetts (www.myspace.com/stonehamlibrary)

F Y I

In October 2010, Myspace introduced a beta version of a new site designed to be more music-oriented and targeted to a younger age group. The site's new logo omits the word "Space" and is stylized as My_____.

Endnotes

1. "Press Room," Myspace, www.myspace.com/pressroom (accessed August 10, 2011).

2. "Myspace," CrunchBase, www.crunchbase.com/company/myspace (accessed August 10, 2011).

3. "Myspace," Wikipedia, www.en.wikipedia.org/wiki/myspace (accessed August 10, 2011).

4. Ibid.

55

Ning
social network
www.ning.com

Overview

Like Facebook (Chapter 22), Myspace (Chapter 54), and Orkut (Chapter 58), Ning offers an easy-to-use service that enables subscribers to create custom-branded social networks. Where this service differs from its three rivals is its ability to attract a target group of users—organizers, activists, and others who want to inspire action—who use this online platform to mobilize, organize, inspire, and connect disparate groups around the topics they are passionate about.

Ning's users have created active Ning Networks in areas such as politics, entertainment, small business, nonprofits, and education. Perhaps the most infamous use of Ning as a powerhouse for advocacy was demonstrated by U.S. senate nominee Scott Brown, who used Ning to create the Brown Brigade, Brown's own unique social network, which allowed the campaign to connect with grassroots supporters in Massachusetts. It is purported that with the use of Ning and other social networking tools, Brown's campaign raised $1.3 million in just one day by publicizing a fundraising blitz using these social platforms, well surpassing his goal of $500,000.[1]

Social network developers have three options available for creating personalized Ning networks: Ning Pro, Ning Plus, or Ning Mini. The first two are paid-for subscription products. Ning teamed up with the education and technology company Pearson to make Ning Mini free for eligible North American K–12 and higher education institutions. Educators who subscribe to Ning Mini can add up to 150 members in a network to facilitate learning in a classroom, encourage best practices, and foster educator-to-educator collaboration or parental support. Ning was founded in 2004 and is based in Palo Alto, California.

Features

The features described below are integrated in Ning Mini, which is available for educational purposes at no cost (about.ning.com/pearson sponsorship):

➤ Up to 150 members eligible to join the social network

➤ 1 GB of storage and 10 GB bandwidth

➤ Blogging capability for every member of the Ning social network created

➤ Ability to create single- or multi-threaded discussion forums to foster collaboration

➤ Photo upload and sharing as well as video embedding

➤ An invitation engine (accessible to network creator only) to invite new members

➤ Twitter and Facebook integration so members can post status updates on these social networks

➤ RSS feed (only one feed is available for this version)

➤ Data gathering for statistics on membership

➤ Ability to add up to two Ning apps

➤ The option of running as ad-free or with ads

➤ Customized network ID

➤ Text boxes integrated on homepage (limited to three)

➤ Content export and archive enabled

➤ Community-based customer support

NING

About Ning   Product   Spotlight   Plans & Pricing

PRICING PLANS

En español | Em português

	MINI	PLUS	PRO
	For Small Groups	Advanced Features	Built for Scale
	The simplest and fastest way to set up a social network for your classroom, community group, small non-profit or family	The tools and features you need to customize your Ning Network with greater design flexibility and control over your members' experience	The ideal solution for building a custom social experience with premium add-ons, integration options, and more bandwidth and storage
	SIGN UP	SIGN UP	SIGN UP
Price	$2.95 Monthly or $19.95/year* (save 44%)	$19.95 Monthly or $199.95/year* (save 16%)	$49.95 Monthly or $499.95/year* (save 17%)
Ning Sponsored Networks	Education	Health	
Members	Up to 150	Unlimited	Unlimited
Storage ❓	1 GB	10 GB	20 GB + upgrade
Bandwidth ❓	10 GB	100 GB	200 GB + upgrade

FEATURES

	MINI	PLUS	PRO
Blog	✔	✔	✔
Photos	✔	✔	✔
Forum	✔	✔	✔
Birthdays	✔	✔	✔
Video embeds ❓	✔	✔	✔
Video uploads with branded players ❓		Continued access to current videos	✔
Music ❓			✔
Chat ❓		✔	✔
Events		✔	✔
Groups		✔	✔
Notes and Pages ❓		✔	✔
Ning Apps ❓	Add up to 2 Ning Apps	Add up to 5 Ning Apps	Add up to 10 Ning Apps

VIRAL TOOLS

	MINI	PLUS	PRO
Invite Page	Network Creator only	Network Creator and members	Network Creator and members
Branded badges ❓		✔	✔
Facebook and Twitter integration ❓		✔	✔
Sign-in with Facebook, Twitter or other authentication services (Coming soon)		✔	✔

Ning Mini is a package available free of charge
for educational institutions.

How Cybrarians Can Use This Resource

Designing and Creating Customized Social Networks

Cybrarians working at school and academic libraries can promote Ning Mini to educators at their institutions as a tool that can be used to design and create customized social networks with little or no technical support needed. Ning is not only a great platform to mobilize your educational institution online, it can also be a tool to introduce innovative online teaching methods to support the curricula. One example of the resource application in education is an English teacher's use of Ning to teach classic literature works to her class (www.pbs.org/wgbh/pages/frontline/digitalnation/learning/literacy/friending-boo-radley.html).

On the Ning website, a section is devoted to spotlighting the creative ways social network developers are using Ning (about.ning.com/spotlight). These have been categorized into seven distinct areas: politics, sports, entertainment, music, nonprofit, publishing, and brands.

F Y I

In July 2011, Ning partnered with Aviary
(Chapter 7) to launch a high resolution online
photo editor (up to 25 megapixels) for Ning
subscribers.

Endnote

1. Sophia Yan, "How Scott Brown's Social-Media Juggernaut Won Massachusetts," Time.com, February 4, 2010, www.time.com/time/nation/article/0,8599,1960378, 00.html (accessed August 10, 2011).

56

OpenID
productivity tool
www.openid.net

Overview

Most web searchers struggle to remember the multiple username and password combinations required to sign in to all of their favorite web resources. When authentication credentials are forgotten, the username or password recovery process can be tedious. With OpenID, searchers can use a single existing account from a growing list of online providers such as Google, Yahoo!, Flickr, Facebook, Myspace, and AOL to sign in and access their web resources, eliminating the need to create multiple usernames and passwords.

On its homepage, OpenID is promoted as a fast, easy, and secure way to sign in to OpenID-enabled websites. Other potential benefits include acceleration of the registration process as basic profile information (name, date of birth, address, etc.) can be stored through your OpenID account and used to prepopulate online forms. Frustration associated with maintaining multiple usernames and passwords is reduced, and user privacy and security risks are decreased by having a centrally administered login and password.

OpenID is administered by the OpenID Foundation, an international nonprofit organization established in June 2007 to serve primarily as a public trust organization representing the open community of developers, vendors, and users.[1] Its main offices are located in San Ramon, California.

Features

The OpenID homepage (www.openid.net) is uniquely designed to assist its community of developers, vendors, and users to achieve three goals:

1. Get an OpenID (www.openid.net/get-an-openid). Clicking on this link provides simple instructions on how to create your own OpenID, or sign in to an OpenID-enabled website, if you already have an account with providers such as Google, Yahoo!, LiveJournal, Blogger, Flickr, WordPress, Myspace, and AOL.

2. Start using an OpenID (www.openid.net/get-an-openid/start-using-your-openid). Clicking on this link provides step-by-step instructions—shown as detailed screen shots—of the process of logging in for the first time to a website that supports OpenID.

3. Add OpenID to an existing website (www.openid.net/add-openid). For website developers wishing to allow users to sign in with an OpenID, this section lists several options (open source libraries, plug-ins, or third-party solutions) that can be used to facilitate this process.

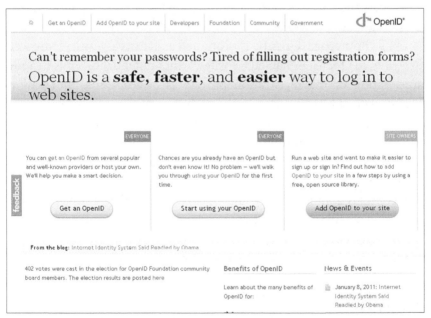

The OpenID homepage is designed to assist users to achieve three goals: get an OpenID, start using an OpenID, and add an OpenID to an existing website.

How Cybrarians Can Use This Resource

Publicizing the Benefits of OpenID and Contributing to the OpenID Community Forum

The OpenID community is passionate about issues of identity, privacy, and security on the web. In addition to promoting the benefits of creating and using an OpenID, cybrarians can join an expanding list of professionals who regularly contribute to the OpenID community webpage (www.openid.net/community) to discuss trending issues and ultimately help shape the future in which all users may have a unified digital identity.

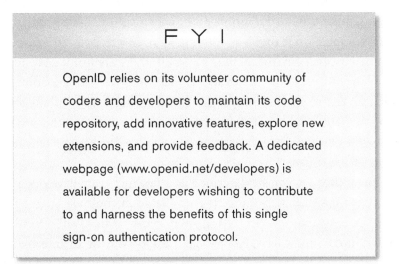

F Y I

OpenID relies on its volunteer community of coders and developers to maintain its code repository, add innovative features, explore new extensions, and provide feedback. A dedicated webpage (www.openid.net/developers) is available for developers wishing to contribute to and harness the benefits of this single sign-on authentication protocol.

Endnote

1. "OpenID Foundation," OpenID, www.openid.net/foundation (accessed August 10, 2011).

57

OpenOffice.org
productivity tool
www.openoffice.org

Overview

OpenOffice.org is the leading open source office software suite used for word processing, spreadsheets, presentations, graphics, and databases. Unlike other rival proprietary office suites (mainly Microsoft Office), OpenOffice.org was developed over the past 20 years in a completely open environment. As a result, there are immediate advantages for end users of this product, including free downloading and quick access to all the programs in the suite, a role in suggesting improvements and requesting new features to enhance the product, and open communication with developers on the current and future status of the software.

OpenOffice.org can be described as a product truly developed with the global consumer in mind. It is available in multiple languages, it runs on all major computing platforms (Microsoft Windows, GNU/Linux, Sun Solaris, Apple Mac), the data is in an international open standard format, and it can also read and write files from other common office software packages.

The latest version of the software is always available for download on the main website (www.openoffice.org). All versions are released under the GNU Lesser General Public License and thus may be used for any purpose—domestic, commercial, educational, and public administration—and installed on more than one computer without limitations. Users can also make copies of the programs to give freely to colleagues, family, and friends. A public wiki provides community-based support for the software (wiki.services.openoffice.org/wiki/Main_Page).

Features

The OpenOffice.org suite contains all the productivity office software commonly used (word processing, spreadsheets, presentations, graphics, databases) bundled in one single package. One quick download and installation of the software delivers the following five products to your desktop:

➤ *Writer* has everything one would expect from a modern, fully equipped word processor or desktop publisher with features such as autocorrect, autocomplete, autoformat, styles and formatting, text frames and linking, tables of contents, indexing, bibliographical references, illustrations, tracking changes, and tables. Writer is ideal for word processing tasks such as creating memos, documents, or blog posts.

➤ *Calc* is the spreadsheet product with functions such as natural language formulas, an Intelligent Sum button (inserts a sum function or a subtotal automatically, depending on context), wizard guides to assist new users when using advanced spreadsheet functions, downloadable templates, styles and formatting options, and support for collaborative work on spreadsheets.

➤ *Impress* is the tool used for creating multimedia presentations. Users have access to features such as 2D and 3D clip art, varying font types, special effects, animation, and drawing tools. Presentations can be shared using multiple formats including PDF, HTML, and Flash.

➤ *Draw* tools allow users to create graphics and diagrams. Useful for drawing and designing quick sketches, flowcharts, organization charts, and network diagrams.

➤ *Base* enables users to manipulate database data seamlessly within OpenOffice.org. Functions include creating and modifying tables, forms, queries, and reports, either using a user custom-built database or the software built-in HSQL (Hyper Structured Query Language) database engine.

On the OpenOffice.org homepage, the latest version of the software can be downloaded.

How Cybrarians Can Use This Resource

Promoting Access to a Suite of Online Productivity Tools

Given the current economic climate, and faced with budget cuts that have been aimed at staff, services, and collections, libraries can consider OpenOffice.org as a free viable alternative to the somewhat expensive Microsoft Office (MS Office Professional is presently priced at $499.99 in the Microsoft Store).

Laura Solomon, the library services manager for the Ohio Public Library Information Network, gave an instructional webinar, "OpenOffice: What Libraries Need to Know" (www.infopeople. org/training/webcasts/webcast_data/351/index.html), outlining how

OpenOffice.org measured up to its main competitor Microsoft Office. She cited the following advantages in support of libraries adopting the software:

> There is comparable functionality between the two systems.

> There is not a huge product shift or steep learning curve moving from one software to the next. Learning OpenOffice core products that are in direct competition with Microsoft Office is not difficult if you are comfortable using Microsoft applications.

> An open source developer community focusing on new features to enhance the product is available.

> OpenOffice is compatible with more file formats.

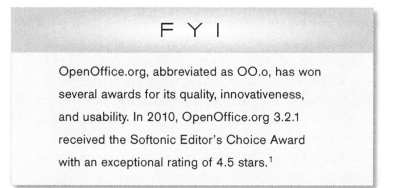

F Y I

OpenOffice.org, abbreviated as OO.o, has won several awards for its quality, innovativeness, and usability. In 2010, OpenOffice.org 3.2.1 received the Softonic Editor's Choice Award with an exceptional rating of 4.5 stars.[1]

Endnote

1. "News From OpenOffice.org," OpenOffice.org, www.openoffice.org/news (accessed August 10, 2011).

58

Orkut
social network
www.orkut.com

Overview

Orkut is a social networking service that is owned and operated by Google. The service as described on its homepage "is an online community designed to make your social life more active and stimulating, by helping you maintain existing relationships with pictures and messages, and establishing new friendships by reaching out to people you have never met before."[1] The service, launched in 2004, is named after its creator, Google employee Orkut Buyukkokten.

By all accounts, Orkut seems to be Google's bid to grab hold of the lucrative social networking market share. If this is true, it still has a long way to go before it unsettles major rivals Facebook and Myspace. The Alexa website currently ranks Orkut as the 108th most popular site on the internet.[2]

Ironically, although Orkut lags behind the competition in the U.S., Wikipedia cites the service as one of the most-visited websites in India and Brazil.[3] As with any online social networking community, Orkut has been troubled with its share of controversy (ethical, political, moral, and legal issues) relating to usage.

Features

➢ To join Orkut, users can simply sign in with their Google account (if one exists) and immediately create a profile (user name, password, birth date). For new users without a Google account, the service provides prompts (www.orkut.com/ presignup) to assist in the creation of a profile.

➤ The scrapbook feature is a way to communicate with friends. You or your friends can write messages in the scrapbook text box and these messages are immediately available for viewing. These scraps or messages can be customized by changing the text color or adding emoticons, images, YouTube videos, and maps. There is a trash can icon to delete unwanted scraps.

➤ Users can create photo albums by uploading photos to Orkut albums using the Picasa plug-in (see Chapter 62).

➤ There is an option to create communities or groups with other Orkut members who share similar interests. Before creating a new community, users can search the database for communities already created—by keywords or by limiting to categories such as arts and entertainment; computers and internet; health, wellness, and fitness; and schools and education—to see if there is an existing community dedicated to their subject interest.

➤ Orkut apps can be used to customize profiles by adding badges, games, music, movies, and tech tools. Although these apps are created by third-party developers, once selected they are integrated into Orkut members' profiles.

➤ The video chat feature is available for users with a webcam and a microphone connected to their computers.

➤ A theme gallery, which is regularly updated, is available for adding a different look to the background of Orkut members' profiles.

➤ Orkut Promote allows members on the network to share YouTube videos, photos, or text with each other to publicize an upcoming event.

➤ Network members can view written testimonials by friends and colleagues within the My Updates section on their personalized homepage.

➤ The Orkut Share bookmarklet makes it easy to share content found on the web with friends. Users can install the bookmarklet to their favorite internet browser.

Orkut users can sign in to the service using an existing Google account.

➤   Orkut mobile (m.orkut.com) allows users to quickly and
    easily access Orkut from an internet-enabled phone or mobile
    device.

How Cybrarians Can Use This Resource

Social Networking

The benefits of Orkut are similar to those of other social networks.
Orkut gives cybrarians the tools to stay connected to their network of
friends and colleagues. Orkut can also offer additional benefits such as
joining Orkut communities with others who share similar library interests and using this forum to promote library events.

F Y I

Orkut was originally hosted in California. In
August 2008, Google announced that Orkut
would be fully managed and operated in Brazil

by Google Brazil. This was decided due to the large Brazilian user base and growth of legal issues.[4]

Endnotes

1. "About Orkut," Orkut, www.orkut.com/about (accessed August 10, 2011).

2. "Orkut.com," Alexa, www.alexa.com/siteinfo/orkut.com (accessed August 10, 2011).

3. "Orkut," Wikipedia, en.wikipedia.org/wiki/Orkut (accessed August 10, 2011).

4. Ibid.

59

PBworks
wiki
www.pbworks.com

Overview

PBworks, formerly known as PBwiki, specializes in helping businesses, nonprofits, and educational institutions collaborate in virtual shared spaces using wikis. The company initially chose the name PBwiki based on the belief that anyone could use the service to quickly and painlessly set up a wiki in less time than it takes to make a peanut butter sandwich.

With features similar to Wikipedia (Chapter 89), Wikis by Wetpaint (Chapter 90), and other wiki hosting services, PBworks offers customizable wiki workspaces with mobile support, document-management applications, security access controls, point-and-click easy editing, and multimedia support. The PBworks Basic Edition is free (for up to 100 persons) for educational institutions, individuals, and nonprofits. It should be noted, however, that the service is now heavily marketed as a "hosted collaboration solution" with features and functions that extend beyond just a wiki and that it relies heavily on fee-based premium subscriptions. These additional applications include knowledge management, project management, and legal or case management.

Given the company's expansion as a business enterprise, it is not surprising that the PBworks Team claims that it has now accumulated a loyal client base and hosts more than 1 million team workspaces. Higher education academic clients include DePaul University, the University of Chicago, and the University of Wisconsin.[1] PBworks was launched in 2005 and has its main headquarters in San Mateo, California, with a branch office in Nashua, New Hampshire.

Features

PBworks is accessible from any web browser with an internet connection. Users can sign up from the homepage (www.pbworks.com), name their workspaces, and start adding content in less than 60 seconds. New users can collaborate in team-based shared spaces with the following features:

- Collaborative editing with a WYSIWYG (What You See Is What You Get) editor

- A complete audit trail of every change made to workspaces, enabling editors to view who made changes and reverse unwanted changes

- Invitation by email functionality to encourage mass user participation in the wiki space created

- Workspace-wide, access-level authorization to control accessibility for different team members (reader, writer, editor, and administrator)

- Multimedia plug-ins for embedding multimedia content such as images, videos, and photo slideshows

- Availability of customizable templates with custom colors (unlimited color choices for premium users, as well as a logo to brand their workspace)

- An online support center with access to user manuals, instructional videos, live training, and a technical support team

How Cybrarians Can Use This Resource

Support for Library Services

Cybrarians have already discovered PBworks and use this resource every day to collect, store, and organize information, coordinate staff activities and schedules, and engage their community. Innovative uses for libraries outlined on the PBworks website (www.pbworks.com/content/edu-librarians) include:

Users can sign up to use the PBworks service, name their workspaces, and start adding content in less than 60 seconds.

➤ Publicizing library services: Publish information about new acquisitions, post library hours and policies, and publicize events such as author visits and special events.

➤ Creating procedures and policy manuals: Use PBworks to collaboratively create procedures and policy manuals.

➤ Scheduling meetings: PBworks can be utilized to publish online reference desk schedules, agendas, meeting notes, and timelines for projects.

➤ Creating a technology support database: Create a collaborative wiki to record technical problems and solutions for ILS hardware and software, online catalogs, databases, and patron computers.

➤ Hosting tutorials: The Baltimore County Public Schools used PBworks as a learning resource to host a series of tutorials for the Learning 23 Things program (www.bcps23things.pbworks.com).

➤ Developing webinars: Rachel Pennig, Director of Support and Services at PBworks, developed a "New Tools for School Librarianship" webinar to demonstrate how wikis can be used by school librarians (www.tinyurl.com/3cmzpra).

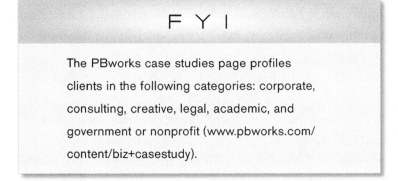

F Y I

The PBworks case studies page profiles clients in the following categories: corporate, consulting, creative, legal, academic, and government or nonprofit (www.pbworks.com/content/biz+casestudy).

Endnote

1. "About Us," PBworks, www.pbworks.com/content/about (accessed August 10, 2011).

60

PDF-to-Word
productivity tool
www.pdftoword.com

Overview

PDF-to-Word is a free service from Nitro PDF Software, a company headquartered in San Francisco, California, trying to entice consumers with a range of software (mainly PDF products) to rival industry leader Adobe Acrobat.

One of the products currently being offered is the freely available PDF-to-Word converter, which enables users to quickly create editable DOC/RTF files from any PDF document, thus making it easier to reuse original PDF documents in applications such as Microsoft Word, Excel, OpenOffice, and WordPerfect. While this PDF-to-Word conversion might not replicate the exact formatting and appearance of the original PDF document, it does produce enough accurate results for users to have a usable working copy.

The PDF-to-Word Converter is just one of a number of free productivity tools available from Nitro PDF. Other products include Nitro PDF Reader (www.nitroreader.com), a viable alternative to the more popular Adobe Reader, PDF-to-Excel Converter (www.pdftoexcel online.com), and Word-to-PDF Converter (www.wordtopdf.com).

Nitro PDF Software products are used by more than 25 million clients worldwide, including American Airlines, Bank of America, Disney, General Motors, Hewlett Packard, IBM, the U.S. Department of Defense, the U.S. Department of Energy, the U.S. District Courts, and Microsoft.[1] Headquartered in San Francisco, California, the company has operations in North America, Europe, Asia, and Australia.

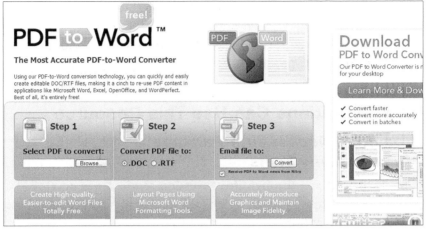

As demonstrated on the homepage, converting
PDF-to-Word documents can be achieved in three steps.

Features

> The software is browser-based, and converting PDF-to-Word documents can be achieved in three steps:

1. Select PDF file to convert.

2. Convert PDF file to DOC or RTF format.

3. Enter an email address to send converted file to and then click on the Convert button.

> The Word document surrogate created accurately reproduces graphics and maintains image fidelity. This results in a file in such a practical format that users need not spend valuable time reformatting content retrieved from the conversion.

> A comprehensive list of features (www.pdftoword.com/features.htm) retained from the original document is itemized on the website. These features are listed under the categories texts and fonts; paragraphs; and layout, tables, and images. For example, under the category text and fonts, the following features are maintained: same size and color text, same font appearance, bold and italic formatting, and rotated text, as well as active hyperlinks.

➤   The Nitro Team maintains a PDF Blog (blog.nitropdf.com) for users wishing to keep up-to-date with product announcements, training events, company news, and tips for using the product.

How Cybrarians Can Use This Resource

Promoting Access to a Package of Productivity Tools

Nitro PDF Software, through its conversion services, has developed a package of productivity tools, which cybrarians can put to practical use in the office and at home:

➤   Nitro PDF Reader (www.nitroreader.com) is a viable alternative to Adobe Reader for creating PDF files.

➤   The PDF-to-Excel Converter (www.pdftoexcelonline.com) can easily create editable XLS (spreadsheets) from PDF files, which can then be imported and used in Microsoft Excel, OpenOffice, Google Docs, and WordPerfect Office.

➤   The Word-to-PDF Converter (www.wordtopdf.com) converts files in DOC, DOCX, and RTF formats to PDF.

F Y I

In May 2010, Nitro PDF Reader was awarded the CNET Editors' Choice award. The site received a stellar five-star review and was applauded for "doing more by default than any free PDF reader currently available ... doing what is advertised ... rocketing it to the top of the PDF pack."[2]

Endnotes

1. "Nitro PDF Software-Corporate Profile," Nitro PDF Software, www.nitropdf.com/corporate/index.htm (accessed August 10, 2011).

2. "Nitro PDF Software's Revolutionary Free PDF Reader Is Deemed Best-in-Class By Leading Technology Portal," Nitro PDF Software, June 9, 2010, www.nitropdf.com/corporate/pr/pr_090610.htm (accessed August 10, 2011).

61

Photobucket
photo hosting service
www.photobucket.com

Overview

Photobucket, like Flickr (covered in Chapter 24), is one of the premier sites on the internet for hosting, finding, and sharing photos, videos, and graphics. Using this free service (with an option to upgrade to the subscription package), users can upload images and videos, have the choice of editing the uploaded photos with the site's photo editor, create slideshows, and share the end products with friends, family, and colleagues by email or on social sites like Facebook, Twitter, and Myspace. Users can also search Photobucket's extensive online library for videos and images to use in presentations or embed in blogs or personal websites.

For iPhone, Android, and Blackberry users, there are apps available for uploading, browsing, and managing photos. Other smartphone users can access the application from the Photobucket mobile website (m.photobucket.com).

Photobucket was founded in 2003 and acquired by Fox Interactive Media, a division of News Corporation, in July 2007. Photobucket merged with Ontela in December 2009. The company has offices in Denver, Seattle, and San Francisco.

Features

➤   New users can sign up to the service from the homepage
      (www.photobucket.com) and immediately start storing and
      sharing photos, videos, and albums created on the
      Photobucket website. Integrated functionality enables photos

to be shared on social networks Facebook, Myspace, and Twitter.

➤ Photobucket facilitates collaboration with friends and colleagues to create group albums of photos and videos that are accessible to all contributors.

➤ There is a database of album themes used to design and personalize photo and video albums.

➤ Access a built-in organizer for managing and organizing photos and videos.

➤ Access a built-in, full-featured photo editor, for editing photos, adding captions, and applying special effects.

➤ Access the Photobucket resource library to search and browse for photos, images, and videos to embed in websites or blogs, or use in presentations.

➤ The site features a scrapbook builder with customized designs that supports drag-and-drop functionality to create and share scrapblogs and collages.

➤ It also features a slideshow builder with customized themes for creating digital slideshows to post and share on websites and blogs.

➤ Visit the online photo gifts and prints store for printing pictures or engraving photos on favorite memorabilia.

How Cybrarians Can Use This Resource

Support for Library Programs and Professional Development

➤ Search Photobucket's online library for images and videos to support a workshop or conference presentation.

➤ Use Photobucket's slideshow builder to create a slideshow to promote your library.

➤ Organize a workshop for patrons to demonstrate how to use Photobucket and other photo sharing applications such as Flickr and Picasa (www.slideshare.net/apeoples/flickr-workshop).

With Photobucket, users can sign up to store, manage, and share photos, videos, and albums.

F Y I

The Photobucket website attracts more than 23 million unique monthly users in the U.S. who upload more than 4 million images and videos per day.[1]

Endnote

1. "About Photobucket," Photobucket, www.photobucket.com/about (accessed August 10, 2011).

62

Picasa
photo hosting service
www.picasa.google.com

Overview

Google's Picasa software is a desktop photo management application that can be installed on a computer to organize and edit digital photos. The allied Picasa Web Albums is the web version of the software used to upload the pictures stored on the computer and convert these pictures into web albums for sharing with friends, family, and colleagues.

Both programs are Google products and freely available online. Picasa software runs on Windows, Macintosh, and Linux platforms. The latest stable release of the software is always available from the Google website (www.picasa.google.com), and can be downloaded from this source. Unlike other photo editing software, once Picasa is downloaded and installed on a computer, it does not transfer and store the photos on your computer within its program. Users have total control over the photos that Picasa displays for editing. The software basically acts as an organizer and editor, only working with photos you search for on your computer. All original photos remain stored in their original folders.

After editing and organizing photos using Picasa, the simplest way to upload these photos to the web is by using Picasa Web Albums (www.picasaweb.google.com), which provides all users with one gigabyte of free storage. This integration between the desktop and web application simplifies the process of taking photos from your desktop and publishing them online for others to view. Picasa Web Albums can be accessed by creating a new account with Google or signing in with an existing account.

Features

This is a summary of features common to both photo sharing applications:

> There are a number of search options for finding photos in the Picasa Web Albums database. Users can click the Explore tab on the homepage (www.picasaweb.google.com/lh/explore) to view a page devoted to hosting public photos from all over the world or browse the Featured Photos selections hand-picked by the Picasa Team or the Recent Photos stream of newly uploaded photos.

> Import or batchload new photos into Picasa software and Picasa Web Albums from multiple devices including smartphones, cameras, CDs, memory cards, scanners, and webcams. Edit these uploaded photos using a range of functions such as adjusting color and lighting, applying special effects, resizing, and adding captions and tags (labeling photos with tags or keywords enables quick searches and easy retrieval). Using the Sync to Web function ensures that edits made to photos in Picasa software are reflected immediately in the corresponding album in Picasa Web Albums.

> Share photos stored in Picasa software on your computer by uploading these directly to Picasa Web Albums. Photos can also be sent directly by email to family, friends, and colleagues, inviting them to view the albums created. The visibility of albums can be determined by setting these as public or private. Picasa's strength as a photo editor and organizer is tied to its unique facial recognition technology. This technology works by automatically grouping similar faces across entire collections of photos.

> Movie Maker allows users to combine photos, videos, and music into digital movies, which can be uploaded to YouTube. Additionally, slideshows and collages can be easily embedded as HTML code on a blog or website.

> Using the Maps tab in the Picasa software, users can embed latitude and longitude information into the EXIF data of

photo files (geotagging). When these photos are uploaded to Picasa Web Albums, geographical information in the photo's EXIF data can be used to drag and drop photos on a map.

➤ The advantage of having a single-login Google account for applications such as Picasa is that any photos uploaded to other Google products such as Blogger (Chapter 10) or Orkut (Chapter 58) are automatically added to Picasa Web Albums.

➤ Picasa Web Albums is accessible from Google's mobile website (picasaweb.google.com/m), and apps are currently available for Android, BlackBerry, Apple, Nokia/Symbian, and Windows smartphones.

Picasa software and Picasa Web Albums are freely available online on the Google website.

How Cybrarians Can Use This Resource

Support for Library Programs and Professional Development

➤ Use Picasa to create a slideshow to promote libraries, similar to the slideshow created at the National Library of Egypt

(picasaweb.google.com/joseph.ph/LibrariesBibliotheca
AlexandrinaEgypt#).

➤ Search for images for a workshop or conference presentation
in the Picasa Web Albums database.

➤ Organize a workshop for patrons to demonstrate how to use
Photobucket, Flickr, Picasa, and other photo sharing services
(www.slideshare.net/apeoples/flickr-workshop).

F Y I

Picasa was runner up in the "Best Digital
Photo Management Tool" category in the Linux
Journal 2010 Readers' Choice Award.[1]

Endnote

1. James Gray, "Readers' Choice Awards 2010," Linux Journal, October 29, 2010,
www.linuxjournal.com/content/readers-choice-awards-2010 (accessed August 10,
2011).

63

Podcast Alley
podcast service
www.podcastalley.com

Overview

Podcast Alley is described on its homepage as the podcast lovers' portal. It may well live up to this description, as it is easily one of the best places on the internet to add new podcasts and search for podcast feeds, news, tutorials, and podcast software. Podcasting as a simple method of distributing audio content over the internet is currently the preferred mode for recording and disseminating information to end-users to download to their iPods or other portable media devices.

Founded by Chris McIntyre, a graduate of Purdue University, Podcast Alley's goal is to index all the podcasts currently available on the internet and in doing so create a central repository or directory for the podcasting community. This is an invaluable service that can also be beneficial to the information community, especially for those libraries working on projects to produce audio and video content to promote innovative programs and services.

Only registered users can add podcasts to the directory. Registration entails supplying an email address, user name, password, and birth date, setting a time zone, and answering a random question. Podcast Alley currently hosts more than 91,000 podcasts.[1]

Features

➤ Podcasts can be added to the Podcast Alley directory in four easy steps:

1. Click on the Add a Podcast tab at the top of the homepage (www.podcastalley.com). In the online form

provided, submit the podcast RSS feed URL (this address should end in .xml as this is the format specific to podcast feeds).

2. Podcast Alley will automatically generate a *validation* of the RSS feed URL supplied, notifying podcasters of possible errors in the URL address submitted.

3. Enhance the podcast submitted by adding descriptive information about its purpose and assigning broad subject categories.

4. Podcasters complete the process by verifying that they own the podcast. Once this is done the podcast is available for broadcast.

➤ For subscribers wishing to search for podcasts on the homepage, there are options to enter keyword searches in a single search box on the left navigation bar, browse featured or newest podcasts, or browse a list of genres and topics.

➤ The Podcast Software tab at top of the homepage links to resources to record and download podcasts from different sources (Windows, Macintosh, Linux, and handheld devices). Under this tab, podcasters will also find links to podsafe music sites and support resources (books, guides, and tutorials).

➤ The forums (www.podcastalley.com/forum/index.php) host discussions on trending issues related to podcasts.

➤ The Podcast Alley blog (blog.podcastalley.com) is the main support center to keep podcasters updated about the service, as it provides links to tutorials, news updates, and product enhancements.

How Cybrarians Can Use This Resource

Innovative Library Services

➤ The Library Success wiki (www.libsuccess.org/index.php?title=Podcasting) provides a comprehensive list of libraries

Podcast Alley has several search options for
finding podcasts on its homepage.

and affiliated organizations that are currently offering
podcast services.

➤ Sarah Long, director of the North Suburban Library System
in Chicago, produces a series of podcasts called "Longshots"

(www.librarybeat.org) that explore the world of libraries through interviews with key library figures and commentary on issues that matter to libraries. For cybrarians, this model could easily be an example of how to use podcasts to tap into the knowledge base of movers and shakers in the library community, while at the same time keeping up with innovative new technologies in the library world.

F Y I

On its homepage, Podcast Alley maintains a monthly list of the Top 10 podcasts on the website as voted by listeners.

Endnote

1. Podcast Alley homepage, www.podcastalley.com (accessed August 10, 2011).

64

Prezi
productivity tool
www.prezi.com

Overview

Prezi, the web-based presentation application and storytelling tool, is in direct competition—and many insiders would not hesitate to say, rapidly gaining ground as a viable alternative—to its main rival Microsoft PowerPoint. This presentation tool introduces totally new and refreshing concepts to the art of creating online presentations. The conceptual model behind the application can be reduced to four words: think, write, arrange, and present. Like a work of art, Prezi users are presented with a blank canvas (editing interface) to create and develop their ideas. They can then use special tools such as the Transformation Zebra, Text Editor, and Zoom buttons to link these disparate ideas into a coherent and cohesive story or presentation to communicate to an audience.

Developer Adam Somlai-Fischer in this statement gives Prezi users an insight into the reasons why Team Prezi developed the application: "We prefer not to follow trends; instead, we learn about culture and respond with technology. We believe in humanity's desire for creativity and self-expression."[1] Somlai-Fischer and co-founder Peter Halacsy commenced working on Prezi in 2007, as an alternative to static slides, which they felt limited their ability to develop and explain ideas. Based on the positive responses from the application's steadily growing community of users, Team Prezi's creation of this tool to solve these limitations was the right idea.

With the free public access version, users can create Prezis from any computer online and download the finished Prezis to present offline, and they are guaranteed storage of up to 100 MB of data. The limitations are that all Prezis created will be published and publicly available online on the company's website (www.prezi.com/explore), and Prezi branding (a small watermark) will be shown on all creations. There is an option to upgrade to a paid subscription and increase storage to 500 MB–2,000 MB. Prezi was officially launched in April 2009 in Budapest, and the U.S.-based office in San Francisco was opened in November 2009.[2]

Features

➣ New Prezi users can sign up for the service by clicking on the Sign Up link on the homepage (www.prezi.com) and filling out the registration form with first and last name, email address (which will be used as your user name), and password. Once registered, members can immediately begin the process of creating Prezi presentations using the free account (100 MB).

➣ For registered users, the Prezi main interface comprises the three main tabs Your Prezis, Learn, and Explore:

- Use the Prezis tab to create new Prezis or access presentations created in previous sessions. A search box at the top of the screen facilitates keyword searching of all Prezis stored in your virtual space, and these can be sorted by Title or Last Opened.

- The Learn tab provides access to instructional learning and teaching tools. This is a resource created by Team Prezi for hosting basic, advanced, and expert tutorials. The Community is a forum for fresh ideas, stories, and tips and tricks from Prezi creators. The Prezi manual is core to the learning center, with a list of FAQs to get new users started on understanding the resource. There is also a support link to report a problem, ask a question, or share an idea with the Prezi staff or with the user community.

- The Explore tab is a showcase of original Prezis created by the user community with the spotlight on popular creations handpicked by Prezi staff. Here users will also find a search box for entering queries to search the entire database of presentations.

➤ The Prezi editor is the main dashboard provided to users to create Prezi presentations. The set of tools described below is central to assisting users in brainstorming, developing, and communicating ideas in a cohesive presentation:

- Zoomable Canvas is the main area for inserting content (text, images, and videos).

- The Bubble Menu (on the top left of the main menu bar) hosts all the tools needed to create and edit Prezi presentations. Tools are available for inserting files, drawings, shapes, images, and YouTube videos from a computer, selecting color and fonts, adding frames, creating a path to connect disparate elements, and selecting the order these elements appear in the presentation. There is also a Show mode to demo the actual presentation.

- Transformation Zebra is the intuitive tool that allows users to easily manipulate objects on the zoomable canvas mentioned above, with functions such as delete, drag and drop, resize, rotate, duplicate, bring forward or backward, or zoom and pan.

- The Navigation Menu has functions to quickly access and save the presentation, editing functions such as undo and redo, and playback controls for viewing completed Prezis.

➤ Unlike Microsoft PowerPoint, Prezi can be used directly from an internet browser such as Firefox, Internet Explorer, Chrome, or Safari and does not require users to install additional software. Prezi Desktop (only available to users who upgrade to the Pro version) can be installed to a desktop and used without internet access.

➤ There is an Export to Portable Prezi function available for presenters wishing to download a noneditable version of a finished Prezi to present offline (without an internet connection) or to copy the Prezi to a CD or DVD.

➤ There are multiple ways for new users to connect with social networks to keep up-to-date with new Prezi features and other newsworthy items. On the homepage there are links to Facebook (www.facebook.com/pages/Prezi/52193296770), the Prezi Twitter account (www.twitter.com/#!/prezi), a community-powered forum (community.prezi.com/prezi), updated blog posts (blog.prezi.com), and RSS feed subscriptions (feeds.feedburner.com/preziblog).

How Cybrarians Can Use This Resource

Creativity Tool for Presentations and Collaborative Group Work

The Prezi Blog (blog.prezi.com) is a great conduit for finding Prezi personal success stories. The reviews so far have been impressive, with users contrasting Prezi's rich visual imagery and interconnected concepts model to Microsoft PowerPoint's text-heavy, outline-based linear style of presentations. Positive comments include how the software helped "visualize thoughts," forced presenters to "think about what my message was, not all of the explanation and detail that supports what I wanted to say," how moving elements around on a canvas "tells a better story," and that the tool "places more emphasis and importance on the speaker's qualities and ideas." In addition to its obvious use in conference and workshop presentations, Prezi

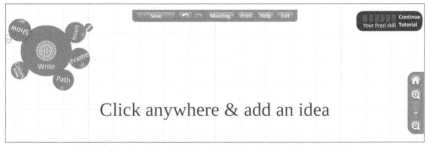

The Prezi editor is the main dashboard provided
to users to create Prezi presentations.

provides support as a creativity tool for collaborative group work, project planning, and brainstorming sessions.

F Y I

Prezi released the new Prezi for iPad app enabling iPad users to easily show Prezis while on the move, thus bringing ideas into everyday discussions. This app can be downloaded from Apple iTunes (itunes.apple.com/us/app/prezi/ id407759942).

Endnotes

1. "Members Adam Somlai-Fischer," TED: Ideas Worth Spreading, www.ted.com/profiles/548262 (accessed August 10, 2011).

2. "About Prezi," Prezi, www.prezi.com/about (accessed August 10, 2011).

65

Project Gutenberg
digital library
www.gutenberg.org

Overview

Project Gutenberg has the enviable reputation of being the first and largest single collection of free ebooks on the internet. The project is host to more than 36,000 ebooks freely accessible to the public on the website (www.gutenberg.org). These free ebooks can be read on a computer (notebook, netbook, or desktop), on ebook readers (iPad, Kindle, Nook, Sony Reader), and on mobile devices (iPhone, iPod Touch, Android). Although the bulk of the collection is comprised of ebooks, which can be easily downloaded, Project Gutenberg also publishes audiobooks, movies, and music.

Founder Michael Hart has published many anecdotal stories of how he started the project.[1] In 1971, he was given $100,000,000 worth of computer time on a mainframe. One of the first projects he undertook was to type the full text of the Declaration of Independence. His idea was that anyone who had access to a computer could have a copy of this seminal document. He continued this project by adding classic American texts, the Bible, and the collected works of Shakespeare. These seed collections provided the foundation for what is now referred to as Project Gutenberg.

Due to copyright restrictions, Project Gutenberg does not publish or make accessible texts still in copyright without permission. Given this restriction, full texts are available for books published pre-1923. Thus, users generally would not find the latest bestsellers or modern computer books in the collection. Instead, they can read original classical works from the start of the past century and previous centuries, from authors like Shakespeare, Poe, Dante, and trusted favorites like the

Sherlock Holmes stories by Sir Arthur Conan Doyle, the Tarzan and Mars books of Edgar Rice Burroughs, *Alice's Adventures in Wonderland* as told by Lewis Carroll, and many others.[2]

Books added to the collection are chosen by volunteers. The entire process—from selection to digitization—hinges on the support of this cadre of volunteers. A volunteer decides on the title of the book that should be added to the collection, obtains a copy of the book, and does the work necessary to turn it into a downloadable ebook. Other volunteer activities include proofreading, recording audiobooks by registering with LibriVox (a project with the goal of creating an audio record of every book in the public domain), burning CDs and DVDs, donating money, and promoting Project Gutenberg on personal websites and blogs. It is noteworthy that there are mirror copies of Project Gutenberg on all seven continents.

Features

➤ No fee or registration is required to access and download the ebooks on the Project Gutenberg website (www.gutenberg.org).

➤ On the homepage, there are a number of options available for searching the collection:

- Use the search boxes on the left navigator bar to enter search queries by author and title.

- Use the advanced search page with filters such as author, title, subject, language, category, Library of Congress class number, file type, and etext number.

- Browse a list of recently added ebooks.

- Browse a list of Top 100 downloaded ebooks.

- Browse the Project Gutenberg offline catalogs using an FTP client.

- Browse a list of audiobooks (human-read and computer-generated).

Project Gutenberg is host to more than 36,000 ebooks
freely accessible to the public on the project website.

➤ For each title found by direct search or from a browse list, the
following features are included:

• A full bibliographic record is returned for each title
searched with the following data: author, translator, title,

language, Library of Congress class number, subject, category, copyright status, release date, and number of downloads from the website.

- A list of supported formats for downloading the ebook includes EPUB, HTML, Kindle, Plucker, QiOO, and plain text. It should be noted that newly supported formats are regularly added to the project.

- Readers can browse a list of related books downloaded by other Project Gutenberg readers.

- A tab with a link to Twitter automatically creates a tweet to alert followers about the title searched and found in the collection (e.g., *Reading: The Notebooks of Leonardo Da Vinci — Complete #free #ebooks @gutenberg_org http://www.gutenberg.org/ebooks/5000*).

- Smartphone users can scan the QR code (two-dimensional code) attached to each book title, and if the smartphone has the appropriate app, it will open the phone browser to the mobile version of the page currently being viewed on the computer screen.

➤ Project Gutenberg periodically generates CD and DVD image files of books from the collection and makes these freely available on the website for users wishing to compile these into CDs or DVDs for their personal use.

➤ The Project Gutenberg Wiki is a community-driven forum for useful information and resources of interest to the ebook community (www.gutenberg.org/wiki/Gutenberg:The_Project_Gutenberg_Wiki).

➤ A mobile version of Project Gutenberg (m.gutenberg.org) is accessible from the homepage.

➤ Access to Project Gutenberg free public domain ebooks is available for iPhone, iPad, and iPod Touch users via the Lexcycle Stanza (www.lexcycle.com/download) ebook reader app.

How Cybrarians Can Use This Resource

Augmenting Library Collections

With more than 36,000 downloadable ebook titles, Project Gutenberg can supplement any library's ebook collection. The Library of Congress is currently promoting the project by including it as a resource in its eresources online catalog (eresources.loc.gov).

Volunteer Work

The success of Project Gutenberg can be attributed mainly to the sterling work of a team of volunteers. Cybrarians can volunteer to be part of this project by participating in the following activities:

➤ Volunteer to be a proofreader at the Distributed Proofreaders site (www.pgdp.net/c). During this web-based proofreading process, volunteers compare a scanned page image and the corresponding OCR text on a single webpage, correct visible errors, and submit the revised version back to the main website.

➤ Volunteer to be a smooth reader at the Distributed Proofreaders site (www.pgdp.net/c/tools/post_proofers/smooth_reading.php). The goal of smooth reading is to have volunteers read the text normally, while notating obvious errors and reporting these errors if they disrupt the main ideas and flow of the book. It is not full-scale proofreading, as comparison with the digitized text is not required.

➤ Volunteer to read and record chapters of books in the project by registering with LibriVox (librivox.org/volunteer-for-librivox).

FYI

Project Gutenberg provides on its website a
listing of partners and affiliates that also offer
access to and promote the distribution of more
than 100,000 free ebooks.[3]

Endnotes

1. "About," Project Gutenberg, www.gutenberg.org/wiki/Gutenberg:About (accessed August 10, 2011).

2. Ibid.

3. "Partners, Affiliates, and Resources," Project Gutenberg, www.gutenberg.org/wiki/Gutenberg:Partners%2C_Affiliates_and_Resources (accessed August 10, 2011).

66

Qwika
search engine
www.qwika.com

Overview

Qwika is a search engine designed specifically for searching wikis. As stated on the homepage, the resource was created to bridge the language gap in Wikipedia, where the growth in English content far outweighs the coverage in other languages. Qwika attempts to fix this inconsistency by indexing content found in wikis in languages other than English and providing access to this machine-translated content in the shortest possible time. Current estimates show that Qwika indexes 1,158 wikis in 12 langauges.[1]

Qwika's unique features are of particular interest to multilingual web researchers who may wish to search for terms in their own language and immediately view matching results translated from content in English and other languages. The founder of the resource, Luke Metcalfe, readily admits that these returned results are not without imperfections, but can "provide a starting point for [researchers] to translate manually into their own language."[2]

Qwika's content is mainly harvested from Wikipedia (www. wikipedia.org; see Chapter 89) and the lesser known publishing platform Wikia (www. wikia.com). Support is provided for the following languages: German, French, Japanese, Italian, Dutch, Portuguese, Spanish, Greek, Korean, Chinese, and Russian. Qwika was launched in February 2006 by search technology company Rapid Intelligence.

Features

➤   A Qwika Toolbar is available on the homepage for download by Internet Explorer and Mozilla Firefox users (www.qwika.com/toolbar/toolbar.html).

➤   A centralized search box strategically placed on the homepage is available for entering search queries. All search queries can be limited by languages selected from a drop-down menu. Search results returned and translated from languages other than the one selected by the user are clearly indicated in bold.

Qwika   Qwika Toolbar for IE and Firefox users!

Home > English

Searching 21,964,380 articles in 1,158 wikis.   Press release (Feb 17): New search engine helps bridge the language gap in Wikipedia
Beta release. Any comments please contact us   Press release (Apr 4): Qwika search engine now indexes 1158 wikis in 12 languages

Search wikis:

[   ] [English ▾] [Search]

In the News - 27 Mar

Guantanamo Bay	Marvin Harrison	Fashion Week	Kate Winslet	Mickey Rourke
Arsene Wenger	Peter Chernin	Sir Alex Ferguson	AR Rahman	Michael Jennings
Jose Mourinho	Gary Locke	Tiger Woods	Danny Boyle	Miguel Cotto
Roland Burris	Jennifer Aniston	Fir Park	Black History Month	Jade Goody

News

BIG UPDATE TO THE FULL WIKI
Fri 1 Oct 10
We are trialling some hot new features at The Full Wiki. You said it's easy to get lost in Wikipedia. We heard you and now have breadcrumbs. And our quizzes are more fun with "What's this picture?" type questions. Like with this Lady Gaga quiz. We also have interesting facts listed on the right hand of articles in our Did you know? section.

View: comments (0)

WE HAVE MORE QUIZZES THAN THE REST OF THE INTERNET COMBINED!
Wed 8 Sep 10
The Full Wiki has released its most interactive feature: quizzes on 44,000 topics. We use Wikipedia as our source to what we believe is the largest quiz source in human history.

Geography Quizzes

- Japan Quiz
- United States Quiz
- Racism in Europe Quiz
- United Kingdom Quiz
- Canada Quiz
- India Quiz

Quizzes about Emotions

- Envy Quiz
- Sympathy Quiz
- Contempt Quiz
- Pity Quiz
- Gratitude Quiz

People Quizzes

- Barack Obama Quiz
- Martin Short Quiz
- Nancy Dolman Quiz
- Ethan Hawke Quiz
- Adolf Hitler Quiz

More Quizzes

- Tornado Quiz
- Serial Killer Quiz
- Fallout 3 Quiz
- Eminem Quiz
- Lady Gaga Quiz

Qwika currently searches 1,158 wikis
translated from 12 different languages.

> The homepage also performs the dual function of an updated wiki-watch news page with postings on new wikis, wiki-related services, and enhancements to existing wikis.

How Cybrarians Can Use This Resource

Research Tool

Currently searching 1,158 wikis translated from 12 different languages, Qwika can be promoted as a resource that complements Wikipedia and can be marketed to multilingual researchers wishing to conduct a singular search across all wiki content in their native language and have immediate access to results translated from English and other languages.

F Y I

Qwika provides a link to the online portal Full Wiki (top-topics.thefullwiki.org), which features a page on trending hot topics in Wikipedia in more than 13,000 categories.

Endnotes

1. Qwika homepage, www.qwika.com (accessed August 10, 2011).
2. "New Search Engine Helps Bridge the Language Gap in Wikipedia," Qwika, February 17, 2006, www.qwika.com/press/en/press_release.html (accessed August 10, 2011).

67

Readerjack.com
online publishing service
www.readerjack.com

Overview

Readerjack.com is a self-publishing service and online ebookstore combining the best of both worlds for authors and readers alike. For aspiring authors, this resource provides the tools to upload and publish their work online, assisting with services such as ISBN (International Standard Book Number) assignment, copyright, and promotion through the internet and print media. Additionally, authors are involved in setting the price of their work and receiving royalties for each book sold.

For readers, the site is promoted as an online portal to search for and buy books by new and established authors as well as browse a selection of more than 16,000 ebooks from the Project Gutenberg digital library (see Chapter 65). Registered members can take advantage of a free service for posting classified ads and promoting literary and other events such as poetry readings, school plays, book fairs, and trade shows.

The service is offered by Readerjack Inc., a company based in Canada. Permanent copies of all published works on the platform are archived at Library and Archives Canada (www.collectionscanada.gc.ca).

Features

➣ An easily navigable search interface is provided on the homepage for readers and authors to search for ebooks by author, title, genre, ISBN, and keywords, or browse for titles arranged under genres such as Children's Literature, Fiction, Nonfiction, and Young Adult.

➤ Free hosting service is available for new authors to upload, promote, and sell ebooks. To initiate the process, members must first register as a Readerjack.com author, sign in, and then use the tools provided to upload their work. The publishers guarantee that authors receive 50 percent of the royalties for each sale and retain 100 percent ownership of the work. Authors can set the book's sale price, obtain a free ISBN, and access free networking tools to assist with promotion.

➤ Readerjack.com's free classified section (www.readerjack. com/homes/classifieds) is available for authors to promote their work. This service is promoted as a valuable resource for finding the professional help required to edit, proof, and translate new works. Additional promotional opportunities are offered by way of podcasts and blogs, and by registering with the Readerjack.com Facebook Group (www.tinyurl.com/ 3c5g4wd).

➤ Registered members also have access to an online events calendar (www.readerjack.com/homes/events) for searching local literary events or publicizing events to promote their work. This database of events is updated regularly and can be filtered by event type, country, city, cost, and date, and also includes postings for book readings, poetry recitals, trade shows, and book signings. Members can take advantage of the Send-to-a-Friend feature in the calendar to notify friends of events posted.

➤ The Awards section on the homepage (www.readerjack.com/ homes/awards) is offered as a free service for authors to search an awards database and enter information on literary and academic awards they have received. This database can be searched by genre, country, or keyword.

How Cybrarians Can Use This Resource

➤ Promote self-publishing platform to local authors.

➤ Utilize Readerjack.com as a collaborative publishing platform.

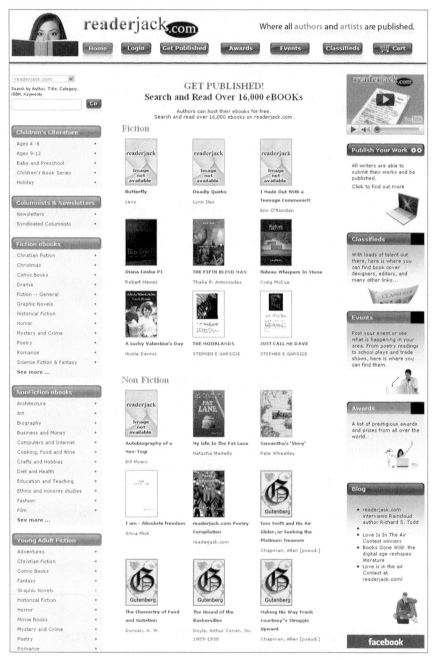

A robust platform is provided on the Readerjack.com homepage
for readers to search for ebooks and for authors to upload their work.

➤   Publicize local library events on the Readerjack.com online
calendar.

➤   Promote the Readerjack.com awards section to encourage
local authors to enter information on literary and academic
awards they have received.

F Y I

A YouTube video (1 minute, 21 seconds)

hosted on the Readerjack.com homepage

(www.readerjack.com) guides authors through

the steps involved in self-publishing their

works.

68

Remember the Milk
productivity tool
www.rememberthemilk.com

Overview

For cybrarians, juggling and managing daily, weekly, and monthly professional and personal tasks are generally time-consuming. Over the years, help has been proffered by way of add-on task management applications in email programs such as Outlook, Gmail, and Yahoo! Mail. Remember the Milk (RTM), which is a play on the adage "don't forget the milk," is a free service created to make managing tasks and creating a to-do list a more enjoyable experience. As the RTM team notes on its About Us page, "As a subscriber to this service, you no longer have to write your to-do lists on sticky notes, whiteboards, random scraps of paper, or the back of your hand."[1]

RTM—when all of its functionality is put to full use—is an all-around electronic planner that offers users the capability to create and manage tasks on the web; send reminders via SMS, email, or instant messages; share or publish lists with contact groups; and obtain support for iCalendar (a standard for calendar data exchange across applications and OS platforms).

The RTM developers began as a small Australian company initially staffed with the two early founders Emily Boyd and Omar Kilani. What started as a project in August 2004 developed into a full-scale web application that was successfully launched in October 2005. RTM now has more than 2.5 million registered users.[2]

Features

> Potential users can sign up for free on the RTM website (www.rememberthemilk.com/signup) by supplying first, last, and user name, password, and email address. Users can also opt to upgrade to a pro account with a paid subscription.

> An intuitive interface makes light work of adding, editing, and managing tasks. All accounts start out with five standardized lists: Inbox, Personal, Work, Study, and Sent. The Inbox is similar to an email inbox, except that instead of email, users receive tasks. Personal, Work, and Study store tasks categorized using the same headings. The Sent list stores the tasks sent to other users. Users have the option of creating new lists, and deleting, renaming, and archiving existing lists.

> For each new task created, RTM users can set a due date, indicate if the task is repetitive, enter an estimated completed date, add a tag to group similar tasks together, add a geographic location to locate tasks on a map, add a URL, or assign a priority. Once created, task lists can be easily printed or shared with a network of friends.

> The RTM iCalendar service allows members to subscribe to and access lists from various calendar software such as Apple iCal, Google Calendar, Mozilla Sunbird, and Microsoft Outlook.

> There are a number of options available for receiving reminders for tasks set with due dates. Reminders can be received via email, SMS, and instant messenger (AIM, Gadu-Gadu, Google Talk, ICQ, Jabber, MSN, Skype, and Yahoo! are all supported).

> Extensive keyboard shortcuts can make task management more efficient. A list of RTM keyboard shortcuts is provided to save users time on typing key strokes (www.rememberthe milk.com/help/answers/basics/keyboard.rtm).

> RTM comes equipped with a task search engine facilitating both basic and advanced searching. The basic search allows members to enter search queries for words that appear in the

name of the task they wish to locate. The advanced search feature allows searching for tasks using matching criteria (such as tags, priority set, and date due).

➤ Using the Add to RTM bookmarklet or button, which can be readily installed in a browser toolbar (Internet Explorer, Mozilla, Opera, Safari, Firefox), RTM members can easily add important events and dates to their RTM tasks lists while browsing the web.

➤ RTM members can manage tasks on the go by accessing the full-featured mobile version of the service (m.rememberthe milk.com). RTM apps are available for the iPhone, iPod Touch, Android, BlackBerry, and iPad.

➤ The RTM API is currently available for noncommercial use by outside developers. As an open source service, this encourages any developer to write applications that interact with RTM.

How Cybrarians Can Use This Resource

Online Scheduling and Task Management

One RTM user blogs about the service as being a time and money saver, and provides examples of how the service can be used to manage

All new RTM accounts have access to five
standardized lists: Inbox, Personal, Study, Work, and Sent.

business, personal, and lifestyle tasks. The list includes using the service for managing blogs (planning and scheduling upcoming postings that have not been written), long-term project management (creating itemized list with due dates), creating grocery lists, managing online coupons, and setting up reminders to pay bills (www.thesimpledollar.com/2007/01/30/remember-the-milk).

F Y I

Google Calendar is a similar (if not more popular) free online scheduling application with similar features and uses. Interested users may sign in with an existing account or create a new account to start the service at the Google website (www.google.com/calendar).

Endnotes

1. "About," Remember The Milk, www.rememberthemilk.com/about (accessed August 10, 2011).

2. Ibid.

69

Rollyo
search engine
www.rollyo.com

Overview

Although categorized as a search engine, Rollyo has a unique distinction when compared with search engines Bing (Chapter 8) and SortFix (Chapter 76). Rollyo (an abbreviation for roll your own engine) puts the power of search in users' hands by giving them the tools to create their own personal search engines, referred to as Searchrolls. This customizable search engine was specifically designed for web researchers who have grown tired of wading though thousands of irrelevant search results to get to the information they want. Using Rollyo, researchers can narrow their searches to only the content of a list of specified websites they already know and trust.

No technical expertise or in-depth knowledge of programming is required to create Searchrolls. The process is quite simple. Searchers are allowed to hand pick the URLs (maximum of 25) of their favorite websites (including blogs and news sources) on any given topic. Rollyo does the intricate work required, creating a custom search engine to search the websites identified. The Searchrolls created are displayed on personalized search pages.

New Rollyo users can explore, save, and edit Searchrolls created by the community of Rollyo users. For example, on the main page, Searchrolls created by so-called high-profile high rollers, including Rosario Dawson (Latino issues), Arianna Huffington (politics), and Debra Messing (favorite online boutiques), are prominently displayed for users to explore or edit.

The Rollyo service is powered by Yahoo!, which provides the basic results returned for websites, news sources, and blog posts searched. Rollyo was launched in 2005 and has its headquarters in San Francisco.

On Rollyo's homepage, users can explore, save, and edit Searchrolls created by the community of Rollyo users.

Features

➤ Registering to use Rollyo is optional but advisable for new users wishing to make Searchrolls public and share with friends. Searchrolls are created by clicking on the Create Searchroll tab on the main page (www.rollyo.com/createroll. html) and completing the onscreen form with the following information:

• Choose a descriptive name for your Searchroll. The limit is 20 characters.

• Enter up to 25 URLs of your favorite websites.

• Choose a subject area (optional), under categories such as computers and internet, entertainment, health, news and media, reference, and science where the Searchroll will be listed in the Rollyo directory.

• Enter any number of tags or keywords (optional) to help other users find your Searchroll and group similar Searchrolls together.

• Check the option to make the Searchroll public so that it can be easily discovered by other users and shared via email with colleagues and friends.

➤ Registered users who have not created their own search engines have immediate access to a dashboard with custom Searchrolls/starter search engines to choose from and display on personalized search pages.

➤ Team Rollyo is constantly adding new tools to make Rollyo more navigable and user-friendly. The RollBar bookmarklet can be used to install a Rollyo search engine in a web browser, enhancing users' ability to add websites to Searchrolls on the fly. The Rollyo widget (www.rollyo.com/searchbox.html) can automatically generate HTML code to embed a Rollyo search box on a personal website or blog.

How Cybrarians Can Use This Resource

Reference and Research

Rollyo is listed as one of the 23 Things to explore in the Learning 2.0 Program (plcmcl2-things.blogspot.com) developed by Helene Blowers. Cybrarians successfully completing the program will be aware of the benefits of the Rollyo service in creating specialized topic-based Searchrolls for quick consultations at the reference desk, or to promote online resources on the library's webpage. The Learning 2.0 Rollyo Program (plcmclearning.blogspot.com/2006/09/12-roll-your-own-search-engine.html) features:

➤ Public domain ebooks search (rollyo.com/onfire4jc/public_domain_ebooks)

➤ Rare book library search (rollyo.com/byblos/rare_book_library_search)

➤ Quick quotes (www.rollyo.com/kizuki-sama/quick_quotes_search)

➤ PLCMC (Public Library of Charlotte Mecklenburg) websites—Searchroll created by Helene Bowers (www.rollyo.com/search.html?q=Search . . . &sid=54436& x=14&y=5&togo-v=1)

F Y I

Rollyo was the winner of the Best Trusted
Search at the 2008 Web 2.0 Awards.[1]

Endnote

1. "2008 Web 2.0 Awards," Seomoz, www.seomoz.org/web2.0 (accessed August 10, 2011).

70

Rondee
productivity tool
www.rondee.com

Overview

Rondee is a free conference-calling service. The developers of the service adapted a truncated form of the French word *rendezvous* (a meeting arranged for a specified time and place), in crafting the name for the service. Rondee offers a convenient way to connect and communicate immediately with colleagues, friends, and family by using a telephone.

The service is promoted as being applicable and relevant to a wide-ranging target group, which includes small businesses, educational groups, nonprofit organizations, and activity clubs. This widespread usage is expected, given Rondee's user-friendly interface, which facilitates quick scheduling of conference calls. Calls can be scheduled in advance or on demand, and all that is required is selecting a date and time for the call and entering the email addresses of invitees. Rondee then emails invitations to each invitee along with a unique access code. At the arranged time, each invitee calls (from a landline or cell phone) an assigned telephone number and enters his or her assigned code to start the teleconference. A maximum of 50 persons are allowed per phone-conferencing bridge.

Rondee offers additional services such as attendance and response tracking; online display of conference title, agenda, and attendees' responses on a webpage unique to the scheduled call; call recording; and automated reminders about recurring conferences. The service is headquartered in Palo Alto, California, and was established in 2006.

Features

➤ Signing up for the service from the homepage (www.rondee. com) is optional for on-demand calls, but users must register to use the service for scheduling conference calls for a later date. Scheduling conference calls is easily achieved in three steps:

1. Click on Schedule a New Rondee, indicate a date and time for the conference call, and provide the email addresses of the participants.

2. Rondee then emails invitations to each invitee. When an invitee responds positively to a request to participate in the call, they are directed to a webpage created specifically for the call and agenda items are provided. If the advanced scheduling version of Rondee is used, the conference call can be integrated directly with Microsoft Outlook, Apple iCal, and Google Calendar.

3. At the prearranged date and time, each attendee dials a preassigned telephone number and enters the assigned code. This call costs no more than any other regular long distance call you make from your home or office phone.

➤ A noncomplex web-based form is available for entering the following data to schedule a conference call:

- Title of conference call

- Date and time

- Duration

- Message (describing the meeting and adding agenda items)

- Email addresses of participants

- Check box with the following options:

  - Indicate if Rondee's conference call is recurring.

- Receive a notification email when participants reply, and receive a copy of the invitation sent.

- Allow participants to invite others.

- Email statistics after the call ends.

- Record audio from the conference call. Rondee records audio from calls in MP3 format, which is available for download for 30 days through a link on the webpage created for the Rondee conference. All attendees will be notified that the call is being recorded, and audio from the call is available about 15 minutes after the last person leaves the Rondee.

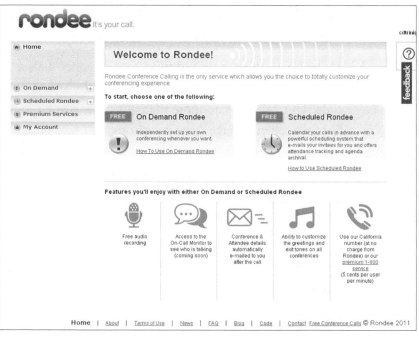

On the Rondee website, calls can be scheduled in advance or on demand by selecting a date and time for the call and entering the email addresses of invitees.

How Cybrarians Can Use This Resource

Scheduling Teleconference Calls

Rondee is ideal as a virtual meeting space where you can hold discussions with a disparate group of people using a telephone. The simple and easily navigable interface is just one of the many benefits for Rondee users. Other benefits include access to primary and back up telephone numbers that can easily be entered as a speed-dial, the flexibility of having access to both web-based advanced scheduling and on-demand calling, the tracking of all attendees' responses, the online display of the name of the person talking during the call, access to the recorded conversation, and access to a full-featured free service when compared to other expensive teleconferencing options.

F Y I

Rondee's Free Conference Calling blog
provides the latest updates about new features
and enhancements to the service (www.rondee.
com/wordpress).

71

Scour
search engine
www.scour.com

Overview

Scour, like all search portals on the web, is on a mission to be branded as a service that delivers added value and the best search experience for end users. It attempts to do this by functioning as a metasearch engine, gathering relevant results from three of the most highly ranked search engines—Google, Yahoo!, and Bing—in response to search queries. These returned results are integrated and displayed on one page. This type of integration enables web searchers to quickly click through to the search engine that, in their opinion, has the most relevant hits.

Scour functionality does not end there. It takes searching the web to the next level by also integrating results from real-time search engine OneRiot (www.oneriot.com), which pulls results from popular social networks like Twitter and Digg, allowing searchers to view in real time what folks are discussing regarding the topic they are currently searching.

Scour thrives on input from its community of users by allowing users to vote search results up (highly relevant) or down (not very relevant) based on the search results' relevance to their query and to add their comments on their experiences with the site. By blending user feedback with proven search algorithms, Scour seems well on its way to its stated purpose to "bridge the gap between searchers and relevant results."[1] The service was established in 2007.

Features

> On the main page (www.scour.com), users are urged to sign up to use the service if they wish to reap all the benefits of

using Scour, such as voting and adding comments to search results.

➤ To search Scour, users can type in keywords in the centralized search box on the homepage with options to limit searches by web, images, video, local, or business. When search results are displayed, searchers will notice that in addition to pulling results from Google, Yahoo!, and Bing, there are also real-time listings from sites like Twitter and Digg. To view real-time results only, users can use the Sort By feature (accessible on the main navigation bar at the top of the search results page), which limits viewed results to one search engine.

➤ Voting and user-generated comments are two important concepts utilized at Scour.com that distinguish the service from other search engines. Although Scour pulls results from the top three search engines, it thrives on and is powered by this feedback from the user community to make the search results more relevant. Searchers must register to add comments and vote. Users are advised that if they obtain a result that does not match their search criteria, they should vote it down by clicking on the thumbs down icon. If a website matches the search criteria, it can be voted up by clicking on the thumbs up icon, and searchers can add positive comments on why they like the site. After enough votes, the website will move up or down in rank, placing the user-reviewed relevant sites at the top. Other searchers can read these reviews when searching Scour and make a more informed decision about selecting the best matching results for their search.

➤ Scour toolbars are available for searching the web from supported browsers. Toolbars are available for Firefox, Internet Explorer, Google, Chrome, and Opera.

➤ Scour is an online searching community built on the contributions of its users. As a result, stringent community guidelines (www.scour.com/communityguidelines) have been created and strictly enforced—especially since the service is open to users 13 years and older—to create a safe search environment.

scour

| Web | Images | Videos | Local | Business |

Web 2.0   Search

Home Goodies Feedback F.A.Q.

Sort by: S G ⚲ b G

Related Searches: web 2.0 templates   web 2.0 sites   web 2.0 design   mobile web 2.0   web 2.0 conference

Results 1-12 for web 2.0   0.245 Seconds

Sponsored Link

Expression Web 4
Buy Directly From Microsoft Store.
microsoftstore.com/expression_web

Hire Web Developers @ $14
Offshore Indian Co. Offer PHP, ASP.Net, ROR,C Programmer on contract.
www.radixweb.com

Build a Website
Build a website in minutes and get your business on the web. Try free
www.homestead.com

Web 2.0 - Wikipedia, the free encyclopedia
A tag cloud (a typical **Web 2.0** phenomenon in itself) presenting **Web 2.0** themes ... Whether **Web 2.0**
is qualitatively different from prior **web** technologies has been ....
en.wikipedia.org/wiki/Web_2.0 Search this Site

G 1
⚲ 1
b 1

What is Web 2.0 - O'Reilly Media
Tim O'Reilly attempts to clarify just what is meant by **Web 2.0**, the term first coined at a
conference brainstorming session between O'Reilly Media and MediaLive ...
oreilly.com/web2/archive/what-is-web Search this Site

19 comments

G 2
⚲ 2
b 2

Web 2.0 Summit 2010 - Co-produced by UBM TechWeb & O'Reilly ...
Nov 29, 2010 ... **Web 2.0** Summit 2010, held at the Palace Hotel, San Francisco, CA,
November 15-17 ..
www.web2summit.com Search this Site

2 comments

G 1
⚲ 4
b

Online tools and applications - Go2web20
Find all Online tools and applications on one page, get a short description, compare, read
reviews, see what people are saying about each one on the **web**....
www.go2web20.net Search this Site

2 comments

G 2
⚲ 7
b 6

Web 2.0
Does "**Web 2.0**" mean anything? Till recently I thought it didn't, but the truth turns
out to be more complicated. Originally, yes, it was meaningless ...
www.paulgraham.com Search this Site

1 comments

G 4
⚲ 10
b 4

Web 2.0 Events: Co-produced by UBM TechWeb and O'Reilly Conferences
Dec 17, 2010 ... **Web 2.0** Expo, co-produced by UBM TechWeb and O'Reilly Media, is a
conference
and tradeshow for the rapidly growing ranks of designers and ...
www.web2expo.com Search this Site

comments

G 3
⚲ 5
b

Web 2.0 - Wikipedia, la enciclopedia libre
Web 2.0 beta. El término **Web 2.0** (2004 presente) está comúnmente asociado con un
fenómeno
Ejemplos de la **Web 2.0** son las comunidades **web**, los servicios **web**, las ...
es.wikipedia.org/wiki/Web_2.0 Search this Site

2 comments

G -
⚲ 3
b -

Web 2.0 Definition from Answers.com
Web 2.0 An umbrella term for the second wave of the World Wide **Web**, which was coined in a
conference
on the subject in 2004 by O'Reilly Media and CMP
www.answers.com/topic/web-2.0 Search this Site

2 comments

G -
⚲ -
b 3

What is Web 2.0 - www.oreillynet.com
Sep 30, 2005 ... The concept of "**Web 2.0**" began with a conference brainstorming session
between O'Reilly and MediaLive International ...
www.oreillynet.com Search this Site

comments

G 5
⚲ -
b -

Web 2.0 Summit 2010 - Co-produced by UBM TechWeb & O'Reilly ...
Web 2.0 Summit 2010, held at the Palace Hotel, San Francisco, CA, November 15-17.
www.web2summit.com/web2010 Search this Site

comments

G -
⚲ -
b 5

web 2.0
Simple web scraping software web 2.0
http://www.mozenda.com/web2.0

Send Text Messages Today
Reach customers on their phones Easy to get started in 5 minutes
http://testing.ly

Custom Website Designing
We help build professional web site with strong
brand value, call now
http://www.dabberdesign.com

web 2.0
Snoozester provides wake up calls and reminder
calls to your phone.
http://snoozester.com

See your ad here...

Scour search results integrate results from Google,
Yahoo!, and Bing, and real-time listings from sites like Twitter and Digg.

➤ The site provides access to a live community statistics window with daily updated figures on the number of users online and daily tracking of the number of comments and votes added by Scour's community of users.

How Cybrarians Can Use This Resource

Promoting Information Literacy

In an effort to promote information literacy, the University of California-Berkeley Libraries created a webpage (www.lib.berkeley. edu/TeachingLib/Guides/Internet/SearchEngines.html) with a table comparing features of the three major search engines, Google, Yahoo!, and Exalead. This one-stop search engine portal is valuable for any researcher wishing to evaluate and understand what each search engine has to offer. Other search engines reviewed include Ask.com, Bing, Dogpile, Rollyo, and Scirus. This is a model that cybrarians can adopt and build on by conducting their own evaluations of other search engines including Scour.

F Y I

In 2009, Scour was a CNET Webware 100 winner under the Search and Reference category.[2]

Endnotes

1. "About Scour," Scour, www.scour.com/about (accessed August 10, 2011).

2. "Webware 100 Winner: Scour," Webware, May 19, 2009, news.cnet.com/8301-13546_109-10237658-29.html?tag=mncol (accessed August 10, 2011).

72

Second Life
3D virtual world
secondlife.com

Overview

Second Life is a 3D virtual world created by Linden Lab in 2003. Since its public launch, the service has grown explosively and today is virtually inhabited by millions of people from around the globe. A free client program, the Second Life Viewer, enables visitors, or "residents," to socialize, interact, and connect with each other through their avatars (a two- or three-dimensional digital representation of a person).

New visitors entering Second Life for the first time start out on Welcome Island. This area is designed to quickly teach users the basics needed to navigate and explore the intricate complexities of Second Life, with the help of guided tutorials on topics such as walking, camera controls, communicating, standing, sitting, flying, and teleporting.

Many libraries and nonprofit organizations have used the Second Life portal to offer innovative services such as lectures, exhibits, book discussions, reference and research assistance, and training to thousands of avatars daily. The Community Virtual Library Foundation is an example of a nonprofit organization formed to support virtual services offered in Second Life through the Community Virtual Library (CVL, www.info island.org). In Second Life, the CVL is comprised of Info Island, Info Island International, Imagination Island, and Cybrary City II, and provides free library resources and services to the residents of Second Life.

Features

➤ From the moment visitors enter Second Life, they will discover a fast-paced digital world filled with people,

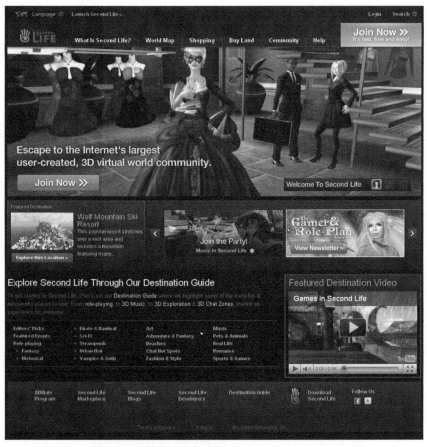

Libraries have used the Second Life web portal
to offer innovative services.

entertainment, experiences, and opportunities. The first
challenge is creating an avatar, which is central to
communicating and connecting with colleagues, friends, and
acquaintances, and necessary for working, shopping,
exploring, learning, or playing in this 3D virtual world.

➢   For the uninitiated, there is a Help page devoted to answering
questions about downloading the Second Life Viewer, system
requirements, tips and tricks, tutorials, personal accounts
and, most importantly, online safety tips for traversing what
can sometimes be perceived as dangerous territory. The
downloadable Quick Start Guide (secondlife.com/support/

quickstart/basic) provides additional information on modifying an avatar's appearance, basic navigation tips, teleporting to a new location, and keyboard shortcuts. Further assistance is available via blogs, community-supported forums, and groups.

> Visitors unsure of what to do when they arrive in Second Life can immediately teleport to Welcome Island and spend some time learning to use the interface and customizing their avatar. The Destination Guide is another source of information useful for discovering and exploring popular spots, allowing visitors to browse and select specific categories such as Featured Events, Role-Playing, Communities, Adventure and Fantasy, Business, Education and Nonprofits, Music, and Real Life. Additionally, there is access to a WorldMap where Second Life residents can find people and explore unique places by clicking on specific spots (represented by green dots on the maps) and teleporting to those destinations.

> In Second Life, residents can purchase land with Linden dollars to build a virtual home or inhabit a scenic location on a private virtual island.

> A personal dashboard is available for all residents to manage accounts and real estate, view which friends are currently online, search for live events, buy Linden dollars, and engage in social activities.

How Cybrarians Can Use This Resource

Socializing by Registering With a Library-Related Community Group

Cybrarians who are bored with their first life can easily register, download the Second Life Viewer, and start exploring Second Life. There are more than 200 groups (secondlife.com/community/groups/?lang=en-US) that congregate over library-related topics. Groups include Digital Libraries, Public Libraries in Second Life, Librarians of Second Life,

Second Life Library 2.0, Florida Librarians of Second Life, and Second Life Medical Library 2.0.

Virtual Library Services

Libraries are using Second Life as the new location for a branch or virtual satellite library. These branch libraries complement their brick-and-mortar counterparts by serving as portals to real-world library collections. Second Life residents are able to:

> ➤ Access library databases, online catalogs, digital archives, and online art exhibits.

> ➤ Obtain live reference assistance at an avatar-manned reference desk.

> ➤ Traverse unknown territory during in-world tours offered to places of interest in Second Life.

> ➤ Attend classes on library instruction, tutorials, and specialized workshops.

> ➤ Network with colleagues.

> ➤ Attend art exhibits, conferences, or lively book discussions.

> ➤ Volunteer to work answering questions at the virtual library reference desk, offer library instruction, catalog virtual collections, or organize special events.

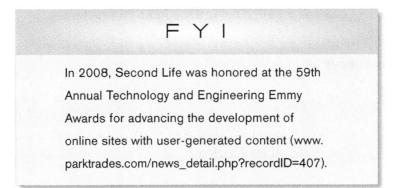

F Y I

In 2008, Second Life was honored at the 59th Annual Technology and Engineering Emmy Awards for advancing the development of online sites with user-generated content (www. parktrades.com/news_detail.php?recordID=407).

73

Shelfari
social cataloging service
www.shelfari.com

Overview

Shelfari, like LibraryThing (Chapter 41), is a social cataloging website for established and aspiring authors, publishers, and avid readers who are looking for a virtual gathering space to connect and share their passion for literary works (fiction and nonfiction), with peers, friends, family, and in some instances, total strangers. The creation of this shared online literary network had its origins in the need by its developers "to enhance the experience of reading by connecting readers in meaningful conversations about the published word."[1]

There are a slew of tools available to support this goal and help this seemingly disconnected global community of book lovers connect with each other in a fun and engaging way. Shelfari's members can search for books; build virtual bookshelves; influence the reading community by rating, adding reviews, and recommending books; join groups to connect with members with similar reading interests; and interact with and learn from published authors.

Based in Seattle, Washington, Shelfari was officially launched in October 2006 and acquired by Amazon in August 2008.

Features

➤ Registration from the homepage (www.shelfari.com) is a requirement for new members wishing to create personalized webpages and immediately start the process of adding book titles to virtual bookshelves.

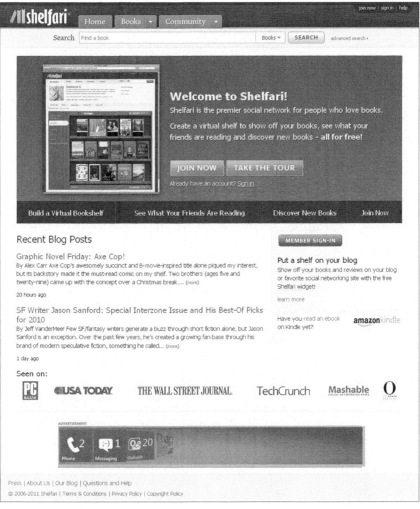

Shelfari homepage welcomes new members wishing to
create personalized webpages and immediately start the
process of adding book titles to virtual bookshelves.

➤ A prominently displayed search box on the homepage enables
readers to search for books in the Shelfari database and add
titles to their virtual bookshelves. For each title, readers can
add rich descriptive metadata to create personalized libraries.
This includes information on whether they have read the
book, plan to read it, or are reading it right now.

➤ Readers can add reviews, ratings (stars), tags, subjects, and classification numbers; mark titles as favorites; write synopses; list favorite quotations; and list book series, authors, and other contributors. They can also add edition details such as date purchased, price, condition of the book, whether the copy is autographed, literary awards received, or if the copy is on loan.

➤ Virtual bookshelves can be designated as private or shared publicly with other Shelfari members.

➤ Resources are available to link to external websites where readers can learn more about the books they are reading, such as related titles, reviews, citations, and suggested reading levels.

➤ Readers can join existing groups or create and lead new groups to discuss their favorite titles with a network of friends and colleagues. Established groups within the Shelfari community (www.shelfari.com/members) include Authors and Writing, Book Clubs by City, Education and Schools, Family and Parenting, Health and Science, Just for Fun, Money and Business, Politics and History, The Reading Life, and World Literature and Culture.

➤ Within the personalized library, readers can view a graphic display of a virtual bookshelf with book jackets showing current titles. This virtual display can be rearranged at will to display a reading timeline by grouping books into the following categories: Books Read, Books Reading Now, Books Plan to Read. This bookshelf (wooden or contemporary design) can be integrated into blogs and personal websites using the Shelfari widget (www.shelfari.com/widget).

➤ By using the Shelfari friend finder, users can connect with friends to see what they are reading. The friend finder scans the user's address book from popular email providers (Gmail, Yahoo! Mail, AOL, Hotmail, Windows Live, MSN) for friends who are members of Shelfari.

➤ Web applications are available on the Shelfari blog (blog.shelfari.com) to integrate the service into two popular social networks, Facebook and Myspace.

How Cybrarians Can Use This Resource

Networking Using Shelfari Library Groups

The group Libraries and Librarians has been established under the category Reading Life in Shelfari (www.shelfari.com/groups/10057/discussions/67762/Uses-of-Shelfari-in-your-library). Several discussion threads have been posted on the success and use of Shelfari in libraries. Innovative uses outlined by community members include:

➤ Creating a webpage with the titles of library books normally listed in the local newspaper

➤ Using the Shelfari widget to integrate a virtual bookshelf with rotating titles on the library's website and Facebook page

➤ Posting blogs that highlight the books reviewed by staff

➤ Including a list of titles in a Reader's Advisory

➤ Utilizing Shelfari apps on Myspace and Facebook pages to feature new books

➤ Integrating Shelfari into a blog or wiki to promote state library reading programs

➤ Integrating the Shelfari widget on the library's homepage with a list of "staff picks"

➤ Posting book reviews to Shelfari

F Y I

Shelfari authors' pages (www.shelfari.com/authors) are devoted to capturing information about established authors and include a comprehensive listing of their literary works, detailed biographies, and accompanying photographs.

Endnote

1. "About Shelfari," Shelfari, www.shelfari.com/Shelfari/AboutUs.aspx (accessed August 10, 2011).

74

Skype
productivity tool
www.skype.com

Overview

Skype is a software application that, when downloaded to a computer, allows users to make free video and voice calls, send instant messages, and share files with other Skype users.

Skype-to-Skype voice, video, and conference calls are completely free, while calls to both traditional landline telephones and mobile phones can be made with paid monthly subscriptions.

If there is one software that can be said to have truly revolutionized PC-to-PC phone calls, enabling global conversations for individuals and corporations alike, it is Skype. Statistical data on the Skype website indicates that Skype had an average of 145 million connected users per month in the fourth quarter of 2010. Skype users made 20+ billion minutes of voice and video calls in 2010, approximately 42 percent of which was video.[1]

The service was launched in 2003. In May 2011, Microsoft and Skype announced an agreement under which Microsoft would acquire Skype for a reported 8.5 billion dollars.[2] One word of caution is advised, and this is that Skype is not a replacement for your ordinary telephone and cannot be used for making emergency telephone calls. Skype-to-Skype calls are always free but with Pay Per Minute and Pay Monthly subscriptions you can call friends and family on any phone.

Features

➤ New subscribers to the service create an account on the Skype homepage (www.skype.com/intl/en/home) by completing the online form with the following information: first name, email address, profile details (birthday, gender, country, city, and language), data on how you intend to use Skype, Skype name, password, and mobile phone number.

➤ The hardware requirements to make Skype-to-Skype voice and video calls are a PC or Mac computer, an internet connection (high-speed broadband is recommended for best quality), a built-in microphone and speakers (or headsets), and a webcam installed on your computer (for video calls). Additionally, subscribers can choose to import friends and contacts from their email providers.

➤ The Skype software (used to make the actual calls) can be downloaded from the website (www.skype.com/intl/en/get-skype) to your computer. Multiplatform versions of the software application are available for Windows, Mac OS X, and Linux. Web applications are also available for mobile phones including the iPhone, iPod Touch, iPad, Android, Symbian, and Nokia.

➤ The Skype software that is downloaded from the homepage has an intuitive, minimalistic, user-friendly interface, and this accounts largely for the service's global popularity. Making calls (PC to PC), is achieved in three steps:

1.   Click the Contacts button (on Skype's main menu). Locate the person you want to call in your contact list and click their name. You will see their details in the main window. There are also graphical icons next to all names in the list of contacts to indicate if the person is on Skype, or if you are calling a phone or mobile number (charges are incurred if calling a landline or mobile phone).

2.   Click the green Call button for voice calls. If you have a webcam installed, click the Video Call button to make it a video call.

3.   When the call is complete, click the red End Call button.

➤ Skype members have access to two types of service models—
a free service and subscription services with costs attached
(monthly, pay per minute, and Skype credit). Features
accessed when using the free service include:

- Skype-to-Skype voice and video calls

- Skype-to-Skype conference calls

- Instant messaging

- File transfer and screen sharing

➤ Features accessed with paid subscriptions include:

- Calls to and from landlines and mobiles

- SMS messages

- Skype-to-go number

- Voicemail

- Call forwarding to landlines and mobiles

- Access via Wi-Fi hotspots

➤ For new subscribers, help is proffered by way of community
and technology blogs (blogs.skype.com) that are maintained
by the Skype Team to keep members updated with company
news and upgraded features.

How Cybrarians Can Use This Resource

Skyping a Librarian

Internet voice and video calling has demonstrated a dramatic rise in
usage with corresponding improvements in features and expanded
functions. Using Skype as an example of a communication technology
that can potentially have a positive impact on society, cybrarians who
are always on the cusp of change and ready to adopt such technologies
for outreach and public services are already evaluating software applications such as Skype as potential sources of innovative services.

The Ohio University Libraries Skype video and internet telephony pilot reference service is an example of such innovative services. Librarians at this university have installed a kiosk in the lobby of the Alden Library with a webcam and a link to Skype in order to provide instant reference service with a live librarian. On the library's webpage, the service is promoted in the following way:

> You can now ask us a question via Skype, the free internet calling service. You can call, videocall, or message us for free using your Skype account—just add ohiolibref, our Skype ID, to your contact list to begin. This service is open whenever

The Skype software is available on the homepage in versions
for Windows, Mac, and Linux, and for mobile devices.

the Learning Commons is—24/5 M–F and long weekend hours. (www.library.ohiou.edu/ask/skype.html)

An updated list of other libraries using Skype is maintained at Library Success: A Best Practices Wiki (www.libsuccess.org/index.php? title=Libraries_Offering_VoIP_or_Video_Reference).

Business Calls to Corporate Clients and Vendors

Cybrarians can download the free business version of Skype (www. skype.com/intl/en-us/business/download) to facilitate free Skype-to-Skype voice and video business calls to clients and vendors anywhere in the world. Features of this service include free instant messaging and free file sharing.

FYI

Skype's integration with Facebook allows users to:

- View Facebook Newsfeed in Skype
- Instant message directly from Skype to Facebook
- Update Facebook status from Skype
- View Facebook friends in your Skype contact list

Endnotes

1. "About Skype," Skype, about.skype.com (accessed August 10, 2011).

2. "Microsoft to Acquire Skype," Skype, about.skype.com/press/2011/05/microsoft_to_acquire_skype.html (accessed August 10, 2011).

75

SlideShare
productivity tool
www.slideshare.net

Overview

If there is a need to promote a new product or service at your library, share PowerPoint slides with an audience who could not attend your conference presentation, or get feedback from colleagues on a slide presentation for an upcoming workshop, then SlideShare is the resource to use to make this happen. SlideShare is by far one of the fastest-growing online networks for sharing slides and other online presentations.

The site's current traffic statistics show that it registers more than 50 million visitors monthly.[1] As a service, it offers users the ability to upload and publicly share PowerPoint presentations and Word, OpenOffice, Adobe PDF, and Apple iWork documents, videos, and webinars. A recently added feature allows users to sync audio with slides. There are obvious advantages to archiving and storing presentations in this way: no need to email the file to recipients, or carry a copy around on a USB drive. Your presentation's URL link on SlideShare can easily be shared with your audience by email for easy access and reference. Add to this the knowledge that there are built-in permission controls to keep your data relatively secure.

For researchers, SlideShare is a great place to find presentations and documents on almost any topic. This is easily done by either entering a keyword search in the main search box on the homepage, browsing by subject categories, or browsing staff picks such as top presentation of the day, featured presentations, or presentations "currently hot" on Twitter, Facebook, and LinkedIn.

Once a presentation is found, researchers can add comments to it, bookmark the URL as a favorite, save and download the file to their computer, or share the content on blogs and social networks such as Delicious, LinkedIn, Facebook, and Twitter. A free account allows users to upload and share presentations. Upgrading to SlideShare Pro offers added features including analytics, ad-free interface, buzz tracking, customized channels, and branding. Launched in October 2006, SlideShare currently has offices in San Francisco, California, and New Delhi, India.

Features

➤   Registration and login is required to post presentations to the service. Similar to all Web 2.0-type services, new SlideShare users can select the sign-up link on the homepage (www.slide share.net), and enter a username, a valid email address, and a password, and click on the Sign Up button. Once the email address is verified, users can enjoy the full benefits of the service.

➤   SlideShare supports the uploading of several formats including Microsoft PowerPoint, Apple's Keynote, Microsoft Word, OpenOffice, Adobe PDF documents, and Apple iWork Pages. Once uploaded, presentations can be kept private or shared publicly by sending the URL to email contacts on Yahoo! Mail, Gmail, Hotmail, MSN, and AOL.

➤   SlideShare is also a great resource to search for presentations and documents on almost any topic. Find presentations by entering search queries in the main search box, browsing specific categories (automotive, business, education, gadgets and reviews, health and medicine, news and politics), clicking on hyperlinked tags, selecting a slideshow spotlighted as the Top or Featured Presentation of the day, or viewing buzzworthy presentations trending on Facebook and Twitter. Slides returned after a successful search can be saved as favorites (using the heart-shaped icon), tagged with keywords that will help to retrieve them in a later search, reviewed with comments added, downloaded to a computer or external drive, embedded in a blog or website by copying and pasting automatically generated HTML code, or sent to a shared group.

➤ Slidecasting is a new multimedia format from SlideShare, where presentations can be mashed up with podcasts. To create Slidecasts, users upload slides to SlideShare, access an audio file (which can be hosted externally on a server or podcasting service), and link the slides and audio together using SlideShare's synchronization tool. When Slidecasts are played, the audio is streamed from its location and plays with the slides.

➤ Under the Events tab on SlideShare's homepage, links are provided to Groups (www.slideshare.net/groups) or forums to host discussions about any common topic or theme. Users can create a new group or join groups already in session to debate issues with colleagues or other SlideShare users. Established groups include Art and Design, Education and E-learning, Literature and History, News and Politics, Tech and Internet.

➤ Events are similar to groups (www.slideshare.net/events), with additional features such as the ability to add a location, date, and time. Events are useful for sharing content related to a conference, seminar, or workshop.

➤ As an open source service, SlideShare APIs encourage developers to create mashups and other customized applications.

➤ SlideShare apps are currently available for Facebook, LinkedIn, and mobile devices (iPhone, iPad and Android). There are plans to make the application compatible with more devices.

How Cybrarians Can Use This Resource

Shared Presentations and Professional Networking

SlideShare is often described as the YouTube of PowerPoint presentations and is currently the best free resource available to promote slides and other marketable presentations on the web. It is a unique medium to share ideas with a global audience, network with others, and generate

SlideShare users can search for presentations and
documents on almost any topic from the homepage.

leads for professional work. Librarians and other professionals have found the service beneficial for:

➤   Conducting research for a conference or for a workshop presentation

➤   Embedding slideshows on blogs or websites

➤   Sharing slideshows publicly or privately

➤   Creating slidecasts by syncing audio to slides

➤   Marketing library programs using SlideShare Events

➤   Joining SlideShare groups to connect with members who share similar interests

F Y I

Rashmi Sinha, founder and CEO of SlideShare, was named one of the 2010 Top 25 Women in Tech to Watch.[2]

Endnotes

1. "What Is SlideShare," SlideShare, www.slideshare.net/about (accessed August 10, 2011).

2. Tony Perkins, "The 2010 Top 25 Women in Tech to Watch," Always On, July 29, 2010, alwayson.goingon.com/AOStory/2010-Top-25-Women-Tech-Watch-0 (accessed August 10, 2011).

76

SortFix
search engine
addons.mozilla.org/en-US/firefox/addon/
sortfix-Extension

Overview

SortFix is described as an intuitive graphical interface that "enhances" searching within Google and other search engines.[1] SortFix aims to do this and, at the same time, surpass search engine rivals Yahoo!, Google, and Bing, by applying what it calls a simple basket concept to its somewhat innovative search technology. In a SortFix search, you literally drag Power Words (keywords most relevant to your search query) into or out of graphical baskets to refine your search and obtain better search results. This new concept is explained by the SortFix Team with the use of an analogy, in that in real life individuals can place different items inside a basket and intuitively opt to add what is relevant and remove what is irrelevant.

In an ongoing effort to boost users' search skills and abilities and stay true to its stated goal of building on existing online search functionality to create a more interactive, refined, and user-friendly search, SortFix is no longer offered as a standalone application on a single website. Instead, it is currently offered as a Mozilla Firefox extension available on Mozilla's Add-Ons page (addons.mozilla.org/en-US/firefox/ addon/sortfix-Extension). Searchers now have the option of easily downloading, installing, and integrating this application to refine search queries conducted within their favorite search engines.

Once installed, users searching Google and other search engines can benefit from SortFix technology—a combination of statistical text algorithms, data mining, and natural language processing algorithms—and obtain improved search results. As noted on the application's download page, "SortFix does not tinker with Google's [or other search engines] results; rather, it offers a collection of words (defined as Power Words) based on the searcher's query, which can then be used to filter the results. The user decides which Power Words are relevant and whether to add them to, or subtract them from, the search."[2]

The SortFix Search Extension is cross-platform and works on Mac OS X, Windows, and Linux systems.

Features

➤ The latest version (2.10 released in March 2011) of SortFix Search Extension can be downloaded from Mozilla's Firefox Add-Ons page.

➤ SortFix's simple and intuitive search user interface (SUI) enables users to easily refine search engine queries to retrieve the most accurate results. (Once SortFix is installed, the SUI automatically displays at the top of the results screen.) For

SortFix's simple and intuitive Search User Interface enables users to easily refine search results from other search engines.

example, to enhance Google's search results, searchers can enter search terms in the main search box on the Google homepage. Within SortFix's SUI, Power Words are displayed in a graphical basket. Searchers can drag and drop words from the Power Words basket to the Add to Search basket, or remove words from the Exclude from Results basket to filter and further refine search results in Google.

➤ SortFix searchers are able to immediately network with friends or colleagues by tweeting search results on Twitter or posting results to their Facebook account.

➤ A Share This widget is available for users wishing to promote this application to friends on Digg, Facebook, Delicious, Myspace, FriendFeed, or Twitter.

➤ New SortFix searchers can access an online tutorial video (1 minute, 11 seconds) on YouTube to obtain useful tips on using this resource (www.youtube.com/watch?v=LPQZug FpJ88).

How Cybrarians Can Use This Resource

Reference and Research

Phil Bradley, information specialist and well known internet consultant who is known in close circles as the "U.K. search guru," is of the opinion that SortFix is an important, if somewhat different, search engine, which warrants not one, but two reviews on his blog. He views SortFix as a simple multisearch search engine, and one that may appeal to children especially given its drag-and-drop functionality and demonstrative use of simple concepts like Power Words, Add to Search, and Exclude from results.[3] It is certainly a search engine worth exploring by young adult librarians in assisting this group of patrons to learn about constructing and refining searches using Boolean operators OR, AND, and NOT using SortFix intuitive and graphical search user interface.

F Y I

SortFix is an Israeli-based company established in 2009. Similar add-ons are planned for
integration with Internet Explorer, Chrome,
Bing, and Amazon.[4]

Endnotes

1. "SortFix Search Extension 2.10," Mozilla Add-Ons, https://addons.mozilla.org/en-US/firefox/addon/sortfix-Extension/www.SortFix.com/#/about (accessed September 28, 2011).

2. "SortFix Search Extension 2.10."

3. "SortFix for easy searching," Phil's Bradley Weblog, March 8, 2010, philbradley.type pad.com/phil_bradleys_weblog/2010/03/SortFix-for-easy-searching.html (accessed September 28, 2011).

4. "SortFix launches Firefox extension," The Next Web, www.thenextweb.com/apps/2011/02/10/sortfix-launches-firefox-extension-enhancing-google-search-get-it-here-first/ (accessed September 28, 2011).

77

Spybot-Search & Destroy
productivity tool
www.safer-networking.org/en

Overview

In an age where data security is threatened by malicious software, often undetected by even the most stringent antivirus programs, Spybot-Search & Destroy has gained notoriety as one of the best privacy softwares available as freeware. The application is described as multifunctional. Two of the main functions immediately available on installation include the ability to scan, detect, and remove spyware (malicious software or malware that silently tracks surfing behavior), and to clean usage tracks (a function useful for protecting private data on shared computers).

Spybot-Search & Destroy creator Patrick Kolla regularly releases updates to this popular freeware, which can be accessed from the download portal on the main website (forums.spybot.info/downloads. php). Subscribers can elect to start the software in one of two modes. Easy mode is available for new users who wish to access just the basic features, and advanced mode is available for professional PC users who may wish more control and access to a variety of customization options. Both modes are available in the free version (www.safer-networking.org/en/features/index.html).

Product support is offered by way of an online tutorial, FAQ page, wiki, online public support forum, and an online dictionary listing terms commonly affiliated with spyware. Kolla's software company Safer Networking Limited is based in Germany and is supported by worldwide user donations and contributions.

Spybot Search&Destroy	⚲ Safer-Networking Forums ➤ Downloads		User Name [User Name] ☐Remember Me? Password [ ] [Log in]		
Register Projects Blogs ▾ FAQ Today's Posts Search			**Home Support Download Donate**		

Download	Forum	Issues	Last Release	Version	Size
Recent updates A list of the past 3 updates.					
Languator© Localization tool that helps translating many of our applications.	✉		0000-00-00	1.1.f	609.2 kB
Advanced Check Library© Updated library for file detections. Not required for 1.5 or above.	✉	💡	0000 00 00	1.0.1	119.2 kB
KnightHop© The easter egg game from Spybot-S&D as a stand-alone application.	✉		0000-00-00	1.0.0	1.7 MB

Download	Forum	Issues	Last Release	Version	Size
Spybot - Search & Destroy©® Everything directly related to keeping your computer clean from malware					
Spybot - Search & Destroy (Installer)©® Protect yourself against spyware.	✉	💡	2009-01-27	1.6.2.46	15.6 MB
OpenSBI Edit Lite© Editor to create malware detection rules.	✉		2009-06-05	1.6.2.16	3.7 MB
Boot CD Creator© A wizard to create a bootable repair CD including Spybot-S&D.	✉	💡	2009-03-10	1.0.4.16	1.1 MB
Distributed Testing© Help improving our updates by letting your computer scan with alpha updates automatically.	✉	💡	2008-11-24	1.6.1	3.4 MB
Subfolder	**Manual updates** Only needed for people who do not use the integrated updater.				
Subfolder	**Mobile Editions** Malware scanners for mobile devices.				
Subfolder	**Beta Versions** The latest versions available for testing purposes.				
Analysis Tools Tools that allow you to digg deeper into files, the registry, &c.					
HandleFilters© Allows to browse a list of system handles.	✉		2009-02-27	1.2.2.7	864.6 kB
RunAlyzer© Shows all the spots where malware tries to hide.	✉	💡	2008-11-24	1.6.1.24	7.6 MB
RootAlyzer© Shows all the spots where malware tries to hide.	✉	💡	2009-04-15	0.3.4.47	1.3 MB
FileAlyzer© Understand files by analyzing their structure.	✉	💡	2008-10-16	2.0.0.10	1.8 MB
FileAlyzer Lite© Understand files by analyzing their structure. This version integrates into the Windows Explorers file properties dialog.	✉		2008-03-11	1.0.1.0	663.8 kB
ProcAlyzer© Process list with ability to browse various process properties as well as a memory editor.	✉		2008-08-04	1.0.0.6	1 MB
RegAlyzer© Browse and search the registry.	✉	💡	2009-04-20	1.6.2.16	1.7 MB
NetAlyzer© Test or query Internet domain details.	✉	💡	2008-10-09	0.4.2.4	2.5 MB
Browser Cache Information© Displays the content of all browsers it detects. Can help as a guide what Spybot-S&D could see and clean, for example.	✉		2010-04-12	1.7.0	1.3 MB
Subfolder	**Command line utilities** Tools that allow you to digg deeper into files, the registry, &c from the command line.				
Goodies Various small helpful helpers					
Tweak Pouch© Registry tweak collection	✉		2010-06-09	0.1	906 kB
AlterEgo© Surf the web from a restricted user account.	✉	💡	2008-04-08	0.3.2.24	846.8 kB
Languator© Localization tool that helps translating many of our applications.	✉		0000-00-00	1 1 f	609.2 kB
Skinner© Allows to adjust the color schemes of Spybot-S&D.	✉		0000-00-00	1.0	296.6 kB
Chrome Anonymizer© Replace the unique Google Chrome ID with a generic one.	✉		2008-09-04	0.1.0.0	951.9 kB
NT native access TC plugins© Browse the filesystem and registry native using Total Commander to locate items hidden by Win32 rootkits.	✉		2008-01-30	0.1.1	839.8 kB

Users can choose to download recent updates and
analysis tools from the Spybot-Search and Destroy download portal.

Features

The following product features are highlighted on a comparative chart on the website (www.safer-networking.org/en/features/index.html):

- ➤ Removal of adware and spyware

- ➤ Removal of dialers, keyloggers, and trojans

- ➤ Removal of usage tracks

- ➤ Permanent blocking of threatening ActiveX downloads, tracking cookies, and Internet Explorer downloads

- ➤ Detailed reports on problems detected

- ➤ Weekly updates including an integrated update function and update notification by email

- ➤ User customized settings to automate scan, removal, and update functions (advanced mode only)

- ➤ Access to detailed system reports (advanced mode only)

- ➤ Customizable interface (advanced mode only)

How Cybrarians Can Use This Resource

Support for Data Security

For cybrarians concerned about data security and securing private information, Spybot-Search & Destroy can be utilized as a free alternative to similar components in costly rival antivirus programs that perform antispyware functions of scanning, detecting, and cleaning malware that may compromise sensitive data.

For example, Emory University's Office of Information Technology, in a bid to increase PC security awareness and secure university community data, began maintaining a FAQ page (it.emory.edu/getfaqs. cfm?catid=1093&fr=1093) that highlights issues related to computer security. This expansive list includes coverage of many topics, including a section on the use of programs such as Spybot to scan, detect, and remove spyware.

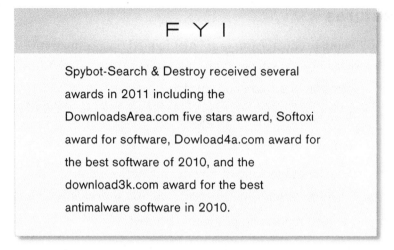

F Y I

Spybot-Search & Destroy received several awards in 2011 including the DownloadsArea.com five stars award, Softoxi award for software, Dowload4a.com award for the best software of 2010, and the download3k.com award for the best antimalware software in 2010.

78

StatCounter
productivity tool
www.statcounter.com

Overview

StatCounter is advertised as a web analytics service, which, like Google Analytics (Chapter 27), offers real-time website traffic statistics. The concept behind using the service is not unlike Google's approach, with users simply inserting automatically generated codes into webpages or blogs, thus facilitating the immediate analysis and monitoring of visitors to the website or blog in real time.

On its homepage, the company claims to screen in excess of 15 billion page loads per month, enabling registered members to improve website traffic by monitoring the number of hits to their website, the geographical location of visitors, popular webpages viewed by visitors, and the keywords used to find the website.[1]

The free service is offered to websites with 250,000 pageloads per month or less with an added bonus offer of summary statistics and a detailed analysis of the last 500 pageloads. For sites that have grown beyond 250,000 pageloads a month, or that require detailed analysis, there is an option to upgrade to the premium services. The company was founded in 1999 by Aodhan Cullen.

Features

New members can start using the service by following four simple steps:

1. Register an account by providing information on username, email, password, name, country, and company.

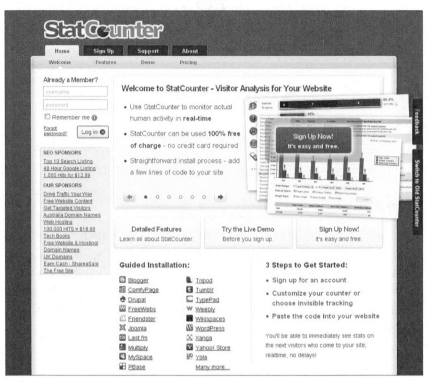

The New StatCounter beta version offers
more features to obtain real-time website traffic statistics.

2. Create a StatCounter Project. With every project a unique code is assigned along with log space for statistics.

3. Insert the assigned code into a website or blog.

4. Analyze the statistics generated.

Other features of StatCounter include (beta-statcounter.com/features):

➤ Option to add a configurable or invisible counter to a website or blog

➤ Customized summary statistics based on visitor traffic

➤ Ability to manage multiple sites from one account

➤ Ability to email reports

➤ ISP statistics that show ISPs (internet service providers) used by visitors

➤ Browser Statistics, a tool that shows which browsers visitors used to view your site

➤ Operating Systems statistics, a tool available to show visitors' operating systems

➤ Ability to block cookies

➤ Detailed analysis of the last 500 pageloads with data provided on:

  • What keywords visitors used to find your site

  • Most popular pages

  • Links used to reach your site

  • Visitors' country of origin

  • How visitors navigate through your site

How Cybrarians Can Use This Resource

Optimizing and Improving Library Website Usage and Design

By using this free website analytics service, cybrarians can take advantage of an opportunity to optimize and improve library website usage and design by monitoring data gathered on areas such as the number of hits to specific pages over a sustained period of time, the geographical location of visitors, the webpages that continue to attract the most patrons views, and the keywords most often typed as search queries to find a library's website. This data can then be analyzed, and over time yield valuable information with regard to developing strategies for increasing web traffic and attracting new visitors; adding service points in new geographic locations; modeling new webpages on existing pages found to be user friendly and easily navigable; and embedding tags and keywords attractive to web searchers.

FYI

The new beta version of StatCounter (beta.
statcounter.com) retains all the functionalities
of the old version while offering new
enhancements and powerful features.

Endnote

1. "News Release: Web Analytics Firm StatCounterAnnounces Free Upgrades,"
   StatCounter, August 26, 2010, statcounter.com/press_release/2010-08-26.pdf
   (accessed August 10, 2011).

79

StumbleUpon
social bookmarking service
www.stumbleupon.com

Overview

Ardent web searchers look to Google and other search engines if they know exactly what they are looking for on the web. But what of novice searchers, who are online and not sure what they are looking for? Researchers, for example, who want to do research on mobile libraries and fervently wish they could draw on the collective wisdom of the crowd (that is, like-minded searchers who have already found and bookmarked the best sites on mobile libraries).

StumbleUpon is a service developed to satisfy this need. As the name implies, the service is a discovery engine that enables web searchers to stumble from site to site and discover new content based on the collective recommendations of a community of users.

Registering on the homepage (www.stumbleupon.com) to use the service is recommended. Once registered, searchers select topics that match their professional or personal interests. There are hundreds of topics to choose from, including broad categories such as books, fashion, art, astronomy, history, and the environment. When a topic is selected and searched, StumbleUpon serves up websites ranked highly by other web surfers to match the topic selected. As searchers stumble—by clicking on the Stumble icon from a downloadable toolbar—from website to website, they can add the served-up website as a favorite, give it a thumbs up or thumbs down, write a favorable review, or share it with friends. The service can be accessed directly from its website, but for the fullest experience, searchers are advised to download and install it to their favorite internet browser toolbar.

This serendipitous way (the service is sometimes branded as a serendipity engine) of discovering websites on the internet has grown by leaps and bounds. StumbleUpon now boasts more than 15 million stumblers (members).[1] Press releases show that it has been recognized as an economically viable service, regularly driving web traffic to online publishers and vendors. So much so that technology juggernaut Google and others have expressed an interest in purchasing it. The service was eventually brought by eBay in 2007, and eBay retained ownership until April 2009. StumbleUpon is now an independent, investor-backed start-up, with offices in San Francisco and New York City.[2]

Features

➤ Once registered for the service, a member is assigned a profile page with links to three tabs:

- Click on the Discover tab to search and find new resources by browsing a list of specific topics (arts, business, computers, health, lifestyle, sports, technology), browsing a list of top-rated resources (resources receiving the best reviews), or reviewing resources recently added to the database in real time by active members.

- The Favorites tab provides quick access to your list of preferred resources—including all formats, websites, blogs, videos, and photos—given a thumbs-up and bookmarked while stumbling from site to site. Here, members can also read reviews they have written and view descriptive tags they have added to individual websites.

- The Stumblers tab connects members (Stumblers) to Facebook friends on StumbleUpon, Stumblers who are following you, or Stumblers you are following.

➤ Access is provided to downloadable StumbleUpon add-ons and bookmarks (www.stumbleupon.com/addon), which can be installed to a web browser to quickly get new members stumbling and discovering relevant content (websites, videos, photos, blogs) tailored to their search interests. For example, the StumbleUpon add-on for Internet Explorer allows users to immediately rate (using thumbs-up or thumbs-down icons) the resource discovered, add tags, bookmark the resource as a favorite, easily share the resource with friends on social networks Twitter and Facebook, or send the resource URL link to friends via email. Add-on support is also provided for Mozilla Firefox and Google Chrome.

➤ Stumblers are encouraged to add or submit websites that are not in the StumbleUpon database. This is done by completing a web-based online form and adding the following metadata: language, the website's URL, tags, a short review, topic, and indicating if the site is safe for the work environment.

➤ Stumblers can join community forums devoted to topics such as arts, history, home, religion, media, commerce, music, and computers (www.stumbleupon.com/groups).

➤ StumbleUpon mobile apps are currently available for the iPad, iPhone, and Android.

➤ Known as a service that generates exposure and drives traffic to publishers' and vendors' websites, StumbleUpon is profiting from this notoriety with the introduction of a paid-for advertising service called StumbleUpon Paid Discovery. Using this paid subscription service, StumbleUpon delivers the right audience to websites based on interest, location, demographic, and mobile device usage.

➤ StumbleUpon also offers a URL-shortening service (su.pr), for online publishers, bloggers, and StumbleUpon users that allows you to simultaneously post content to multiple social networks while automatically shortening posted URLs.

➤ The StumbleUpon Blog provides regular posts on new features, current releases, and general updates on the service (www.stumbleupon.com/sublog).

Registered Stumblers are assigned a profile page with
three tabs: Discover, Favorites, and Stumblers.

How Cybrarians Can Use This Resource

Increasing Web Exposure by Driving Traffic to Library Websites

Cybrarians can add StumbleUpon badges to blogs, library websites, and resource guides so that patrons who use these web spaces can easily submit the content to the StumbleUpon database. Adding badges requires copying and pasting a few lines of code generated by the StumbleUpon widget (www.stumbleupon.com/badges). This action potentially increases traffic and exposure—for free, as there are more than 15 million Stumblers who have access to these resources and can potentially share them with others. The badges also show a real-time count of how many times the webpages have been viewed by StumbleUpon users.

Searching and Finding Content Tailored to Specific Subject Interest

It becomes increasingly difficult to keep up with resources being added daily to the ubiquitous web. StumbleUpon, as a crowdsourced recommendation engine, filters through this vast amount of information to direct subscribers to high-quality websites that are relevant to their personal interests. Cybrarians can use this resource to discover valuable, premium web content instead of relying on search engines and hunting through what are often irrelevant pages of results. Once the StumbleUpon toolbar is integrated into a web browser with the click of a button, StumbleUpon delivers limitless access to the most relevant content (websites, videos, blogs, photos), which has been tailored to your specific interests. These resources can be saved as favorites and shared with a network of friends with similar interests or compiled in a resource guide and made accessible to library patrons.

F Y I

As a discovery engine that finds the best peer-sourced content on the web, StumbleUpon records one billion personalized recommendations per month (www.stumble upon.com/press).

Endnotes

1. "Press Center," StumbleUpon, www.stumbleupon.com/press (accessed August 10, 2011).

2. "StumbleUpon," Wikipedia, en.wikipedia.org/wiki/StumbleUpon (accessed August 10, 2011).

80

SurveyMonkey
productivity tool
www.surveymonkey.com

Overview

In today's competitive environment, where customer satisfaction is invariably tied to a library's success, there is nothing more critical to success than keeping customers satisfied and engaged. Unfortunately, measuring an abstract concept such as customer satisfaction can be a daunting, costly, and somewhat time-consuming task. Free web-based survey solutions such as SurveyMonkey and Zoomerang (Chapter 100) can offer financially strapped libraries cost-effective solutions to quickly and efficiently gather quantitative and qualitative consumer data.

SurveyMonkey is one of the more user-friendly web-based survey tools available for gathering every type of feedback possible—from customer satisfaction and course evaluations to event scheduling and employee performance reviews—and viewing these results as graphical and real-time data. This online productivity tool successfully combines survey methodology and web technology to offer a suite of features suitable for advanced researchers and survey rookies alike.

The basic plan is free, with no additional software to install, and includes the ability to create and administer multiple surveys, long-term maintenance with no automatic deletions of surveys created, and free online storage. Advanced features and customization are available for a low monthly fee. Customers using the service include libraries, businesses, academic institutions, and nonprofit organizations. Founded in 1999, SurveyMonkey is a multinational company with offices in the U.S. (California and Orgeon) and Madeira, Portugal.

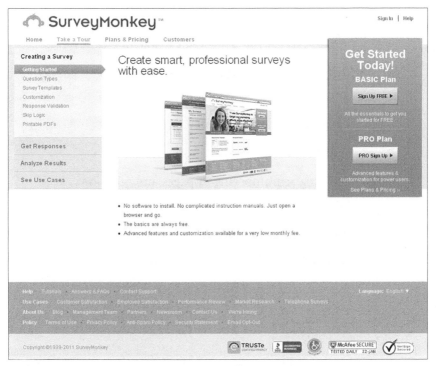

New SurveyMonkey subscribers must register on the homepage.

Features

➤ New users can register on the SurveyMonkey homepage (www.surveymonkey.com) by entering a username, password, and contact email to create a basic (free) account. This free account can be upgraded at any time to a professional plan. For new users, the self-guided tutorials explore the service's basic design elements and provide the steps necessary to start using the service in a matter of minutes.

➤ The basic account also offers 24/7 customer support.

➤ The basic plan provides immediate access to the following features:

• Survey Design

  - Creation of an unlimited number of surveys

- Ability to add up to 10 questions per survey

- Option to choose from 15 available question types

- Access to basic survey templates and prebuilt survey themes

- Support for multiple languages, including Unicode

- View of survey completion progress bar

- Automatic numbering of pages and questions

- Ability to validate/require survey responses from respondents

- Randomization/sorting of answer choices

- Access to 508 compliant and certified surveys (U.S. only)

• Data Collection

- Limit of 100 responses per survey

- Collection of responses via weblinks, email, and Facebook and Twitter accounts

- Embedding of surveys within websites or blogs

- Creation of a maximum of three collectors per survey

• Analysis

- Option to view live results as they are recorded

How Cybrarians Can Use This Resource

Marketing Research

While many libraries are still using printed questionnaires to obtain valuable consumer data, many have discovered that online questionnaires are just as effective, and, in fact, may offer additional advantages. Online surveys are more convenient for time-conscious respondents, may reach more respondents and yield better response rates, and can be less expensive to create and manage.

Registering for a free basic account on SurveyMonkey or investing in an upgraded version of the service can offer the online tools required to conduct market research, gain valuable insights, and make more informed decisions in the following areas:

- ➤ Conducting course evaluations, quizzes, and tests online

- ➤ Gathering patrons' feedback on new collections and services

- ➤ Measuring customer satisfaction with current services

- ➤ Conducting employee performance reviews

- ➤ Measuring employee satisfaction

- ➤ Gathering feedback on programs and events

- ➤ Measuring brand perception

F Y I

In March 2010, the SurveyMonkey application was added to the profitable Google Apps Marketplace (www.google.com/enterprise/marketplace/home). The move is considered a lucrative one, making it "easier for Google Apps customers to access an extremely powerful feedback tool that can be utilized in any business, organization, or academic institution."[1]

Endnote

1. "SurveyMonkey Now Available Through the Google Apps Marketplace," Survey Monkey Newsroom, March 9, 2010, www.surveymonkey.com/PressRelease 03092010.aspx (accessed August 10, 2011).

81

Technorati
search engine
www.technorati.com

Overview

Technorati is heralded as the first blog search engine on the internet. Founded by software entrepreneur Dave Sifry in 2003, the service was initially created to give blogs more online promotion, or as the Technorati Team writes on its about page, to "help bloggers succeed by collecting, highlighting, and distributing the global online conversations."[1] For web searchers, it is a useful tool for searching for blogs on their favorite topics in the ever-expanding blogosphere.

Technorati's claim to be the leading blog search engine holds true according to statistical evidence. At the time of this writing, the service has indexed more than 1 million blogs. The site has become the definitive source for tracking blog posts in real time. It serves up a regularly updated front page with trending top stories of the day, opinion pieces, and photos and videos across several topical categories including entertainment, technology, lifestyle, sports, politics, and business. It has also gained recognition as an authoritative source and up-to-date directory of the top bloggers and the most popular blogs with daily postings of the Top 100 blogs (www.technorati.com/blogs/top100).

Since its start-up, the California-based company has expanded into a full-service media company offering advertising and other services to blogs and social media sites. Most noteworthy among these value-added services is the publication, since 2004, of the annual Technorati State of the Blogosphere report (www.technorati.com/state-of-the-blogosphere), which chronicles growth and revolutionary trends in the blogosphere. The name Technorati is a blend of the words technology and literati (intellectuals).

Features

➤ The service announced a relaunch and redesign of the website Technorati.com in October 2009 in a bid to reinforce its original goal of helping searchers find great blog content. The front end of the site is completely new to regular followers, and much of the search technology has been significantly changed as well. The homepage has several sections that are much more organized and user-friendly than the original version, and it now includes sections such as Today on Technorati (trending, newsworthy, breaking news posts), Top Blogs, Top Tags Today, Latest Articles Across Technorati, Hottest Blogosphere Items, Most Popular Videos, and Currently Hot.

➤ There are multiple search strategies for searching for blogs on Technorati's homepage:

- Enter your search term in the main search box (above the main menu on Technorati's homepage). Searchers are immediately offered options to refine search results; first by restricting results to blogs or news sites, then filtering by specified categories from a drop-down menu, and finally sorting results by relevance or dates. Technorati displays the results of your search by listing the blog posts that have been tagged with your search term. Each result displays an "authority" number that represents the number of blogs linking to each site displayed in the result set during the past six months.

- Browse Technorati tags (a keyword or short phrase that writers assign to articles to describe or identify the content). Users can view a list of popular tags used in Technorati articles over the last month arranged in an A–Z list. Mousing over any tag shows the number of articles that have used the tag.

- Browse the blog directory organized by broad subject areas such as technology, business, entertainment, lifestyle, sports, politics, and videos. Each category has the number of blog posts specific to that category enclosed in parentheses.

- Browse Technorati Top 100 blogs as ranked by Technorati Authority. This list is updated daily. Searchers can also browse a directory of *all* blogs hosted (more than 1 million) and their rankings.

  - Browse the People tab, which is an alphabetical (A–Z) listing of bloggers by name.

➤ An added service on the search engine is a feature to promote your blog by *claiming* it on Technorati. Claiming your blog will add it to Technorati's blog directory, in the categories you specify, and in the tags directory based on the tags you assign. Only registered users of the service can claim blogs. This can be done by signing up, signing in, and entering your blog URL in the personal profile page.

➤ On the homepage, a link is provided for Twittorati (www.twittorati.com), which tracks the tweets from those who are considered the most influential bloggers listed in the Technorati Top 100 and may soon include more of the web's authoritative voices.

➤ The Technorati blog (blog.technorati.com) is updated regularly with blog postings on news and information on new features and enhancements.

How Cybrarians Can Use This Resource

Tracking Trending Topics on the Internet

Use Technorati on a daily basis to track various trends and topics on the internet. With regularly updated sections such as Today on Technorati (trending, newsworthy, breaking news posts), Top Blogs, Top Tags, Latest Articles, Hottest Blogosphere Items, Most Popular Videos, and Currently Hot, the search engine returns relatively good results and offers good insight into the main talking points in the blogosphere.

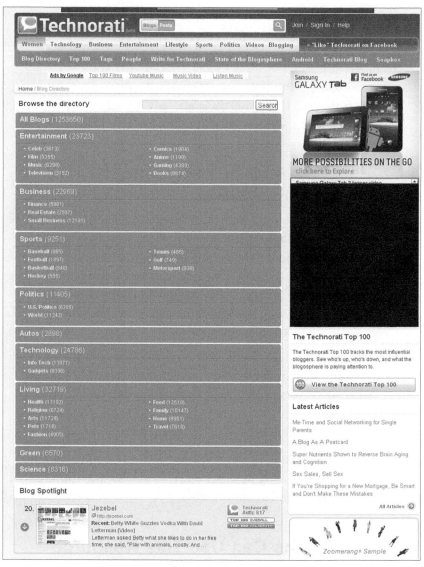

There are multiple search strategies for
searching blogs on the Technorati homepage.

Becoming a Technorati Writer

Technorati has an established writing community (www.technorati.
com/write-for-technorati), which publishes original content on a wide
variety of topics. These are focused in the areas of blog reviews, breaking

news, trend pieces, and opinion-focused posts. The criteria are that submissions must be timely, news-focused, interesting, well written, and in English.

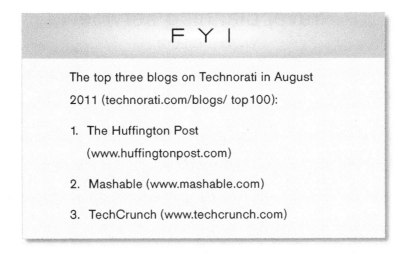

FYI

The top three blogs on Technorati in August 2011 (technorati.com/blogs/ top100):

1. The Huffington Post (www.huffingtonpost.com)

2. Mashable (www.mashable.com)

3. TechCrunch (www.techcrunch.com)

Endnote

1. "About Technorati," Technorati, www.technorati.com/about-technorati (accessed August 10, 2011).

82

TripIt
travel planning service
www.tripit.com

Overview

Booking travel online has become so popular that it is estimated that half of U.S. travelers plan trips using an online service. Today, a typical trip may include a flight booked at Orbitz (www.orbitz.com), a hotel room booked at Expedia (www.expedia.com), and a rental car booked at Hertz (www.hertz.com). Even the most experienced traveler will tell you that in order to have a successful trip—business or pleasure—one must oversee all the minute details of the impending trip: booking airline tickets, hotels, and rental cars; booking restaurant reservations in advance; printing maps for directions; and getting updates of the weather forecast. It is not unusual to see frustrated travelers at the check-in counter, feverishly hunting through a folder with leaves of paper with this required information.

Branded as an online service using technology to simplify the internet travel experience, TripIt (www.tripit.com) helps users organize all of their travel plans—flights, hotels, and rental car reservations—regardless of the source site used to make the bookings. This is achieved by travelers simply forwarding all their travel confirmation emails to plans@tripit.com. The TripIt Itinerator—TripIt's patent-pending and proprietary technology for automatically creating itineraries from travel confirmation emails—processes and combines all of the related bookings into a master itinerary.

Then, TripIt goes a step further, using the trip data to automatically pull information from other websites: daily weather forecasts from the National Oceanic and Atmospheric Administration (NOAA), local maps and driving directions from Google, and unique city guides from Wikipedia, Flickr, and Eventful. Travelers can access travel information online or via a mobile device, print itineraries, share their travel plans online with family and friends, and collaborate with colleagues on planning trips. The service, based in San Francisco, California, was established in October 2006 and officially launched in 2007.

Features

➤ New subscribers must register and log in to use the basic service. New TripIt members can create accounts on the homepage (www.tripit.com) or sign up with existing accounts from Facebook or Google. TripIt Pro is available as a paid-for subscription upgrade with added features.

➤ Master itineraries are automatically created from the confirmation emails forwarded by travelers from their online booking services such as airlines, car rentals, and hotels.

➤ The option is included for TripIt members to edit itineraries, adding personalized notes and photos. Itineraries can be shared with friends, family, and colleagues for collaborative travel and users can request their comments about impending trip plans.

➤ Weather and map information for the destination city is automatically added to itineraries by the service.

➤ Members have the option to manually add bookings from websites and services not yet supported by TripIt.

➤ Travelers can check flight status, check in for flights, monitor itineraries for changes, and receive travel alerts and text messages about flight delays, cancellations, and gate changes. TripIt Point Tracker tracks frequent flyer miles and hotel points.

➤ TripIt mobile site (m.tripit.com) is available online, and travelers can access itineraries from mobile devices with free TripIt apps for the iPad, iPhone, Android, and BlackBerry.

➤ A gallery of online travel widgets and tools is available on this itinerary platform (www.tripit.com/uhp/tools) for easy

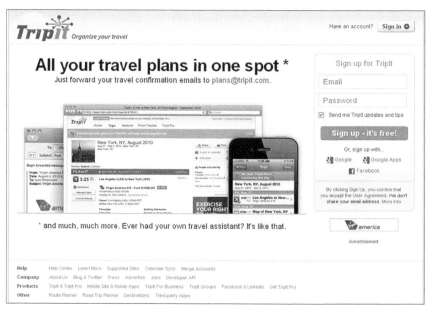

Registration and login is required to use the basic TripIt service.

integration and organization of travel plans. For example, the Blog badge can add upcoming trips to a blog, and the Facebook app automatically publishes updates on trips planned.

How Cybrarians Can Use This Resource

Organizing and Managing Travel Plans

TripIt applies the power of social networking to improve the travel experience. For cybrarians, this service can turn chaotic trip planning into some semblance of order by organizing disparate trip details into one master online itinerary that includes airline bookings, car rentals, and hotel reservations. Additionally, the service can be marketed to library patrons as a useful tool that can be accessed online or on mobile devices to plan out-of-town travel, and share travel plans with their network of friends and family.

TripIt was voted as one of Time.com's 50 Best
Websites of 2009.[1]

Endnote

1. "50 Best Websites 2009," Time.com, www.time.com/time/specials/packages/completelist/0,29569,1918031,00.html (accessed August 10, 2010).

83

Twitter
social network/
microblogging service
www.twitter.com

Overview

Since Twitter's launch in 2006, the social networking and microblogging service that allows users to create, send, and read messages or posts known as *tweets* has steadily gained notoriety and popularity worldwide. This widespread appeal is reflected in figures released by the company in March 2010 on the growth spurt of the service. Cofounder Biz Stone comments: "Twitter has recorded a 1,500 [percent] growth in the number of registered users, the number of employees has grown 500 percent, while over 70,000 registered apps have been created for the microblogging platform." Stone touts Twitter as "more than a triumph of technology"; he views it as a "triumph of humanity."[1]

There is plenty of anecdotal evidence to support his claim. One only has to look at recent events where Twitter has indeed presented a new and unique way to communicate online, helping to foster and connect communities during major crises. In April 2008, a journalism graduate student at UC Berkeley was arrested for taking photographs at a public demonstration in Egypt. In jail he had the foresight to tweet one word, *arrested*, which triggered his network of followers into action as they contacted the U.S. embassy and university in Egypt, resulting in his early release. Iranian elections protests were extended to a global stage due to coverage on Twitter in June 2009.

In January 2010, following the aftermath of a 7.0 magnitude earthquake in Haiti, in which an estimated 3 million people were affected, tweets were sent to alert families of the well-being of loved ones, describe the progress of relief efforts on the ground, and appeal to donors who wanted to assist legitimate charitable organizations. In January 2011, Twitter accounts served as sources of riveting up-to-date information on the protests in Egypt. These and similar events have catapulted Twitter into what can best be described as a genuine media tool that has become a major player in the geopolitical and social landscapes.

So how does Twitter work? All you need to use Twitter is an internet connection or a mobile phone. Once you are on the homepage (www.twitter.com), choose a username and password, and you are signed up (for free) in a matter of seconds. Log on and type your first update, or post or tweet into the What's Happening box at the top of the screen. Tweets entered must be 140 characters or less and once typed are immediately posted to your profile or your blog and sent to your followers. Why 140 characters, many have asked? The short answer is this: The 140-character limit on message length was initially set up for compatibility with SMS (short message service) and has brought to the web the kind of shorthand notation and slang commonly used in SMS messages.

Features

> Twitter offers many ways to post updates: from the web in the update box, from your mobile phone, from your web browser using m.twitter.com, or from any third-party application (APIs).

> On the Twitter homepage's side navigation bar, you will find a record of the number of tweets you have posted since you joined the service, the number of persons you are following (i.e., you are receiving their Twitter updates), and the number of persons following you (every time you post a new message, it will appear on their Twitter homepage).

> A search box allows searching by keyword to find news, people, and other real-time information coursing through the service. Operators help to filter a search or make it more exacting. For example, users can group posts together by topic or type by use of hashtags—words or phrases prefixed with the symbol #, for example, #ALA 2010. The @ sign

Twitter's homepage has all the features
characteristic of a microblogging service.

followed by a username is used for mentioning or replying to
other users. If users wish to repost a message from another
Twitter user and share it with their own followers, they use
the retweet function symbolized by RT in the message.

➤ Trending, buzzworthy, or popular topics are listed as Trends
on the navigation sidebar and can be limited by countries or
cities. The recommendation feature suggests Tweeters for you
to follow.

➤ Through its partnerships with other startups such as Flickr,
Justin.tv, TwitVid, TwitLens, Ustream, Vimeo, and YouTube,
Twitter users can now view photos, videos, and other
embedded media content directly on the service.

➤ Discover related content by clicking on a tweet and viewing a
detailed pane with additional information related to the
author or subject, such as @replies, related tweets, and a map
showing from where a geotagged tweet was sent. Mini profiles
with account information, biodata, and recent tweets are
accessible by clicking @username.

➤ Twitter's Tweet With Your Location is one of the service's
popular features and allows users to selectively add location
information to tweets as composed on Twitter.com and with
other applications or mobile devices that support this feature.
Due to privacy concerns, this feature is off by default and
users will need to opt in to use it. The geolocation
information that is shared publicly can be either your exact
location (coordinates), or a place (like a neighborhood or
town). Tweeting with location information can add context to
your updates as you join local conversations or share
interesting information such as weather reports, traffic
conditions, restaurant wait times, and supermarket deals.

➤ Twitter's APIs easily allow other web services and applications
to integrate with Twitter. These apps include Echofon,
TweetDeck, Twitterrific, Seesmic, and Twitter for Android,
iPad, Windows Phone 7, iPhone, and BlackBerry. A list of
other third-party applications can be found on the Twitter
Fan Wiki (twitter.pbworks.com/w/page/1779796/FrontPage).

How Cybrarians Can Use This Resource

On Twitter's About Us page (www.twitter.com/about), this statement
(appropriately in less than 140 characters) describes the service as "a
real-time information network powered by people all around the world
that lets you share and discover what's happening now."[2] As a social
medium, there is no doubt that Twitter has become a permanent part
of the Web 2.0 landscape and librarians may be well advised to explore
all opportunities to use social tools such as Twitter—to experiment
with new ideas, share resources, keep updated, and socialize. Here are
some examples of how this can be done.

Current Awareness Service

To keep patrons up-to-date and informed about services available at
the library, librarians at the Alvin Sherman Library, Research, and
Information Technology Center at Nova Southeastern University in
Florida (www.twitter.com/alvinshermanlib) post tweets to promote

new library materials, current events, training opportunities, systems alerts, changes in policy, book sales, library statistics, and links for evaluating new resources.

Creating Customized News Feeds

Using Twitter's list feature, librarians can search for and follow bloggers and movers and shakers in the library world who regularly post about topics of interest for library patrons. Lists on Twitter are the quickest, most personalized news filter readily available to obtain an unadulterated stream of news on any given topic at any moment in time.

Attending a Conference Virtually While Connecting With Attendees On-Site

Most webinars and conferences now promote a Twitter hashtag to encourage virtual and on-site attendees to post information about presentations and give feedback. At the 2010 Computers in Libraries annual conference in Arlington, Virginia, attendees added *#CIL2010* to their tweets. By searching *#CIL2010* on Twitter, virtual followers read the latest conference updates (saving on printing costs and reducing carbon footprints due to travel.

Promoting Virtual Reference Service

The Nebraska Library Commission (NLC) is using Twitter to enhance its virtual reference service. NLC posts all incoming reference questions as they are submitted directly to Twitter through its Ask a Librarian service (www.twitter.com/NLC_Reference). As of this writing, this service has registered more than 400 followers. Similarly, the Maryland Ask Us Now! (www.twitter.com/askusnow) online reference service for Maryland library patrons has registered more than 1,000 followers and is also creating virtual reference tweets.

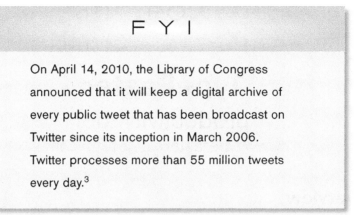

F Y I

On April 14, 2010, the Library of Congress announced that it will keep a digital archive of every public tweet that has been broadcast on Twitter since its inception in March 2006. Twitter processes more than 55 million tweets every day.[3]

Endnotes

1. "Twitter Registers 1,500 Percent Growth in Users," New Statesman, March 4, 2010, www.newstatesman.com/digital/2010/03/twitter-registered-created (accessed August 10, 2011).

2. "About Twitter," Twitter, www.twitter.com/about (accessed August 10, 2011).

3. Biz Stone, "Tweet Preservation," Twitter Blog, April 30, 2010, blog.twitter.com/ 2010/04/tweet-preservation.html (accessed August 10, 2011).

84

TypeFaster
productivity tool
www.typefastertypingtutor.com

Overview

TypeFaster is a free, online typing tutor program that teaches users how to touch-type on a simulated keyboard. The immediate benefit of completing this touch-typing course is that it eliminates the need to constantly keep one's eyes focused on a computer keyboard when typing documents or accessing data on the web, thus increasing efficiency and lessening mental and physical fatigue. The program is available in three versions: standard, accessible, and Spanish. All three versions are available for download from the program's homepage (www.typefaster typingtutor.com).

TypeFaster is categorized as an open source program, licensed under the GNU General Public License. The source code is immediately available when the program is installed and there is an open appeal for developers to assist with further enhancements of the product (www.typefastertypingtutor.com/developers.html). All versions of the program are hosted on the SourceForge (www.sourceforge.net) website. The latter is renowned as one of the leading resources for open source software development and distribution of free open source software.

Features

➢ Users accessing the homepage (www.typefastertyping tutor.com) can navigate to the main menu on the left navigation bar and download one of the three versions of the software (standard, accessible, and Spanish) offered.

> There is a link on the homepage (www.typefastertypingtutor. com/screenshot.png) to a screenshot showing the keyboard layout and functions.

> The following features are available in the standard version:

- Support for keyboard layouts in multiple languages as well as support for nonrectangular keys

- Guided instructions on which fingers to use for touch typing

- A 3D typing game for lesson enhancement

- Access to typing statistics for teachers and students, and the option of practicing the least accurate, slowest, and custom keys

- Availability of a lesson progress indicator

- Resolution-independent keyboard (does not conform to a fixed size standardized)

- Support for multiuser version including teachers

- Interface for editing lesson files and game settings

- Backspace support, right to left text support and support for variable text size

How Cybrarians Can Use This Resource

Promoting Access to the Multiuser Version of the Program at School Library Media Centers

The multiuser version of TypeFaster was designed specifically for use in a shared setting, ideal for school library media centers. This version provides full access for two types of visitors to simultaneously use the program: students and users with teacher privileges. Users with teacher privileges can create and edit lesson files, edit the game settings for students, and view statistics on accuracy and speed.

TypeFaster Typing Tutor

Standard Version
Accessible Version
Spanish Version
Developers / How to help

About TypeFaster

This free typing tutor teaches you how to touch-type. Once you can touch-type you will not need to look at the keyboard to find the letters you want to type. The program comes in three versions: Standard, Accessible and Spanish. Use the menu on the left to navigate to the version you are interested in. Take a look at a screenshot. Free download of the fully functional standard version typing tutor at the bottom of this page.

Standard Version Features

- Supports multiple keyboard layouts and more can be added easily (see the developers section). Includes support for non-rectangular keys. The following keyboard layouts are currently supported:
  - Danish
  - Finnish
  - French
  - French-Belgian
  - German
  - Hebrew (no lesson files)
  - Italian
  - Norwegian
  - Numeric Keypad
  - Portuguese
  - Spanish
  - UK-English
  - US-Dvorak
  - US-English
- A clear indication of which fingers to use. This is the essence of touchtyping.
- A 3D typing game.
- Typing statistics and the option of practising the least accurate/slowest /custom keys.
- Keyboard is not a fixed size (resolution independent).
- Multi-user support.
- Teacher support (view student statistics).
- Interface for editing lesson files and game settings.
- Backspace support.
- Right to left text support.
- Variable text size.
- Lesson files can be prose or poems.
- Lesson progress indicator.
- Completely free with full source code availability.

Multi-user aspects of the Standard Version

The version of TypeFaster Typing Tutor that is installed can be set when the installer is run.

Single-user

This is for one user on one computer.

Multi-user

This is for several users on one computer. For example, each of your family members can have their own login. The settings and progress of each user is stored.

Multi-user with teacher support

This version is designed for use in a school. It must be installed in one place only, for example in a shared, writable network folder. Ideally in its own fairly small partition but with some space for new users. In this version there are two types of users: ordinary users and users with teacher privileges.

When ordinary users (pupils) login, they must select a teacher. The pupil will

On the TypeFaster homepage, you can choose among the Standard Version, Accessible Version, and Spanish Version.

The Accessible Version of Typefaster Typing
Tutor is available for visually impaired or blind
users. It uses the excellent, free, text-to-speech
engine Flite to provide continuous voice
support. Currently, only the U.S. English
keyboard layout is supported (www.typefaster
typingtutor.com/accversion.html).

85

Ustream
broadcasting service
www.ustream.tv

Overview

Unlike other webcasting services that favor broadcasting prerecorded static video content over the internet, Ustream is one of the few web-based video broadcasting platforms that enables anyone with a camera, computer, and internet connection to broadcast live video to a global audience. Using Ustream's one-to-many model (one user broadcasting to an audience of unlimited size), in less than two minutes, anyone can become a broadcaster with the creation of customized channels on Ustream or by broadcasting through a personal website.

Established in March 2007 by John Ham, Brad Hunstable, and Dr. Gyula Feher as a way to help overseas soldiers connect and communicate more efficiently with their families, this live streaming platform has become an instant success as broadcasters from all over the world have been empowered and are finding new and innovative uses for it every day. Ustream has been used to broadcast exclusive live events like movie premieres and other red carpet events, conferences and concerts, school and business events, live workshops, and interactive games for viewers to watch or join. Web searchers can also explore Ustream's networks for recorded live content ranging from talk shows, sporting events, political debates, speeches, rallies, and personal milestones such as holiday gatherings, weddings, graduations, and parties.[1]

Unique features such as multiple streams on a single show page, designated show networks, interactive chat, broadcasting from mobile devices, recorded broadcasts, and customizable show features make broadcasting live video on Ustream a somewhat dynamic and rewarding experience for broadcasters and viewers alike. Ustream network reaches more than 50 million unique viewers each month.[2] The company has its headquarters in San Francisco, California.

Features

➤ Signing up for a Ustream account (www.ustream.tv/login-signup) is free and allows registered users to immediately broadcast shows and interact with other broadcasters and viewers. New users can also log in with an existing Facebook, Google, Yahoo!, or OpenID account.

➤ To start broadcasting on a live show, potential broadcasters need a computer, internet connection, microphone, and a webcam or video camera. The show can be started immediately using the following steps:

- Log in with username and password.

- Click on Create a Show.

- Type the name of the show in the Create New Show box and click on Create.

- Add show information such as subject category (entertainment, sports, animals, music, how-to, gaming, religion, events, technology, news, 24/7) from the drop-down menu provided. Add tags and a short descriptive summary.

- Click on Broadcast Now to start broadcasting. A broadcast window will appear and request permission to autodetect a camera or microphone. Select Allow. Click Start Broadcast or Start Record. The show immediately begins recording to create a prerecorded show or to broadcast to a live global audience.

➤ All registered Ustream broadcasters have access to a personal dashboard, which can be customized by enabling the following features:

- Manage account information such as name, email, location, biodata, and password.

- Manage connections between Ustream and other applications. This allows broadcasters to login with Facebook, Twitter, Myspace, AIM, OpenID, and YouTube accounts, and find and update friends on what they are currently watching or when a live show will be broadcasted.

- Collect statistics on your live and recorded shows including number of viewers.

- Customize the show page theme by changing the background and color.

- Customize prerecorded videos.

- Manage people you follow (Crowds You Are In) and people who follow you (People in Your Crowd).

➤ To search and find shows from the Ustream homepage, searchers can browse spotlighted or featured broadcasters or the section with newly added broadcasts (Now Broadcasting). There is also a main search box (on the main navigation menu) for entering keyword searches.

➤ Ustream is currently available for viewing and broadcasting on mobile devices (iPad, iPod Touch, Android, and Windows Phone).

➤ Live forums are available for community help (www.ustream. tv/forum/index.php) and the Ustream blog (www.ustream.tv/ blog/2010/10) keeps members updated on company news and enhanced features.

➤ Ustream Open Pay-Per-View service allows Ustream broadcasters to apply for their own pay-per-view program where viewers must pay a fee to view premium content.

From the Ustream homepage, searchers can browse
spotlighted/featured broadcasters or newly added broadcasts.

How Cybrarians Can Use This Resource

Continuing Education and Professional Development

Webcast technology has provided benefits for radio stations, news corporations, and nonprofit organizations. Libraries are also taking
advantage of this medium, using webcast technologies to host conferences and training sessions, broadcast live messages, and connect with
local communities.

The following are examples of the use of this innovative technology
for continuing education and professional development for the library
community:

> ➤ Cybrarians were afforded the opportunity to view prerecorded
> content from a LITA (Library Information Technology
> Association) Nation Forum held in October 2010 in Atlanta.
> The session "Using the Cloud to Please the Crowd," presented
> by Roy Tennant, is currently available on Ustream
> (www.ustream.tv/recorded/9952172).

> ➤ Many of the sessions from the Smithsonian speaker series on
> the future of libraries have been recorded from live broadcasts
> and are available on Ustream. One such session is the
> presentation "Democracy 2.0: A Case Study in Open
> Government" with U.S. archivist David Ferriero
> (www.ustream.tv/channel/smithsonian-institution-libraries).

F Y I

In September 2010, Business Insider named
Ustream in its list of Digital 100: The World's
Most Valuable Startups.[3]

Endnotes

1. "About Ustream," Ustream, www.ustream.tv/about (accessed August 10, 2011).

2. "Ustream Media Kit," Ustream, www.ustream.tv/mediakit (accessed August 10, 2011).

3. "Digital 100: The World's Most Valuable Startups," Business Insider, September 23, 2010, www.businessinsider.com/digital-100 (accessed August 10, 2011).

86

Vimeo
video hosting and sharing service
www.vimeo.com

Overview

Vimeo (a play on the word *video*) is comparable to YouTube (Chapter 98), providing a platform for hosting, viewing, and sharing original video content created by a community of users with a wide range of video interests. However, according to an article on Time.com, this is the only similarity that the two platforms share. "Vimeo is the video-streaming service of choice for creative types—the indie darling to YouTube's blockbuster. For casual viewers, Vimeo is the place for shorter, artsier clips. Search for *President* and you'll find yourself watching a humorous animated pop-up book that catalogs George W. Bush's presidency. Enter the same term into YouTube and you'll find relevant music videos and old news clips."[1] This description is apt and very much in sync with Vimeo's mission to provide users with a space to be inspired and showcase their creativity.[2]

Launched in November 2004, and with operations in New York, the service supports video uploads and storage of high-definition videos, the creation of community groups and channels, video player customization, and the creation of password-protected videos. In order to upload content to Vimeo, registered users must own or hold all necessary rights (copyright) to the work, and users are urged to upload only videos that they create and not to upload videos that are commercial in nature.

In August 2010, Vimeo released a long-awaited universal player that allows viewers to watch embedded Vimeo videos on mobile devices such as the iPhone or iPad using HTML5. The site has also added a new Watch Later feature into all versions of its player that allows viewers to bookmark a video for future viewing.

Features

➤ New users can sign up for the Vimeo free basic service from the homepage (www.vimeo.com). Vimeo Plus subscription service is available for an annual or monthly paid subscription fee.

➤ Features in the free basic service include:

- 500 MB per week storage space

- Standard video quality

- Banner ad displays

- No priority uploading, standard wait time for uploading and converting video on Vimeo's platform

- One HD video upload per week

- Access to basic customization of the video player

- Creation of group (limited to one only) or community forum where members chat, share videos with others who share similar interests, and learn about using the service

- Creation of channels (innovative platforms for showcasing videos; limited to one only) and albums (useful for organizing and managing videos; limited to three only)

- Video conversion to the Vimeo format and option of uploading original files (removed after one week, leaving only the Vimeo version)

- Robust privacy controls so that users can choose who they wish to share videos with

- A wide range of widgets to allow users to customize their videos to fit seamlessly into any website, or post videos on social networking sites like Facebook, Twitter, Myspace, Flickr, or Digg

➤ Users can explore a number of options in searching for videos on Vimeo's homepage:

- Enter a search term in a centrally positioned search box.

- Click on the Explore tab to browse Vimeo's videos in categories arranged A–Z: activism and nonprofits, art, animation and motion graphics, comedy, education and DIY, experimental, everyday life, films, music, nature, sports, travel and events, web series, and Vimeo projects.

- On the homepage, browse Team Vimeo selections by clicking on the tab Videos We Like.

- Click on the Right Now tab to view videos as they are uploaded in real time.

➤ Once found on the service, videos can be added as favorites, embedded in a blog or website by copying and pasting HTML code, queued to be watched later, or shared via email or web services like Flickr, Delicious, StumbleUpon, Facebook, Myspace, Twitter, and Digg.

➤ A Help Center (www.vimeo.com/help) provides first-time users with a FAQ page and video tutorials. Users can also post questions to Vimeo's community forums (www.vimeo.com/forums) or read a regularly updated blog (www.vimeo.com/blog).

How Cybrarians Can Use This Resource

Library Activism and Advocacy

Vimeo can be utilized as a platform to record, air, and share supportive speeches and actions by politicians, community leaders, or library patrons who are strong advocates for libraries, with views on protecting library budgets and avoiding closures and cutbacks in hours and services during turbulent economic times. The use of videos as tools for library activism and advocacy is exemplified in the following videos hosted on Vimeo:

➤ At the annual meeting of the Boston Municipal Research Bureau, Boston mayor Thomas Menino discusses the future of the Boston Public Library (www.vimeo.com/9921675).

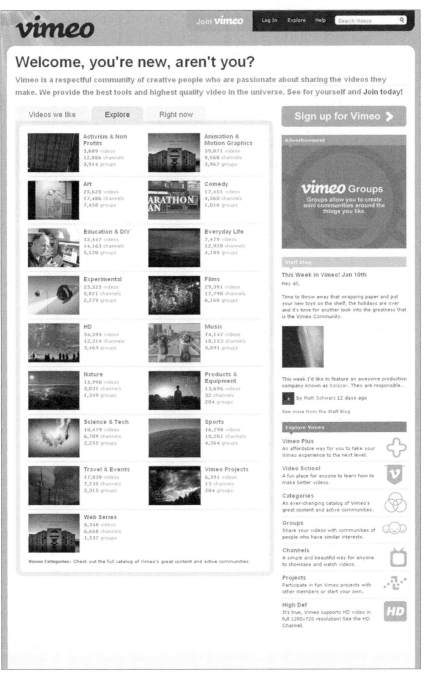

Users can explore a number of options in
searching for videos on Vimeo's homepage.

> Supporters of the Boston Public Library (BPL) speak out against cutbacks and branch closings at a BPL Trustees meeting (www.vimeo.com/10072515).

> The president of the City-Wide Friends of the BPL gives an interview about possible service cutbacks and branch closings (www.vimeo.com/10036838).

> A New York Public Library patron talks (in Spanish) about the importance of library services (www.libvid-awards.com/ 2010/ 02/24/more-library-advocacy-through-video).

FYI

In 2009 and 2010, Vimeo was voted as one of Time.com's 50 Best Websites.[3]

Endnotes

1. "50 Best Websites 2010," Time.com, www.time.com/time/specials/packages/article/ 0,28804,2012721_2012728_2012746,00.html (accessed August 10, 2011).

2. "About Vimeo," Vimeo, www.vimeo.com/about (accessed August 10, 2011).

3. "50 Best Websites 2010," Time.com.

87

VuFind
open source ILS
www.vufind.org

Overview

Villanova University's Falvey Memorial Library developed VuFind, a search-and-discovery portal (library.villanova.edu/Find/Search/Home) to enable library patrons to browse through all of the library's resources (books, journals, audiovisual materials, eresources, digital resources) using a single interface. Many libraries are following this path and adopting similar prototypes—or what are commonly referred to as next-generation catalogs—in an attempt to make their collections and services visible and attractive to patrons, who by all accounts can be easily categorized as 2.0 users, familiar with and somewhat addicted to Google's one-stop-shop search box and the personalization and social networking features of commercial sites such as Amazon.

VuFind is open source software, offered free through an approved General Public License by the Open Source Initiative. Many libraries have chosen to implement VuFind, adding customizations tailored to their users' needs. A VuFind installations wiki page (www.vufind.org/ wiki/installation_status) lists libraries and allied institutions that have taken advantage of this free resource.

The appeal of the software can be attributed to many factors: modular design allowing a variety of implementations; a driver-oriented communication interface that allows it to interact with library management software of any type for access to item status, holdings, and other similar information; the fact that it runs on the Apache Solr search engine, which offers quick response times; its scalability and flexibility; and the availability of social networking features such as adding tags, comments, and creating a Favorites list.

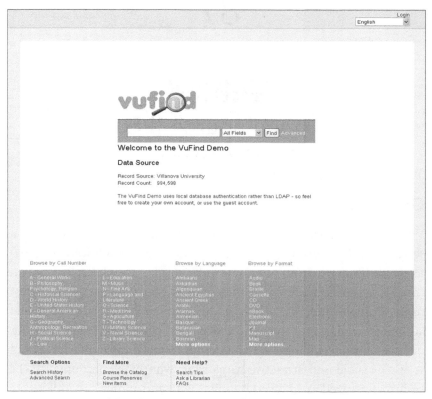

Libraries can use the VuFind demo site
before downloading the latest version of the software.

VuFind has translations available in Brazilian Portuguese, Chinese, Dutch, English, French, German, Japanese, and Spanish, with plans to add more languages. On July 15, 2010, VuFind's extended beta period was declared over, and VuFind 1.0 officially released. A demo of VuFind and links to download the software are available on the homepage (www.vufind.org).

Features

➤   Availability of basic and advanced search with faceted results: The system allows the user to search from a basic or advanced search box and then narrow the results by clicking on the various facets such as format, language, genre, region, and call number.

➤ Live record status and location with Ajax querying: The search results page is able to display the live status of a record through the use of Ajax programming.

➤ Similar Items suggestions: When viewing a retrieved record, searchers are offered suggestions of resources that are similar to the resource they searched for.

➤ Save resources to organized lists: Users have the ability to save the resources from both the search results page and from the record view page to personal, customizable lists. These lists can be retrieved later when saved.

➤ Persistent URLs: This allows searchers to bookmark search results, thus giving permanent access to pages retrieved from a search.

➤ Personalization and social networking features: Users can create an account with a username and password and log in to the VuFind OPAC to add tags, add comments, and bookmark items to their Favorites list. Additionally, end users can view bibliographic citations in multiple styles; view cover art; export to reference management tools Refworks, Endnote, and Zotero (see Chapter 101); text bibliographic information to their mobile phones; forward searches via email; and view authoritative reviews on works retrieved from services like Amazon and Syndetic Solutions.

➤ Availability of nonbeta release: In July 2010, VuFind released its first nonbeta version VuFind 1.0, which included several features missing from the previous beta versions such as improved stability and security, flexible support for non-MARC metadata formats, a mobile interface, Dewey Decimal support, and integration with Serials Solutions's web-scale discovery service Summon. The August 2011 release included support for expanded ILS integration (holds, renewals, etc.), a brand new alternate mobile theme based on jQuery Mobile, more accurate advanced search, and enhanced translation support. The latest releases and updates to the

software are always available on the download page
(www.vufind.org/downloads.php).

How Cybrarians Can Use This Resource

Access to a Next-Generation Search-and-Discovery Portal

VuFind as a library resource portal, designed and developed for
libraries by libraries, has been enjoying some success with a wave of
new installations (live or public beta) at the following institutions:

> ➤ Colorado State University Libraries, discovery.library.
> colostate.edu

> ➤ London School of Economics and Political Science Library,
> catalogue.lse.ac.uk

> ➤ National Library of Ireland, sources.nli.ie

> ➤ University of Georgia Libraries, gilfind.uga.edu

> ➤ University of Michigan Libraries, mirlyn.lib.umich.edu

> ➤ York University Libraries, www.library.yorku.ca/find

F Y I

Downloads for the latest stable releases of the
VuFind software are hosted on the SourceForge
(www.sourceforge.net) website—one of the
leading resources for open source software
development and distribution of free open
source software.

88

Widgets
programming code service
www.widgets.yahoo.com/gallery

Overview

Widgets (pronounced WIH-jits) are being integrated into webpages and social networking sites at such an alarming rate that 2007 was declared the Year of the Widget in a *Newsweek* article.[1] Richard MacManus, in a post on the highly rated technology blog ReadWriteWeb, agrees that widgets are indeed popular tech tools and he goes further to suggest that they should be considered "the new black."[2]

Widgets are chunks of programming code that can be easily dragged onto a desktop or pasted into a personal webpage, where they can be constantly updated with whatever information you want. Many bloggers, social network users, and day-to-day office workers are now adding bling (i.e., adding enhancements) to their blogs, web spaces, or desktops with these easy-to-use mini applications.

They are relatively easy to download and add to personal pages, because the user does not need to know the markup language (HTML) or programming language (JavaScript or Flash) used to develop the code. In most instances, the coding is created automatically and all users have to do is copy and paste the required information into their blog or website, or drag the application onto their desktop. For example, widgets included on a personal blog or Facebook page could allow a visitor to listen to a song when the page is loaded, automatically listen to an audio message, view the word of the day (English or Spanish), view photos as a slideshow, check an online calendar, check email, or view the latest weather report.

The usefulness and portability of widgets have not gone unnoticed by online content providers. Web portals like Google and Yahoo! offer customizable pages for their users by way of iGoogle (www.google. com/ig) and My Yahoo! (www.my.yahoo.com). Mainstream media houses like the *New York Times, Wall Street Journal,* and ESPN have allowed users to design the page they see when they log on. Flickr (www.flickr.com; see Chapter 24), the photo sharing site, encourages its members to create a Badge that they can post on their blogs and personal homepages to let friends know when they have uploaded new snapshots.

Features

Here are some common characteristics of widgets:

➣ Shareable: Users can easily obtain the widget's embed code and add the widget to their website or blog. This code can then be shared with others who visit their site.

➣ User Customizable: It is often possible for users to pick the size, color, and other features of a widget when getting the embed code. This ensures that the widget has been customized to match the design of their website or blog.

➣ Interactive: Widgets by nature are dynamic portable chunks of codes that when integrated into static websites and blogs give these an interactive look and feel. Widgets that fit these characteristics include maps, quizzes, and updated RSS feeds.

How Cybrarians Can Use This Resource

Promoting Library Services

This is a good example of a resource that, if incorporated seamlessly in library catalogs, blogs, and main webpages, can result in a more user-friendly and attractive interface, ultimately increasing user traffic to these portals and promoting library services.

The following are links to some popular downloadable widgets. For the majority of the resources listed here, no technical knowledge or expertise is required; simply follow the instructions for copying and pasting the chunk of code that is automatically generated:

At Yahoo! Widgets, you can search a
database of widgets or create your own.

➤ LIB Widgets developed by the University of Texas Libraries
(www.lib.utexas.edu/tools): This webpage lists a number of
widgets that patrons may find useful while conducting
research. The widgets are organized into three categories:
search widgets, information organizing widgets, and
collaboration widgets. Popular downloads include the
CD/DVD Search Plugin, Library Catalog Search Plugin,
University of Texas Digital Repository Search Plugin,
WorldCat for iPhone, Delicious Web Browser Add-On, Flickr
Uploadr, and Facebook App. The webpage also hosts a
Spotlight or Widget of the Day and a suggestion box for
patrons to recommend widgets for the library.

➤ The SEOmoz list of Web 2.0 Awards top websites for finding
and downloading widgets (www.seomoz.org/web2.0)

> Yahoo! widgets gallery for downloading or creating widgets (www.widgets.yahoo.com/gallery)

> Google Desktop widgets (www.desktop.google.com/plugins)

> Word of the Day widget (www.dictionary.reference.com/help/linking/wordoftheday-simple-widget.html)

> WorldCat.org widgets (www.worldcat.org/wcpa/content/affiliate/default.jsp)

F Y I

Widgets are also known as modules, gadgets, badges, capsules, snippets, minis, flakes, and plug-ins.

Endnotes

1. Brian Braiker, "The Year of the Widget?" *Newsweek*, December 22, 2006, www.newsweek.com/2006/12/21/the-year-of-the-widget.html (accessed August 10, 2011).

2. Richard MacManus, "Widgets Are the New Black," ReadWriteWeb, June 23, 2006, www.readwriteweb.com/archives/widgets_are_the.php (accessed August 10, 2011).

89

Wikipedia
wiki
en.wikipedia.org

Overview

Since its creation in 2001 by founders Larry Sanger and Jimmy Wales, Wikipedia has grown rapidly into one of the largest and most popular collaborative reference websites on the internet, attracting an average of about 400 million visitors monthly. There are more than 82,000 active contributors working on more than 19 million articles (about 3.7 million in English) in more than 270 languages.[1] Given this massive collaborative effort, it is not surprising when one learns that the name Wikipedia is a combination of the words *wiki* (a technology for creating collaborative websites, from the Hawaiian word *wiki*, meaning "quick") and *encyclopedia*.

All Wikipedia articles are written collaboratively by anonymous volunteers around the world, who write without remuneration. Contributors can choose to submit anonymously, under a pseudonym, or with their real identity. In such an open environment, anyone with internet access can make changes to Wikipedia articles (except in certain cases where editing is restricted and a page becomes fully protected to prevent disruption and vandalism).

This openly editable model, in stark contrast to conventional print encyclopedias, is often cited as a weak link by Wikipedia's critics, who have leveled accusations of systemic bias and pointed to inconsistencies and inaccuracies in contributed articles. A case in point is that of an anonymously written article claiming a link between former journalist John Seigenthaler and the assassinations of Robert Kennedy and John F. Kennedy.[2] Many university lecturers have joined the chorus of dissenters, discouraging students from using Wikipedia, and going so far as to threaten censure to students bold enough to use the resource for academic assignments.

To bolster credibility, the Wikipedia community has tried to promote five fundamental principles, referred to as the five pillars, by which the encyclopedia is governed: Wikipedia's function is as an encyclopedia only; articles must have a neutral point of view, and authors must strive for verifiable accuracy by providing references; all contributions are freely licensed to the public, and no editor owns any article; Wikipedians should interact in a respectful and civil manner; and Wikipedia's rules are not carved in stone.[3]

The Wikipedia project is managed by the nonprofit organization Wikimedia Foundation, which also manages the operation of Wikipedia's sister projects, including Wiktionary (a wiki dictionary) and Wikibooks (textbooks), discussed later in this chapter.

Features

➤ Users do not have to log in to read Wikipedia, nor is a registered account required to edit the articles. However, users are encouraged to register for the service (username and password required) as they are afforded the following advantages:

- Start new pages, including their own user page

- Edit semi-protected pages, once they have made 10 edits and their account is at least 4 days old

- Rename pages, upload images, and send and receive email from other users

- Customize the appearance and behavior of the website, including signatures

- Keep a watch list to track changes made to articles of interest

- Access more advanced editing tools

- Vote in Arbitration Committee elections and Wikimedia Board elections

- Edit without their IP address being visible, except to a few highly trusted users who have the "check user" permission

- Log in to other Wikimedia projects

➤ Wikipedia's homepage employs a familiar layout with the main navigational links on the left sidebar and a Google-like search box to search for Wikipedia articles (en.wikipedia. org). Researchers can browse broad subject categories or click through to the following subsections: Today's featured article (exemplifying the best articles written), In the news, Did you know … , On this day … , and Today's featured picture.

➤ All Wikipedia articles are well organized using a consistent template. Each entry is characterized by similar tabs:

- Article page: This is the article's main page, with user-contributed content including a title, an introduction, table of contents, main headings and subheadings to assist users in finding information quickly within the article, and images. Also included are in-text hyperlinked references linking to a list of notes and references at the end of the article, hyperlinks within the text leading to other Wikipedia articles, and a section at the bottom of the page showing external links or additional resources.

- Discussion page: The purpose of the discussion page accompanying each article is to provide space for editors to discuss and coordinate changes required for the associated article. Articles needing additional work are marked with prominent alerts often worded as "This article needs attention from an expert on the subject." The discussion page is often linked to the WikiProject page used to coordinate changes across single or multiple topics.

- The Edit tab: Anyone who has edited an article is immediately referred to as a Wikipedia editor. Editing most

Wikipedia pages is easy and requires using simple markup language. To edit articles, users click on the Edit tab at the top of any Wikipedia article. This will automatically open a new window with a text box containing the editable text of the current page. All editors are advised to write a short summary of their actions after editing is complete. Changes made can be previewed and compared with previous versions by clicking the Show Changes button. Clicking the Save Page button completes the editing process and the changes are immediately visible to all Wikipedia users. Articles considered to be well-authored, lacking inaccuracies, and with valuable content are marked with a star in the upper-right corner of the article page and are often promoted as a featured article on the homepage. Wikipedia maintains a style guide, the Manual of Style (en.wikipedia.org/wiki/Wikipedia:Manual_of_Style).

- The View History page: This page records past revisions of all articles, making it easy to compare old and new versions, undo changes that an editor may consider undesirable, or restore lost content.

How Cybrarians Can Use This Resource

Promoting Libraries in Users' Social Spaces

Notwithstanding its critics, Wikipedia is often cited as an example of a Web 2.0 service that, along with YouTube, Myspace, and Facebook, has been successfully implemented and has steadily gained acceptance across a diverse group of community users. For some, this resource has become one of the top reference resources for searching for information on a particular topic, and it is often one of the first references in a results list in a Google or Yahoo! search. The explosive growth of Wikipedia has made it a prime partner for cybrarians in their efforts to push library services to users, deliberately invading their social spaces where they conduct their research.

All Wikipedia articles are well-organized and use a consistent template with the following tabs: Article, Discussion, Read, Edit, and View History.

The following is a list of libraries with articles written in Wikipedia. All of the articles, for the most part, are modeled on the same pattern: presenting concise and factual information on the library's history, the use of its catalogs, access to digital or special collections, library holdings, innovative services, and a list of library events.

➤   Library of Congress (en.wikipedia.org/wiki/Library_of_
    Congress)

➤   University at Buffalo Libraries (en.wikipedia.org/wiki/
      University_at_Buffalo_Libraries)

➤   University of Florida Digital Collections (en.wikipedia.org/
      wiki/University_of_Florida_Digital_Collections)

➤   University of Washington Libraries (en.wikipedia.org/wiki/
      University_of_Washington_Libraries)

Free Resources for Reference and Research

Wikipedia also hosts a number of sister projects that can easily be
added to a library's subject guide of free internet resources to assist
patrons with reference and research:

➤   Commons: Repository of media files (commons.
      wikimedia.org)

➤   Wikinews: Source of user-contributed news (en.
      wikinews.org)

➤   Wiktionary: Online dictionary and thesaurus
      (en.wiktionary.org)

➤   Wikiquote: Collection of quotations (en.wikiquote.org)

➤   Wikibooks: Repository of textbooks and manuals
      (en.wikibooks.org)

➤   Wikisource: Online library of free ebooks and other
      epublications (en.wikisource.org)

➤   Wikispecies: Directory of species (species.wikimedia.org)

➤   Wikiversity: Online repository of learning resources
      (en.wikiversity.org)

F Y I

Wikipedia is ranked the seventh-most-visited
website in the world according to Alexa traffic
rankings (statistics for August 2011,
www.alexa.com/siteinfo/wikipedia.org).

Endnotes

1. "Wikipedia: About," Wikipedia, en.wikipedia.org/wiki/Wikipedia:About (accessed August 10, 2011).

2. Daniel Terdiman, "Growing Pains for Wikipedia," December 5, 2005, CNET News, news.cnet.com/Growing-pains-for-Wikipedia/2100-1025_3-5981119.html (accessed August 10, 2011).

3. "Wikipedia: Five Pillars," Wikipedia, en.wikipedia.org/wiki/Wikipedia:Five_pillars (accessed August 10, 2011).

90

Wikis by Wetpaint
wiki
www.wetpaintcentral.com

Overview

Wetpaint is a company that provides a broad range of social publishing services, but it is best known for its wiki hosting service. Wikis by Wetpaint is a tool of choice for nontech-savvy users who wish to create a wiki in less than five minutes and immediately start the process of collaborating online.

Using the Wetpaint wizard located on the homepage (www.wet paintcentral.com), users can create a wiki in three simple steps, and then use the Click and Type tools to add text, photos, URL links, and other user-generated content to the wiki. There is no limit to the number of wikis that can be created on the service. The majority of wikis created have a web address or domain name of wetpaint.com (for example, yoursite.wetpaint.com); custom URLs can be purchased from third-party vendors such as GoDaddy (www.go daddy.com), Dotster (www.dotster.com), or Network Solutions (www.networksolutions.com).

Although wiki hosting and the creation of free websites remain part of its core services, Wetpaint underwent a strategic shift in its business model in 2010, according to the technology startup blog TechCrunch.[1] What began as a simple social publishing platform took a new direction by launching Wetpaint Entertainment (www.wetpaint.com/#no), a TV news site that covers news and gossip from major TV shows such as *Glee, Grey's Anatomy,* and *Gossip Girl.*

This shift in focus has led many to surmise that this was the same line of thinking used in coming up with the rather unique name Wetpaint, which refers to the fact that Wetpaint sites are never really complete—the content is always changing. The shift has led to an expanded base of the community of users, running the gamut from individuals and companies to shared groups building websites on every imaginable topic. Established in 2005, the company's main headquarters is located in Seattle, Washington.

Features

➤   The Wikis by Wetpaint service is free and supported mainly by contextual advertising links strategically placed on wikis created using the service. Users wishing to remove ads from their wikis can upgrade to the premium service.

➤   New users can create wikis from the homepage in three simple steps:

1.   Register for a Wikis by Wetpaint account from the homepage (www.wetpaintcentral.com) by supplying a username and password.

2.   Choose a site name and URL (web address) for your Wetpaint site by completing the online form provided. All wiki creators must also write a concise explanation of what the site is about, select a subject category that best describes the wiki, and indicate if the site will be public (edited by everyone) or private (edited by persons you invite to collaborate).

3.   Pick a design from the selection of preformatted templates. Wikis are now ready for immediate use and creators can start sharing content.

➤   The following features are available for customizing and improving wikis after the three steps have been completed:

•   Creation of a personalized profile page

•   Access to the easy edit toolbar that facilitates click-and-type page editing for adding content such as text, images, videos, music, polls, and tables

- Clickable keyword tags

- Ability to manage pages (move, delete, rename, revert pages)

- Maintainance of site statistics: Google Analytics, SiteMeter, and questionable language report

- Access to a menu of popular widgets

- Customizable content modules (choose from: the new member spotlight, new gallery photos, recent site activity, top contributors, hot discussions, related content, and featured content)

- RSS updates, email notifications, and full address book upload

➤ New users are encouraged to interact with other wiki developers through discussion forums (www.wetpaintcentral. com/thread). Here users can ask questions, comment on features, make suggestions, post tips and tricks, and discuss a wide range of topics related to Wetpaint websites.

How Cybrarians Can Use This Resource

Promoting Information Literacy

Wetpaint has publicly stated its commitment to helping educators bring the power of wikis to the learning process. Toward this end, it has established the Wetpaint Wikis in Education Community forum (wikis ineducation.wetpaint.com), an organized network of close to 3,000 educators working collectively to document and share their experiences about experimenting with wikis in the classroom. Their success stories, which cybrarians can emulate, are outlined on the Wetpaint website under categories such as:

New Wetpaint users can register to use the
service and create wikis in three simple steps.

➤ Classroom Wikis (wikisineducation.wetpaint.com/page/
Wikis+in+the+Classroom)

➤ Student Created Wikis (wikisineducation.wetpaint.com/page/
Student+Created+Wikis)

➤ Higher-Ed Wikis (wikisineducation.wetpaint.com/page/ Higher-Ed+Wikis)

➤ Group Project Wikis (wikisineducation.wetpaint.com/page/ Group+Project+Wikis)

➤ Global Connections Wikis (wikisineducation.wetpaint.com/ page/Global+Connections+Wikis)

➤ Parent-Teacher Organizations Wikis (wikisineducation. wetpaint.com/page/PTO+Wikis)

➤ Teacher Peer Wikis (wikisineducation.wetpaint.com/page/ Teacher+Peer+Wikis)

F Y I

The Wetpaint Golden Paint Can Awards (goldenpaintcanawards.wetpaint.com) is an annual online event in which wikis are nominated, chosen, and voted for by the community of Wetpaint users.

Endnote

1. Leena Rao, "As It Moves Away From the Wikis, Wetpaint Launches TV News and Entertainment Site," TechCrunch, September 5, 2010, techcrunch.com/2010/09/05/ as-it-moves-away-from-the-wikis-wetpaint-launches-tv-news-and-entertainment-site (accessed August 10, 2011).

91

Wolfram | Alpha
search engine
www.wolframalpha.com

Overview

On its FAQ page, the developers of Wolfram|Alpha are quick to point out that the service is not a search engine. It is described instead as a computational knowledge engine. When a search query is plugged into the search box on the main page, Wolfram|Alpha generates output by analysis and complex computations, using its built-in knowledge base and algorithms to provide specific answers.

Instead of searching the web and returning links to documents, like other search engines, Wolfram|Alpha computes answers to questions that have factual responses or involve mathematical calculations or formulas. For example, What is the capital of Turkey? How many protons are in a hydrogen atom? What is the average rainfall in Vancouver? What is $450 + 10%$?

Wolfram|Alpha contains "trillions of pieces of data, more than 50,000 types of algorithms and models, and linguistic capabilities for more than 1000 domains."[1] All data in Wolfram|Alpha is centrally curated and audited by its developers. Some of the data in this computational knowledge base is derived from public or private websites, primary sources, reference libraries, and handbooks. The team also uses a portfolio of automated and manual methods to check data, including statistics, visualization, source cross-checking, and expert review.

Computer scientist Stephen Wolfram, lead developer of the service, readily admits that it is an ambitious and long-term project. The Wolfram Mathematica system (on which Wolfram|Alpha is built) has been in continual development for more than 20 years.[2] The service was officially launched in May 2009.

This seemingly supercomputational engine does list some of its main limitations as follows: The knowledge engine can only compute facts that are known and are somehow public, it can only deal with facts (not opinions), there may be long lapses in computation time for each query, and the service is in continual development (continuous beta).

Features

➤ There is a customizable search box on the homepage (www.wolframalpha.com) to type in search queries. Searchers can select one of seven different background themes to change the look of the search box. There is also the option to show hints while typing searches.

➤ Wolfram|Alpha's output or results screen is divided into different labeled sections referred to as pods. In response to the question "What is the median annual salary for librarians," the following responses were returned within labeled pods (as shown in figure):

- Input interpretation shows Wolfram|Alpha's interpretation of the question and a definition of key search terms.

- Result shows data based on a search of the knowledge base.

- History is a graph showing historical data relevant to the query.

- Employment summary shows U.S. employment summary based on 2001–2008 data.

- Related occupations shows mean wage of related occupations such as archivists, curators, museum technicians, and library technicians.

- At the bottom of each results page there is a Source Information button, which when clicked shows a pop-up window listing primary and secondary sources and references.

➤   Searchers can download WolframlAlpha toolbars to install to a browser (Internet Explorer, Mozilla Firefox, and Google Chrome are supported).

➤   Links on the right sidebar show related search results on the web (Google and Wikipedia), as well as tools for bookmarking and sharing results on social networks, blogs, and via email. Tools include Facebook, Twitter, Delicious, Myspace, LinkedIn, Reddit, Digg, Blogger, WordPress, and TypePad.

➤   The WolframlAlpha homepage has several resources to help new users in navigating this somewhat innovative resource, including an overview video by Stephen Wolfram, a FAQ page, and preworked examples or random searches arranged by topic and as a visual gallery. Additional resources include the WolframlAlpha blog (blog.wolframalpha.com) and community discussion forum (community.wolframalpha.com).

➤   There are WolframlAlpha apps for the iPad, the iPhone, and Android. A mobile version of the WolframlAlpha website is also available (m.wolframalpha.com). Widgets or mini-apps built on top of WolframlAlpha queries are coalesced into a Widget Gallery (developer.wolframalpha.com/widgets/ gallery/featured), and developers are encouraged to use the API available to build their own widgets and other supportive apps.

How Cybrarians Can Use This Resource

Reference and Research

The lofty goal of this computational engine is to take as much of the world's knowledge as possible and make it computable and accessible to everyone. The target group is wide-ranging, spanning all professions and education levels. Any level, from kindergarten to graduate school to a practitioner in the field, can use this expansive knowledge base to get answers. Cybrarians can readily promote this resource as a reference and research tool for their patrons by adding it as a free resource link on webpages and subject guides.

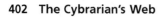

WolframAlpha computational... knowledge engine

What is the median annual salary for librarians

Input interpretation:

librarians	median wage	annual wage United States

Definition »

New to Wolfram|Alpha?
TAKE THE TOUR »

Result:

$52 530 per year (US dollars per year) (2008)

Wolfram|Alpha
App for iPhone
and iPod touch

History:

(from 2001 to 2008)
(in US dollars per year)

Employment summary: More | Show hourly

people employed	151 170 people
yearly change	+2370 people (+2%)
workforce fraction	0.1% (1 in 864)
median wage	$52 530 per year (US dollars per year)
median wage yearly change	+$1560 per year (US dollars per year) (+3%)
50% range	$(42 240 to 65 300) per year
80% range	$(33 190 to 81 130) per year

(2009 data)

Related occupations:

	people employed	mean wage
archivists, curators, and museum technicians		
library technicians	113 510 people	$30 130 per year

Definition »

Standard occupational classification information:

SOC code	25–4020
SOC parent occupation	librarians, curators, and archivists

Computed by Wolfram *Mathematica*   Source information »   Download as: PDF | Live *Mathematica*

Give us your feedback: send

About | Products | Mobile Apps | Business Solutions | For Developers | Resources & Tools

Blog | Forum | Participate | Contact | Follow:

© 2011 Wolfram Alpha LLC—A Wolfram Research Company | Terms | Privacy | Entity Index

The Wolfram|Alpha output or results screen is divided
into different labeled sections referred to as pods.

There are other WolframlAlpha projects beneficial to reference and research services in libraries:

➤   Wolfram Demonstrations Project is a database of interactive, open-code innovative demonstrations that can be used to teach in a classroom setting, assist in visualizing tough concepts, or share cutting-edge ideas to help in research (demonstrations.wolfram.com).

➤   Wolfram Mathworld is a resource created and developed with contributions from the world's mathematical community (mathworld.wolfram.com).

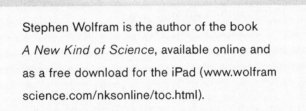

F Y I

Stephen Wolfram is the author of the book
A New Kind of Science, available online and
as a free download for the iPad (www.wolfram
science.com/nksonline/toc.html).

Endnotes

1. "About WolframlAlpha," WolframlAlpha, www.wolframalpha.com/about.html (accessed August 10, 2011).

2. Ibid.

92

Wordle
visualization tool
www.wordle.net

Overview

A tag or word cloud is a visual depiction of user-generated tags typically used to describe the content of websites. Tags are usually single words, listed alphabetically, and the importance of a tag is shown with font size or color.[1] Tag clouds are becoming increasingly popular in blogs, websites, and online catalogs.

Created by Jonathan Feinberg, Wordle is a useful tool for generating word clouds from text that you provide. To create a word cloud on the Wordle website (www.wordle.net/create), users have the option of pasting text into an editing window or entering the URL for a website or blog, and Wordle turns the words into tag clouds (visualizations) of the input text. The more times a certain word is mentioned throughout the source text, the more prominently it is displayed in the cloud. Word clouds can be customized with different fonts, layouts, and color schemes.

Wordle is a Google App Engine application. The images created by the Wordle application are licensed under a Creative Commons Attribution license and can be printed, saved as PDFs, or saved to the website's public gallery (www.wordle.net/gallery) to share with friends or colleagues. The developer does advise, however, that if users utilize a screen-capture, PDF, or other image representation of a Wordle from the database, it should be attributed to Wordle.

Features

➣ A user-friendly, intuitive, well-designed interface is available for quick generation of word clouds in three simple steps:

1. Click on the Create tab to paste source text in the window provided; enter the URL of any blog, blog feed, or webpage that has an atom or RSS feed; or enter a Delicious user name to see their tags.

2. Word clouds are generated and appear in an editing window that allows some customization. Customization includes options to display words in lower or upper case, show word count, remove numbers and common words, change font and layout, choose color palette, and randomize words.

3. Word clouds can then be printed, saved as PDFs, saved to Wordle's public gallery, or uploaded to a blog or personal website.

➤ Visitors to the website have access to a public gallery (www.wordle.net/gallery), which is updated in real time with

A user-friendly, intuitive, well-designed interface is available in Wordle for quick generation of word clouds in three simple steps.

visual examples of Wordles created by the community of users.

➤ A moderated discussion forum (groups.google.com/group/wordleusers/topics), hosted by Wordle creator Jonathan Feinberg, is useful as a resource for users to ask questions and share experiences about using the service.

How Cybrarians Can Use this Resource

Library Marketing and Promotion

➤ Create Wordles as cover art for book covers.

➤ Add word cloud art to T-shirts, posters, business cards, and brochures to promote programming and services in the library.

➤ Spruce up the library's blog or homepage with a Wordle generated for electronic and other resources in the library's collections.

F Y I

Wordle creator Jonathan Feinberg hosts a Wordle blog (blog.wordle.net) and writes regular postings on other visualization tools.

Endnote

1. "Word Clouds," Wikipedia, en.wikipedia.org/wiki/Tag_cloud (accessed August 10, 2011).

93

WordPress.com
blog hosting service
www.wordpress.com

Overview

WordPress.com is a free blog hosting service managed by Automattic, developers well-known for their foray into open source blogging content management systems. WordPress.com was developed as an easy-to-use, browser-based alternative to the self-hosted version of the same package known as WordPress.org. The latter, although freely available, is considered a barrier to some, because it requires a hosting account, an online database, FTP, and other add-on software to function. By creating WordPress.com, Automattic effectively achieved its goal of bringing the WordPress experience to a larger audience.

Comparable to other hosted blogging services such as Blogger (Chapter 10) and Movable Type (Chapter 53), subscribers to WordPress.com can start a blog in minutes without any technical knowledge. The usual features, familiar to bloggers, such as custom design templates, integrated statistics, and automatic spam protection, are integrated into the service. Always in active development, new features and services are driven by community feedback and rolled out as updates almost every day. The basic service is free, and there is a paid upgrade option for advanced features such as CSS editing, custom domains, ad-free blogs, unlimited users, extra storage, and video hosting.

Bolstered by claims of being as solid as a rock regarding storing and securing data, the company has been hosting content mounted on hundreds of servers in three datacenters (Chicago, Dallas, and San Antonio) since it was launched in 2005. It currently offers native versions of WordPress.com in more than 50 languages and is the blog

The WordPress homepage makes it easy
to sign up for a WordPress.com account.

hosting service used by premier clients such as CNN's Political Ticker,
Time Inc.'s The Page, People Magazine's Style Watch, and the Flickr blog.

Features

➤ Users can have a blog up and running in less than five
minutes by registering for the service from the homepage

(www.wordpress.com) and following the 10-step walk-through guide (learn.wordpress.com). Registering requires creating a username and password, and supplying an email address. Subscribers have the option of having a personal WordPress. com address (for example, johnsmith.wordpress.com) or switching to a custom domain. All new users are assigned 3 gigabytes of file storage space.

➤ There is a wide selection of free and customizable designs or themes for bloggers to choose from, and these themes can be changed instantly with just the click of a button.

➤ One of the more popular features offered by WordPress is a robust integrated statistics system. This is designed to give bloggers up-to-the-minute statistics (raison d'être for amateurs and professional bloggers alike) on the number of visitors to a blog, where these visitors reside, which posts are popular, and which search engine keywords are driving traffic to the blog.

➤ Bloggers can create and edit posts with an easy to use WYSIWYG (What You See Is What You Get) editor and built-in spell checker. Bloggers can also upload photos using services like Flickr or Photobucket and embed videos from YouTube or Hulu. As relevant tags or keywords are added to each posting, WordPress automatically adds these to a global tag system or tag browser housed on a separate page (en.wordpress.com/tags), which is fully searchable.

➤ WordPress.com uses Akismet (www.akismet.com), considered one of the best comment and trackback spam technologies, which automatically blocks spammers from leaving comments on a blog.

➤ Technical support and help is offered by way of user forums (en.forums.wordpress.com), the WordPress support team, and online documentation (en.support.wordpress.com).

➤ Migration of existing blogs is supported and subscribers can easily import content from other blogging services such as Blogger, LiveJournal, Movable Type, and TypePad. Conversely, bloggers wishing to leave WordPress.com can receive a complete XML export of all their blog content.

➤ WordPress.com allows subscribers the option of hosting wholly public blogs, partial public blogs (blogs that are public but not included in search engines or public listings), or private blogs that only invited members can access. There are no restrictions on the number of blogs created or the number of authors who are allowed to post or to contribute. A "track replies to comments" feature notifies bloggers of follow-ups to comments posted on their blogs.

➤ Users can easily add or rearrange widgets on their blogs' sidebars using WordPress drag-and-drop functionality. Widgets (en.support.wordpress.com/apps) are available for sharing Twitter posts, adding Flickr photos, or integrating a host of web applications available from other social software.

➤ To support the continuation of the free service, WordPress blogs are embedded with and show Google text ads. The premium service (en.wordpress.com/products) is ad-free.

➤ WordPress has developed supporting apps for the Android, iPhone, iPod Touch, iPad, BlackBerry, Windows Phone 7, and Nokia.

How Cybrarians Can Use This Resource

Promotion of New Library Services and Community Engagement

Libraries are taking advantage of this free blogging service to create blogs to engage in conversations with their community, initiate internal dialogue by encouraging contributions from library staff, and promote new collections and services. The following is an active list of libraries providing access to blogs created using the WordPress software:

➤ Erving Public Library, Massachusetts (ervingpubliclibrary. wordpress.com)

➤ Benedictine University Library, Illinois (benlibrary.word press.com)

➤ Barrier Reef TAFE Library and Information Services, Queensland, Australia (britlibraries.wordpress.com)

➤ Sullivan Library, Dominican College, New York Veritas Blog (sullivanlibrary.wordpress.com)

➤ The University of Manchester, John Rylands University Library (jrulenginfo.wordpress.com)

F Y I

Freshly pressed statistics are displayed live on the WordPress.com homepage daily. As of August 2011, more than 350,000 bloggers had used the service to create blogs.

94

WorldCat.org
next-generation online union catalog
www.worldcat.org

Overview

Internet-savvy users are now well accustomed to one-stop searching for content on the internet. This search habit is characterized by plugging in search terms into a single, prominently placed, Google-like search box on almost every homepage. Users have become attuned to this search pattern because, according to an OCLC report, vendors are now in the business of unbundling content from traditional containers (books, journals, CDs, videos). Today, information seekers are no longer concerned with where information "lives" or who owns it, only that they can get to it quickly and effortlessly.[1]

In recognition of this, OCLC has created WorldCat.org, an end-user discovery interface that delivers single-search access to the WorldCat union catalog, which contains bibliographic records and holdings contributed by libraries in 170 countries and territories around the world. Current estimates show that this union catalog provides access to more than 236 million different records for materials in all formats—physical (books, journal articles, music CDs, and video) and digital assets (ebooks, downloadable audiobooks, digital photos)—in more than 470 languages.[2]

Searching for items (print, nonprint, digital) in the WorldCat catalog can originate by entering a search in the search box on the WorldCat.org homepage (www.worldcat.org), or searchers can serendipitously discover these items among their search results for regular web content by doing a keyword search on partner sites such as Google and Yahoo!.

Successful searches in this web portal lead to a detailed item record page, with bibliographic information (author, title, format, language, and publisher), access to social networking features (user-generated reviews, ratings, and tags), views of cover art, full-text previews (if available), and links to local or regional libraries that own the required item.

As a nonprofit membership organization created in 1967 with the goal of furthering access to the world's information, OCLC is continuously looking for ways to promote libraries.[3]

Features

➢ WorldCat accounts require only registration of user name, password, and email address, so users can quickly establish their identity and move on to member-driven activities such as creating lists and bibliographies and reviewing library materials.

➢ Searchers on the WorldCat.org homepage can use the centrally placed search box to find popular books, music CDs, videos, ebooks, audiobooks, article citations with links to their full text, and digital objects (photographs, PDF documents).

➢ When an item of interest is found, WorldCat's Find a Copy in a Library feature shows the distance from the user's current location (based on ZIP code and geomapping function) to the nearest local library that owns the item. By clicking on the link to the nearest library, a user may be able to view the item's availability and, after authenticating as a library member, perform any number of circulation activities, including the placement of a hold, remote checkout, or having the item remotely delivered to their current location. Access is also provided to the library's virtual reference services and to general information on their homepage about branch locations, operating hours, and contact information.

➢ Facets are available to refine search results by author, format, year, content (fiction, nonfiction, biography, dissertation), audience, language, topic, and related subject areas.

➢ The Find More Information About Author tab previews data such as publication timeline, works about the author, other works by the author, audience level of the item searched, and the author's related identities (including pseudonyms). The WorldCat Identities service (www.worldcat.org/identities) provides the framework for this feature.

➤ Click-through links to book vendors Amazon and Barnes & Noble Online facilitate purchase of items retrieved in a search.

➤ Clicking on the Preview This Item link leads searchers to the Google Books search interface (books.google.com) where they can read a book's full text or snippets of text depending on the item's copyright status.

➤ WorldCat.org also offers these social features designed to appeal to a new generation of searchers interested in contributing user-created content that further enhances discovery and access:

- Maintain a public profile that lists interests, occupation, personal websites, and email addresses.

- Build a personalized list of books, videos, and other library-owned items that can be designated as public or private and shared with friends.

- Add ratings, reviews, tags, and contextual notes to the displayed items.

- Create automatic citations in one of five standard styles (APA, MLA, Harvard, Chicago, Turabian) and export citations to EndNote, RefWorks, and EasyBib.

- Share library materials with social networks through sites such as Digg, Delicious, Twitter, Facebook, StumbleUpon, and Blogger.

- Install one of many WorldCat.org widgets (www.worldcat. org/wcpa/content/affiliate/default.jsp) available on the website. For example, modular search boxes are available for integrating into blogs and personal webpages or to a browser toolbar.

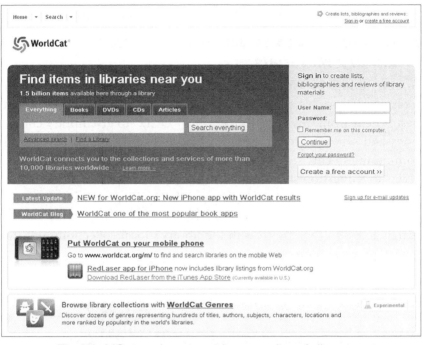

The WorldCat.org homepage is a search-and-discovery portal for popular books, music CDs, videos, ebooks, audiobooks, articles, and digital objects.

➤ For the open source developer there is free access to WorldCat.org developer tools (www.worldcat.org/wcpa/content/affiliate/default.asp), including the WorldCat Search API, which allows any business or organization to integrate WorldCat information into a web-based application such as an ecommerce site or search engine.

➤ A WorldCat mobile interface (www.worldcat.org/m) is available for searches on mobile devices.

➤ WorldCat.org is available in multiple languages, including English, German, Spanish, French, Dutch, and Chinese.

How Cybrarians Can Use This Resource

Providing Access to an Online Catalog of Library Materials

By integrating the WorldCat search box (www.worldcat.org/affiliate/ tools) on library blogs, webpages, and subject guides, cybrarians can best benefit from this herculean effort by OCLC to give library collections and services greater exposure and use among local and global communities. This search box will provide library patrons with free access to a one-stop shop of the world's most comprehensive database of library materials. The University of Washington Libraries have added WorldCat Local to the library's homepage to provide single-search access to the resources in the library's local collections and the global library community.

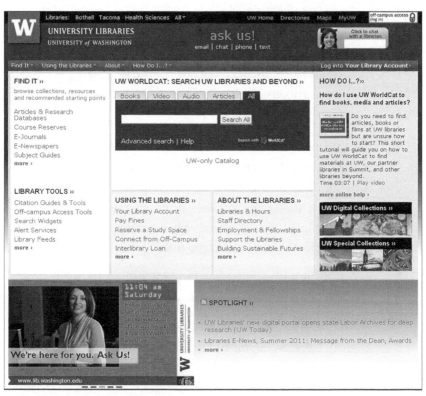

UW WorldCat allows patrons to search local and global library collections.

FYI

It is estimated that one new record is added to
the WorldCat global catalog every 10 seconds
(www.oclc.org/worldcat/statistics).

Endnotes

1. "Information Format Trends: Content Not Containers," OCLC, www.oclc.org/reports/2004format.htm (accessed August 10, 2011).

2. WorldCat Facts and Statistics, OCLC, www.oclc.org/worldcat/statistics (accessed August 10, 2011).

3. "OCLC Mission and Vision," OCLC, www.oclc.org/about/mission/default.htm (accessed August 10, 2011).

95

XING
social network
www.xing.com

Overview

XING (formerly Open Business Club) is a professional networking service based in Hamburg, Germany. Like the professional networks Ecademy (Chapter 21) and LinkedIn (Chapter 43), this service offers its members a platform to conduct business and promote their careers by creating personal profiles, hosting discussion forums, promoting events, and other common social community functions. Basic membership is free. But many core functions, like searching for members with specific qualifications or messaging members who are not in your current network, can only be accessed by subscription to the premium paid package.

In September 2010, XING announced that it passed the 10 million registered members mark, 4.2 million of whom are from German-speaking countries and use the service to manage their business contacts and boost their career.[1] In March 2011, this figure increased to 10.8 million registered members.[2]

In a bid to attract more international members, support is given to multiple languages including English, German, Spanish, Portuguese, Italian, French, Dutch, and Chinese. While the company headquarters is in Hamburg, there are key strategic offices in Barcelona, Spain, and Istanbul, Turkey.

Features

Free basic membership to the XING service requires registering from the homepage (www.xing.com) and entering personal and professional information to create a profile. With basic membership, users have full access to the following features:

- ➤ A basic network toolkit provides access to Microsoft Outlook, event planning tools, and RSS feeds.

- ➤ Members can establish contact with XING members, join groups, and participate in events.

- ➤ The member's professional profile page is viewable on the internet.

- ➤ There is a "people" search function by first name, last name, town, and industry.

- ➤ Advanced search functions have filters for company, position, university, ZIP code, and country.

- ➤ Members have limited access to search for jobs on XING or submit job openings.

- ➤ XING users with basic memberships have a trial premium membership for six days. Added features in the premium package include: unlimited job postings, ability to contact XING members directly with private messages, access to information about visitors to their profile page, ad-free profile page, document upload, and access to XING special offers on products and services.

- ➤ There are more than 17,000 groups on XING on a wide array of topics. Members can use this forum to host and moderate discussions with experts in similar or related professions.

- ➤ The XING Event tool is available for members wishing to organize events and schedule appointments or meetings.

- ➤ Members can access their business network on the go by visiting the XING mobile site (www.xing.com/mobile), developed for smartphones and other mobile devices. The network has also developed apps for the iPhone, BlackBerry, Android, and Windows Phone 7.

From the XING homepage, you can sign up for an account,
begin networking, and search for jobs.

How Cybrarians Can Use This Resource

Professional Networking

With XING at more than 10 million members and growing daily,
cybrarians can take advantage of the free XING membership to generate contacts and stay connected with an international network of professionals who share the same interests. This network may prove useful
to career development by providing new contacts, offering job leads, or
generating new ideas to assist you in your current job.

Recruitment Service

Professional networks such as Ecademy, LinkedIn, and XING are fertile ground for recruiters to post job openings and for unemployed cybrarians to search for lucrative positions within a professional environment.

F Y I

In June 2011, XING released a new version of its professional networking platform. New features include increased focus on users' own networks, a standardized and intuitive structure, and more mobile apps.

Endnotes

1. "XING Passes 10 Million Member Mark," XING, September 27, 2010, corporate.xing.com/english/press/press-releases/details/article/press-releasebrxing-passes-10-million-member-ma/572/a7e38b85f0c2326e911cd491dd6e686b/?tx_ttnews[pointer]=1 (accessed August 10, 2011).

2. "Corporate Pages," XING, corporate.xing.com/no_cache/english/company/xing-ag (accessed August 10, 2011).

96

Yahoo! Answers
question-and-answer service
www.answers.yahoo.com

Overview

In May 2010, Yahoo! Answers reached an important milestone by receiving its 1 billionth answer. With this important objective covered, the service claims that it has now become the largest and most popular knowledge-sharing community on the web, receiving more than 800,000 questions and answers per day, with 21 million unique users in the U.S. and 90 million worldwide.[1] Arguably, this would seem like quite an achievement for a question-and-answer service that originated from humble beginnings in December 2005 when it offered the first answer to a question posted on the service. This question was: Why are yawns contagious?

Not unlike other Q&A services covered in earlier chapters (for example, About.com, Chapter 2), Yahoo! Answers is an online community that connects people to the information they are seeking by getting answers from those who know it. The inner workings of the service are based on the premise that everyone has life experiences and knowledge about something, and Yahoo! Answers provides a way for people to share this experience and knowledge on a wide variety of topics.

Anyone registered with the service can ask a question on any topic and receive a timely answer from someone knowledgeable within the Yahoo! Answers community. Questions remain open for others to answer for four days before they are deleted. This period can be extended or shortened. An evaluative ratings system is built in to allow the best answers to be rewarded. These best answers can be selected either by the person asking the question (asker) or by Voters' Choice for Best Answer (Yahoo! Answers community vote). Users also have the option of browsing the database to find questions that have already been answered.

To encourage participation and reward great answers, Yahoo! Answers has a system of points and levels (www.answers.yahoo.com/ info/scoring_system). The number of points received will depend on the specific action users take. Begin participating on Yahoo! Answers and you are rewarded 100 points, answer a question and get rewarded with two points, or have your answer selected as the best answer and get 10 points; deleting an answer results in a *deduction* of two points.

Features

➤ New members register on the homepage (www.answers. yahoo.com) to create an account to log in and use the service. There is also the option to automatically sign in using an existing Yahoo! ID. Registering for a Yahoo! Account entails supplying personal information (name, gender, birthday, country of residence, postal code), and selecting a login ID and password.

➤ The main page for the question-and-answer service is divided into three sections:

• Ask section: Registered users must type questions into an online form. Questions must be 110 characters or less. The service is intuitive enough to display similar questions as you type and to point to misspelled words. There are options to choose the most relevant category for your question (arts and humanities, business and finance, computers and internet, education and reference, news and events), add details for clarification, and indicate if you wish Yahoo! Answers to send you an email whenever someone answers your question. Once an answer is selected as Best Answer, the question is considered resolved.

• Answer section: Open or unresolved questions are listed in this section. Experts on specific topics can browse

The Yahoo! Answers homepage is divided into
three main sections: Ask, Answer, and Discover.

unanswered questions and share their knowledge by providing answers. The In Voting tab previews a list of questions that have been answered but not yet resolved. The Resolved tab shows questions considered resolved with the selection of a best answer. There is an option here to also browse questions listed in specific subject categories.

- Discover section: Users can browse this section to view resolved questions, which in most cases are the best answers chosen by the Yahoo! Answers Community.

How Cybrarians Can Use This Resource

Reference and Research Services

Libraries have been competing with Q&A services such as Yahoo! Answers since these services gained acceptance as a permanent part of the reference and research landscape in the 1990s. Approval within the library community is understandably not widespread. The debate revolves around the question of why library users would want to ask unqualified strangers or pay for answers when they could ask a trained librarian with access to a wealth of authoritative resources. Convenience, habit, and lack of promotion for similar library Q & A services may be some answers. Libraries have responded positively by offering some form of synchronous or chat reference services to users to supplement reference services offered from a central desk. A list of libraries offering these virtual reference services can be found on the LISWiki website (www.liswiki.org/wiki/Chat_reference_libraries).

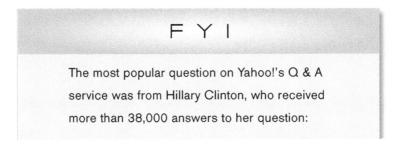

F Y I

The most popular question on Yahoo!'s Q & A service was from Hillary Clinton, who received more than 38,000 answers to her question:

"Based on your own family's experience, what do you think we should do to improve health care in America?" This is closely followed by Oprah Winfrey's question with more than 37,000 responses: "If you were given $1,000 to change the life of a perfect stranger, what would you do?"

Endnote

1. "What Is Yahoo! Answers?" Yahoo! Answers, help.yahoo.com/l/us/yahoo/answers/ overview/overview-55778.html (accessed August 10, 2011).

97

YouSendIt
file hosting and sharing
www.yousendit.com

Overview

YouSendIt offers a timely solution for sending, receiving, and tracking large files and other digital content. YouSendIt facilitates the process of sending large files without the limitations of email attachments or FTP connections, or having to mail critical data using a costly courier service.

The service makes sending and receiving large files fast and easy in three simple steps: 1) Subscribers to the free service (there is an option to upgrade to YouSendIt Pro for a fee) can start the process of sending files by uploading these through a web browser from their desktop or from within an application such as Microsoft Outlook, 2) the YouSendIt service stores the file securely and emails the recipient a notification that the file has been sent, and 3) the recipient receives the email notification, clicks on the link in the email, and downloads the file.

Designed for individual use or for business, YouSendIt claims on its homepage (www.yousendit.com) that it has more than 15 million users with more than 20 million transfers monthly across 192 countries and is the "most widely used solution for sending, receiving and tracking large files used by large corporations and independent professionals alike."[1]

Corporate clients such as Levi's, Ritz Camera, VMware, Salesforce, Reuters, and Kelly-Moore Paints rely on YouSendIt for the secure delivery of their time-sensitive data. Launched officially in September 2006, YouSendIt is a privately held company based in Campbell, California.

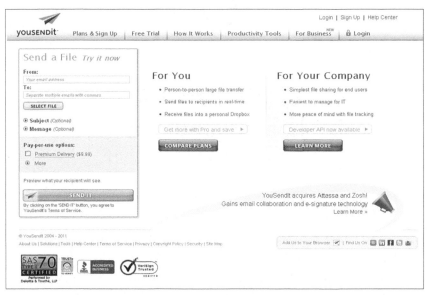

With YouSendIt, users can send and receive large files.

Features

➤ A YouSendIt Lite package is available free for individuals.
Users must register to use this free service from the homepage
(www.yousendit.com) by completing the web-based form
with an email address, full name, and password.

➤ Files can be sent immediately from a web browser by
following these steps:

- Add your email address.

- Add recipient's email address.

- Click the Select File button to select a file from a computer
or other device.

- Add Subject or Message (both are optional).

- Select from the following pay-per-use options (optional):

  - Premium Delivery

- Password-protected file

- Return receipt

• Preview the file you are sending.

• Click the Send It button.

➤ Lite account users are restricted to storage space up to 2GB, a maximum file size of 50MB, and the maximum number of downloads per file is set to 100. The site offers free access to the knowledge base for technical support. Lite users do have the option of pay-per-use for advanced security options and to receive notifications when files are downloaded.

➤ In addition to the free Lite service for individuals, YouSendIt offers three business subscription plans YouSendIt PRO, PRO Plus, and Corporate Suite. As expected, there are more features and added functions for these fee-based services, such as incremental increases in the size of files sent or received, additional storage for saved files, the ability to send multiple files, advanced security options, a dropbox or YouSendIt-hosted page where others can send files to you, detailed tracking of files sent, branding and customization, and email and live chat support.

➤ Plug-ins such as YouSendIt for Microsoft Outlook facilitate seamless sending of large files and folders within Microsoft Outlook.

➤ YouSendIt Tracker is available for the iPhone for on-the-go convenience with plans to add an app for Android devices in the immediate future.

How Cybrarians Can Use This Resource

Access to a File Transfer Service

YouSendIt is employed by a wide range of users seeking a productivity-boosting application for transferring and sharing all types of files. Cybrarians can use the service in the following ways:

> Upload and transfer files to be used in conference presentations and workshops.

> Conduct an archival transfer of files off-site to conserve hard drive space.

> Enhance collaboration with colleagues in real time by uploading large files in different formats (images, videos, audio, documents) required to complete a group project.

F Y I

YouSendIt has won a number of awards as a web-based, digital file-delivery company, including being successful in the 2010 Tech Awards Circle and winning the 2010 CODiE Award for Best Software-as-a-Service.[2]

Endnotes

1. "About You Send It," YouSendIt, www.yousendit.com/aboutus (accessed August 10, 2011).

2. "YouSendIt Awards," YouSendIt, www.yousendit.com/aboutus/press/awards (accessed August 10, 2011).

98

YouTube
video hosting and sharing service
www.youtube.com

Overview

To put a twist on a popular phrase used in the world of video sharing, YouTube has gone viral! Acquired by search engine giant Google in November 2006, with an average of more than 2 billion views per day, and ranked by Alexa[1] as the third-most-visited website on the internet (behind Google and Facebook), YouTube is the undisputed, world-leading video hosting and sharing service on the internet.

Based in San Bruno, California, the service is renowned for allowing users to create, upload, share, and view videos online. This repository of user-generated content includes movie clips, TV clips, music videos, and original videos. Videos run the gamut from firsthand accounts of current events and renditions by new artists and filmmakers to the quirky and unusual. All evince the passion and enthusiasm that people from all corners of the globe feel in the need to find a forum—in this case, a centralized video sharing distribution platform—to connect, inform, and share compelling videos.

The YouTube service is free, with most of the service's revenue generated from advertising. The first YouTube video was uploaded on April 23, 2005. It is entitled Me at the Zoo, uploaded by YouTube co-founder Jawed Karim and shot by Yakov Lapitsky at the San Diego Zoo. The 19-second video can still be viewed on the site (www.youtube.com/watch?v=jNQXAC9IVRw).

Features

As videos are the main focus of YouTube, the video page—the page where you watch clips—was redesigned and improved for simplification

431

and ease of use in March 2010. Users are encouraged to create an account and sign in to enjoy the following enhanced features on this page:

➤ A search box is strategically placed as one of the more prominent elements on the page for searching all video content by using keywords related to your interests. The Suggestions Feature shows videos that have a connection to the one you are currently watching.

➤ The Subscribe link allows you to subscribe to the channel of the video you are currently viewing and be alerted of new videos on the same subject. The account profiles of registered users are referred to as *channels*.

➤ The Add To button adds the video to an existing playlist or list of favorites.

➤ Each video is accompanied by a short summary, descriptive keywords or tags, and viewers' comments.

➤ The Share button allows users to send videos via email; copy and paste embed code to sites such as Blogger, Facebook, Twitter, Google Reader, Orkut, Myspace, Live Spaces, Bebo, and StumbleUpon; and obtain a permanent URL link to the video being viewed on screen.

➤ Each video features statistical data such as first views, total view count, links to referrals about the video, audience genre, and honors associated with a video.

➤ Users have the ability to rate videos viewed with *like* (thumbs up) and *dislike* (thumbs down) icons.

➤ Video files can be uploaded from desktops, mobile devices, or recorded live from a webcam. Uploaded videos can be high definition, but must be no more than 2 GB in size or 10 minutes in length. YouTube also supports a wide variety of video formats but recommends using H.264, MPEG-2, or MPEG-4 for best results.

➤ There are various modules that have been added to the interface to customize a YouTube user viewing experience. These include the Recommended for You module, which picks videos based on your viewing history, Spotlight Videos where YouTube members rate videos they like and staff editors select highly rated videos for the spotlight, What's New, Most Viewed, Top Favorites, and Featured Videos.

➤ Video embedding allows users to insert a YouTube video into Facebook and Myspace accounts, blogs, or other websites.

➤ Users can elect to broadcast their videos publicly or share them privately with friends and family upon upload.

➤ Users with a webcam and Flash software are able to instantly record videos and add to YouTube rather than having to prerecord and then upload the video.

➤ TestTube (www.youtube.com/testtube) is an area where YouTube engineers and developers conduct alpha testing for new features in development. Users are encouraged to participate in the development process and are welcome to evaluate the feature.

➤ Part of YouTube's goal is to extend its reach beyond the internet browser and enable users to discover and share compelling video content. Toward this end, YouTube has provided access to an API for developers (www.youtube.com/dev) to access parts of the YouTube site and integrate it with their own site.

How Cybrarians Can Use This Resource

Marketing Library Services

Before the launch of YouTube in 2005, there were not many options available for users of the internet to post videos online. YouTube has made it possible for anyone (including cybrarians) with an internet connection to post a video and be guaranteed the possibility of a global audience watching within minutes.

Here is a list of libraries using innovative methods via YouTube to market library services:

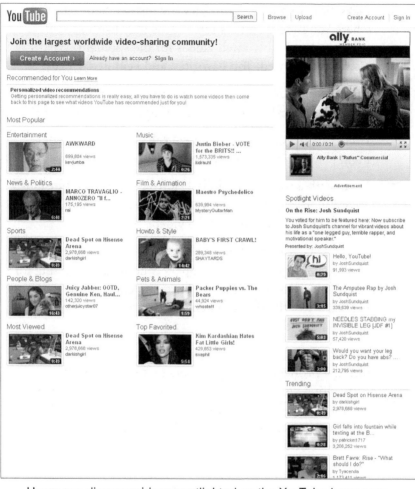

Users can discover videos spotlighted on the YouTube homepage.

➤ The Library of Congress YouTube Channel showcases the national library's timeless treasures and contemporary presentations (www.youtube.com/user/LibraryOfCongress).

➤ A promotional video (36 seconds) titled Adventures of Super Librarian was recorded by the McCracken County Public Library in Kentucky (www.youtube.com/watch?v=Bu-T ijjVs_g).

➤   The Georgia Institute of Technology has an instructional
     guide (6 minutes, 13 seconds) to citation searching using Web
     of Science (www.youtube.com/watch?v=3Y_8dvPixe4).

➤   Students and faculty from the University of Washington's
     Information School promote the use of online catalogs and
     databases by doing a parody of Lady Gaga's song "Poker Face"
     (4 minutes, 23 seconds; www.youtube.com/watch?v=a_uzUh1
     VT98).

➤   The Teen Summer Reading @ Birmingham (Alabama) Public
     Library video (39 seconds) was used to promote summer
     reading at several library systems across the U.S.
     (www.youtube.com/watch?v=hWlicnl3HII).

F Y I

YouTube users upload 35 hours of video every
minute. More videos are uploaded to YouTube
in 60 days than the three major U.S. networks
created in 60 years.[2]

Endnotes

1. "YouTube.com," Alexa, www.alexa.com/siteinfo/youtube.com (accessed August 10,
   2011).

2. "YouTube Press Room," YouTube, www.youtube.com/t/press (accessed August 10,
   2011).

99

Zoho
productivity tool
www.zoho.com

Overview

Zoho is a suite of online office applications and productivity tools developed by the U.S.-based company of the same name, Zoho Corporation. These applications were developed with the goal of providing users (identified as students, educators, nonprofits, small- and medium-size businesses) with the most comprehensive set of applications available anywhere (breadth), and for these applications to have enough features (depth) to make the user experience worthwhile.

This goal has been realized, as Zoho is easily the most extensive set of online applications offered by any one company on the internet and can easily rival proprietary productivity applications suites such as Microsoft Office or open source applications like Google Docs (Chapter 29) and OpenOffice.org (Chapter 57). Online collaboration and sharing tools include email service, word processing, online spreadsheets, presentation software, document management, note taker, wiki collaboration, organizer, chat, and a centralized repository for sharing content in different formats.

In addition to the obvious advantage of having access to a free suite of productivity tools for working online from within your browser (all Zoho apps are cloud-based), Zoho also offers free online storage, quick access to Zoho data from any computer, and collaboration and sharing of information on group projects. For Microsoft Office Suite users, there is the availability of the Zoho Plug-in for MS Office, which offers the flexibility to work offline with Microsoft Word (documents) and MS Excel (spreadsheets) and have these changes reflected and synced directly into your Zoho Writer and Zoho Sheet account online.

New Zoho users can have immediate access to the suite
of productivity applications by creating an account.

Editions of all the applications (described in the features section) are
offered free for personal use, but business and corporate users must pay a
subscription fee, offered at somewhat competitive rates. There are discounts for nonprofit organizations.[1] Zoho currently supports web access
to all of its tools from a mobile version of its website (mobile.zoho.com)
on the iPhone, Android, Blackberry, Windows Mobile, and Nokia devices.

Features

➤   New Zoho users can have immediate access to the suite of
    applications by creating an account (email address, password,

and a verification code to prevent spam) in the online form provided on the homepage (www.zoho.com). There is support for single sign-on across all Zoho applications, so once subscribed to one service, members have access to all the services using the same user name, email address, and password.

➤ Once signed in to the basic service, users have free access to the Zoho applications summarized here under the categories Collaboration, Productivity, and Business.

- Collaboration applications:

  - Zoho Chat: Supports live chat, group chat, embedding of chat boxes on blogs and websites, search of chat history, and shared desktops

  - Zoho Docs: Supports online document management, useful for storing and sharing files securely and accessing these files from any computer

  - Zoho Discussions: Software that supports the creation of community forums for open discussions and exchanging ideas

  - Zoho Mail: Web-based email service with no display ads, offers offline support for composing and reading email, spam protection, creating personalized email addresses and folders, and integration with instant messaging

  - Zoho Meeting: A tool for hosting web conferences and online meetings

  - Zoho Projects: A web-based project management, collaboration, and issue tracking software that allows teams to collaborate on shared projects

  - Zoho Share: A centralized public repository for sharing content (PowerPoint presentations, PDF documents, Word documents, spreadsheets, and images)

- Zoho Wiki: Supports creation of online portals for content sharing and group collaboration

- Productivity applications:

  - Zoho Writer: Online word processor that supports the sharing of documents with colleagues, collaboration on group projects in real time, offline document editing (edits will be synchronized with online version of software), posting documents created to blogs, importing and exporting documents, and use of customized templates available from a template library

  - Zoho Sheet: Online spreadsheet that supports creating, editing, and sharing spreadsheets from any computer, with option available to allow multiple users to work on a spreadsheet simultaneously; can be imported and exported as Excel files (Microsoft Office format), and for advanced users there is access to advanced features like VBA (Visual Basic for Applications) Macros and Pivot Tables

  - Zoho Show: Online tool for making presentations that includes prebuilt themes, clipart, and drag-and-drop functionality; can import, access, edit, and share presentations from any computer and embed to a blog or website

  - Zoho Notebook: Online note taker for typing text or embedding content such as images, audio, and video

  - Zoho Planner: Online organizer that enables users to create to-do lists with due dates and email reminders built in; capability to add notes and images before sharing lists with a network of friends or colleagues

  - Zoho Calendar: Enables scheduling, managing, and tracking meetings and events

- Business applications:

  - Zoho Assist: Simple user interface with online remote support; useful for online technical support

  - Zoho Books: Online accounting software

  - Zoho Business: Email hosting and office suite for businesses (basic free version gives access to only three users)

  - Zoho Challenge: Software that automates and streamlines online test creation, including distribution and evaluation of scores

  - Zoho CRM: Tools that can build and strengthen customer relationships by tracking and analyzing sales and marketing trends and managing inventory

  - Zoho Creator: Database management software for creating online databases (basic free version gives access to only three users)

  - Zoho Invoice: Online invoicing software that creates invoices for expenses and tracks payments received

  - Zoho Marketplace: Free business web applications listed in categories such as IT management, sales, marketing, human resources, education, and nonprofits (also used to showcase and sell professional services)

  - Zoho People: Human resources information system

  - Zoho Recruit: An easy-to-use applicant tracking system that assists staffing agencies and recruiting departments in tracking job openings, resume submissions, and candidates' applications

  - Zoho Reports: An online reporting and business intelligence service

How Cybrarians Can Use This Resource

Productivity Tool for Reference Statistics

Ellyssa Kroski, the emerging technologies and web services librarian at Barnard College, New York, and author of *Web 2.0 for Librarians and Information Professionals*,[2] has been using Zoho for its word processing and spreadsheet programs. On her blog iLibrarian (oedb.org/blogs/ ilibrarian), there is an evaluative post[3] and several screenshots demonstrating how to use the application Zoho Creator and its suitability for creating a database to keep track of statistics for the library's reference department. She admits that despite not having "much background with database creation," she was able to create a reference statistical analysis database in about 20 minutes and attributes this mainly to the application's drag-and-drop functionality. This is one example of the practical application of the Zoho productivity suite in libraries.

Research Tool

Librarians at the University of Texas Libraries created a widget page to assist faculty, staff, and students when conducting research. Included in the list is Zoho Notebook, which is cited as "a great tool for collaborating on team projects or starting a group notebook."[4] To further assist first-time users, librarians included a short description of the widget, instructions on getting started, a link to the Zoho Notebook homepage, and a video demonstration.

F Y I

Zoho.com has received numerous awards, including the Infoworld 2009 Product of the Year and the 2008 PC World 25 Most Innovative Products Award (www.zoho.com/ company.html).

Endnotes

1. "Zoho Pricing," Zoho, www.zoho.com/pricing.html (accessed August 10, 2011).

2. Ellyssa Kroski, *Web 2.0 for Librarians and Information Professionals* (New York: Neal Schuman, 2008).

3. "Reference Statistics With Zoho Creator," iLibrarian www.oedb.org/blogs/ilibrarian/ 2007/reference-statistics-with-zoho-creator (accessed August 10, 2011).

4. "LIB Widgets," University of Texas Libraries, www.lib.utexas.edu/tools/info.html (accessed August 10, 2011).

100

Zoomerang
productivity tool
www.zoomerang.com

Overview

Zoomerang and SurveyMonkey (Chapter 80) are viewed as industry leaders and pioneers in the development and delivery of web-based survey tools. Zoomerang, like SurveyMonkey, provides businesses, nonprofits, and educational institutions with a cost-effective alternative for conducting comprehensive online surveys to make informed decisions.

The service offers customizable survey templates for the creation and distribution of some of the most common online surveys, including customer and employee satisfaction, meeting and product feedback, event planning, online voting, and market research. By accessing Zoomerang's free online survey software, users can build surveys in minutes, then analyze and share the results as customized charts posted to a blog or website, or they can export the data to Excel spreadsheets, PowerPoint presentations, or PDF documents. Zoomerang's 2-minute tutorial videos and recorded webinars are designed to assist new subscribers to quickly create and send online surveys and analyze the results in the shortest possible time.

A unique feature that gives Zoomerang a slight edge over its main rival SurveyMonkey and similar products is customer accessibility—with the payment of a modest fee—to Zoomerang Sample. Zoomerang Sample is a consumer survey panel of more than 2 million people who have been profiled on lifestyle, demographic, and occupational attributes and are immediately available to take surveys. Introduced by the company MarketTools in 1999, Zoomerang headquarters is based in San Francisco, California.

Features

The basic service is free and available to all registered users from the homepage (www.zoomerang.com). The list of features available for this basic introductory service includes:

> Twelve questions per survey and one hundred responses per survey

> Access to online polls

> Deployment of surveys to Facebook and Twitter accounts

> Access to survey creation, reporting, and analysis tools

> Creation of surveys in a secured environment

> Email survey link to contacts

> Email support and access to online knowledge base, resource center, and online training

> Share results publicly

How Cybrarians Can Use This Resource

Data Gathering Tool

Zoomerang's free basic account can provide the impetus needed by cybrarians to obtain feedback on key strategic areas. Research has shown that engaging library patrons in customer satisfaction surveys can yield valuable insights and assist in making informed decisions, offering all the advantages of operating libraries on quantitative and qualitative "real data" and not simplistic and sometimes unrealistic theories. Some key strategic areas for data gathering are:

> Discovering what customers think about current services and collections

> Garnering customer feedback on new products and services

> Evaluating and reviewing which services or new products drive customer satisfaction and loyalty

On the Zoomerang homepage, users can
learn about features, pricing, and related news.

➤ Learning about the organization's strengths and weaknesses when compared with competitors

➤ Demonstrating a commitment to customer satisfaction by enlisting the service of and listening to the collective wisdom of a loyal customer base

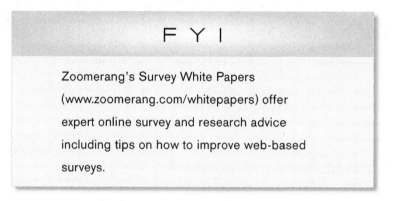

F Y I

Zoomerang's Survey White Papers (www.zoomerang.com/whitepapers) offer expert online survey and research advice including tips on how to improve web-based surveys.

101

Zotero
productivity tool
www.zotero.org

Overview

Ask most researchers to name the most tedious aspects of their work and it is guaranteed that creating citations and managing bibliographies will be at the top of their list. Zotero easily and effortlessly solves this problem. Described on its homepage as a next-generation research tool, Zotero is a free, easy-to-use reference management tool. It helps researchers collect, manage, cite, and share resource sources—books, journal articles, bills, cases, statutes, webpages, images, sound recordings—used when conducting research and writing essays or articles.

Zotero is comparable to other reference management tools CiteULike (Chapter 13) and Connotea (Chapter 14). It incorporates similar features, such as allowing users to bookmark websites for future retrieval by storing author, title, and publication information; add personal notes; attach different file types such as PDFs, Word documents, and Excel spreadsheets to citations created; assign descriptive keywords or tags; share research data with likeminded experts; export saved data as formatted references; and create and search group and personal libraries.

Zotero has the added advantage of being available to users as an extension for the popular open source web browser Firefox. Since the software is installed and runs within Firefox it can integrate seamlessly with other web services and online applications. For example, if a user is on a research website such as Google Scholar, or browsing a search service like Amazon, the Zotero capture icon automatically appears in the address bar. Zotero then intuitively detects if a book, article, webpage, or image is being viewed, and finds, captures, and saves the data required to create a full reference citation for the item.

Zotero's Word and OpenOffice plug-ins allow users to insert citations and create bibliographies directly from their word processing software. Most of the major bibliographic styles such as APA, MLA, Chicago Manual of Style, Harvard, National Library of Medicine, and Turabian are supported.

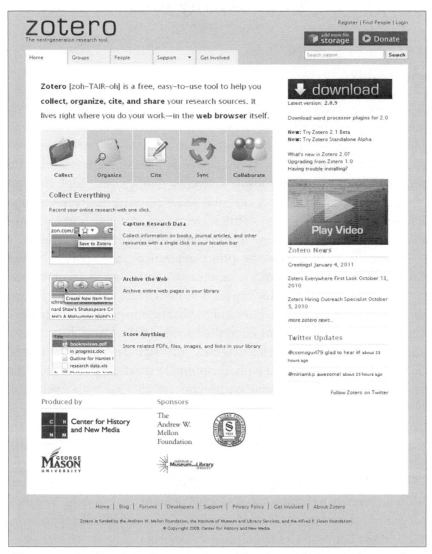

Users can download the latest version of Zotero right from the homepage.

Zotero is the brainchild of the Center for History and New Media at George Mason University and is funded by the Andrew W. Mellon Foundation, the Institute of Museum and Library Services, and the Alfred P. Sloan Foundation.

Features

➤   An online registration form is available on the homepage (www.zotero.org) to create a Zotero account to log in and use the service.

➤   A download button is available on the homepage for quick-and-easy installation of the latest free version of Zotero. To install the software, visit the Zotero homepage using the Firefox browser and click the red Download button. Restart Firefox after completion of the installation. You should see the Zotero logo in the status bar in the bottom-right corner of your Firefox browser window.

➤   Seamless integration with Word and OpenOffice gives researchers the option to download plug-ins for these applications and create in-text citations when writing essays or articles. A drag-and-drop bibliography function allows researchers to instantly add bibliographies to email, blogs, wikis, or webpages.

➤   On the homepage, there are clickable on-screen help icons with brief instructional guidelines on how users can use Zotero to Collect, Organize, Cite, and Sync resources, and Collaborate with other users.

➤   How-to videos are posted on the website, giving step-by-step demonstrations on how to use Zotero. A video tutorial, live Twitter feeds, and a regularly updated Zotero news page spread the word about using Zotero features and functionalities.

➤   An Add More File Storage feature on the homepage links to information on Zotero's cloud-based file storage solution for PDFs, images, web snapshots, and other files stored in personal and group libraries. This is a tiered pricing model based on user storage needs; only storage of up to 100 MB is free.

➤ If you are regularly using more than one computer in your research, Zotero's Sync Your Library functionality can keep your library up to date on multiple computers. Zotero stores a copy of your library on the Zotero.org server and checks it for updates whenever you open your library on a different computer. For this feature to work efficiently, all computers must be running the same version of Zotero and be configured to sync to the server.

➤ Links are provided on the homepage to other Zotero services:

- Groups: Zotero users can create collaborative or interest groups (www.zotero.org/groups). These are useful forums to share resources and references you have discovered with others who are working in similar fields and to collaborate with colleagues, publicly or privately, on ongoing research.

- People: Once an account is created, users can create a Zotero profile to help other researchers discover their publications and research interests (www.zotero.org/people). Users can also search within the Zotero community for people working on similar projects or browse other researchers' shared libraries for a quick view of their current projects.

- Support: This service provides links to technical support and online documentation.

- Get Involved: Information is given on ways to volunteer and become involved with the Zotero project. For example, volunteers can contribute code, assist with documentation and support, give a demonstration of Zotero at their workplace, or write a review on their blog.

How Cybrarians Can Use This Resource

Providing Library Workshops on Zotero

The Harvard Kennedy School Library and Knowledge Services (Cambridge, Massachusetts) developed a workshop to promote the use of Zotero (www.hks.harvard.edu/library/blog/?p=630) to faculty and students. Cybrarians can follow this model and extend the use of the application in the following ways:

➣   Use Zotero's customizable My Library feature to create subject guides, reading lists, web resources lists, and Reader's Advisory resources.

➣   Search by ISBN, Digital Object identifier, or PubMed ID to find and bookmark resources aligned with subject areas and research interests of patrons and that are supportive of the curricula.

➣   Automatically generate and insert citations and bibliographies for essays, term papers, and journal articles. Zotero uses Citation Style Language to properly format citations and it supports all major citation styles.

Online Public Access Catalog Integration

The Copac library catalog (www.copac.ac.uk), which gives free access to the merged online catalogs of many major university, specialist, and national libraries in the U.K. and Ireland (including the British Library), has been remodeled to work seamlessly with Zotero. Users have the option of exporting bibliographic citations to titles searched in the OPAC to Endnote or Zotero citation managers.

Collaborative Research and Keeping Up-to-Date with New Research

Librarians can use this tool to work collaboratively with colleagues on projects and conference presentations by saving and sharing relevant resources within the same iTunes-like interface. Zotero is also a great tool for keeping up-to-date with the latest library literature and technology news in a designated subject area. An added advantage is that Zotero saves (includes dragging and dropping files) and supports resources in multiple formats including journal articles, PDF documents, PowerPoint presentations, images, webpages, podcasts, and videos.

F Y I

In October 2010, a post on the Zotero Blog[1] announced the development of Zotero Everywhere, a new initiative aimed at increasing the accessibility of Zotero to a wide range of users. This new application has two components: a stand-alone desktop version with full integration in most web browsers, and an expanded API to provide web and mobile access to Zotero libraries. This application, released as Standalone Zotero Alpha, is available on the website (www.zotero.org/support.standalone).

Endnote

1. "Zotero Everywhere," Zotero, October 13, 2010, www.zotero.org/blog (accessed August 10, 2011).

Appendix I

Tips and Teaching Tools for Keeping Up-To-Date With Web 2.0 Technologies

Having demonstrated in the preceding chapters that Web 2.0 technologies can be beneficial to libraries, the question of cybrarians keeping abreast of the quick-fire developments that characterize these resources needs to be addressed. How do we *keep up* with all the fast-paced changes, and how do we find the time to learn about new tools and practices applicable to our work environment, given our busy schedules?

Reading this book and similar publications on this topic are logical places to start. Personally, I have discovered over the years that the core of any education strategy is commitment to learning, experimenting with what you have learned, and sharing this with your network of friends and colleagues. This can be readily articulated in one simple formula: *Learning + Experimenting = Sharing + Innovation.*

Here are six useful pointers:

1. Make a personal commitment to conduct your own research; learn about the new technologies and follow through on this commitment.

2. Take advantage of the continuing education opportunities; many of them are free and available on the web (on my blog Caribbean Connector I often provide links to these opportunities).

3. Network with colleagues because they are often aware of what is available.

4. Network with industry players at the forefront of developing Web 2.0 technologies. This may require a *can do* attitude, because in some instances you must be brazen and intervene in areas that may be outside your comfort zone.

5.   Have the capacity to learn constantly and quickly.

6.   Read professional literature—especially outside your field—
     and be prepared to conduct research and publish your results.

Finally, here are links to resources such as blogs, wikis, books, and
journals that will help you in your quest to keep up-to-date. Good luck!

Recommended Resources for Keeping Up

General Resources

Centre for Learning and Performance Technologies, www.c4lpt.co.uk

Internet Public Librarian, www.ipl.org

Internet Scout Project, scout.cs.wisc.edu

Library Success: A Best Practices Wiki, www.libsuccess.org

Library Technology Guides, www.librarytechnology.org

Lifehacker, lifehacker.com

Mashable, mashable.com

The Pew Research Center's Internet & American Life Project,
     www.pewinternet.org

ReadWriteWeb, www.readwriteweb.com

SirsiDynix Institute, www.sirsidynix.com/community/sirsidynix-
     institute/overview

TechCrunch, www.techcrunch.com

TechSoup for Libraries, www.techsoupforlibraries.org

WebJunction, www.webjunction.org

Wired, www.wired.com

Blogs

ACRLog, acrlog.org

ALA TechSource Blog, alatechsource.org/blog

Free Range Librarian, freerangelibrarian.com

iLibrarian, oedb.org/blogs/ilibrarian

Information Wants to Be Free, meredith.wolfwater.com/wordpress

Librarian in Black, librarianinblack.net/librarianinblack

Library Stuff, www.librarystuff.net

LITA Blog, litablog.org

Stephen's Lighthouse, stephenslighthouse.com

Steven Bell's Keeping Up Web Site, stevenbell.info/keepup/librarianship.htm

Tame the Web, tametheweb.com

Appendix II

Web 2.0 Tools and Other Resources: A Glossary

AbiWord: a free, open source, cross-platform word processor suitable for performing basic tasks.

About.com: an online source of how-to guides, articles, and commentaries written by experts in a particular field.

Academic Earth: a website that offers free online video lectures from select Ivy League universities.

Amplify: a social blogging service.

Animoto: a web-based application that automatically produces videos from user-selected photos, video clips, and music.

Audacity: an open source software for recording and editing sounds.

Aviary: a browser-based suite of creative graphic design applications.

Bing: Microsoft's web search engine marketed as a decision engine designed to help searchers with targeted topics such as shopping, travel, local business information, and health-related research.

Blio: an ereading application created by Ray Kurzweil.

Blogger: a blog publishing tool from Google.

Bloglines: a web-based news and feed aggregator.

BusinessCard2: an online service for creating virtual business cards.

CiteULike: an online service for storing, managing, and discovering scholarly references.

Connotea: an online reference management and sharing service for researchers and scientists.

CuePrompter: a web-based teleprompter/autocue service.

Delicious: a social bookmarking web service for storing, sharing, and discovering web bookmarks.

Digg: a community-driven social news website.

Dogpile: a metasearch engine that returns combined search results from leading search engines Google, Yahoo!, Bing, and Ask.com.

Doodle: a web application for scheduling group events.

Drupal: an open source content management system for organizing, managing, and publishing web content.

Ecademy: a social network for professionals.

Facebook: a social networking site that connects people with friends and others who work, study, and live around them.

FaxZero: a web-based free faxing service.

Flickr: a photo and video hosting service.

Foursquare: a location-based social networking website for mobile devices.

GIMP (GNU Image Manipulation Program): an image manipulation program.

Google Analytics: Google's free website statistics service.

Google Books: a service from Google that searches the full text of books digitized and stored in a digital database.

Google Docs: Google's web-based office software application, which can be used to create online documents, spreadsheets, drawings, flowcharts, forms, and presentations.

Google Reader: Google's web-based news and feed aggregator service.

Google Sites: Google's free wiki and webpage creation tool.

HathiTrust: a shared digital library jointly owned and operated by major research institutions and libraries from the United States and Europe.

Hulu: an online video hosting service.

Internet Archive: a nonprofit digital library offering free universal access to ebooks, moving images, live music, audio recordings, software, and archived webpages.

iTunes U: a free audio and video hosting service offered by Apple via the iTunes Store for educational institutions and lifelong learners.

Jing: a screen-casting program for capturing and sharing onscreen images and videos.

Justin.tv: a platform available for creating and broadcasting streaming live video to a global audience.

Khan Academy: a hosting and sharing service for educational videos.

LibGuides: SpringShare's hosted content management and publishing system marketed to libraries to create multimedia content, subject guides, course guides, and information and research portals.

Library Success: A Best Practices Wiki: a one-stop shop wiki created for librarians to share innovative ideas and best practices.

LibraryThing: a social cataloging web application for creating, storing, and sharing personal library catalogs online.

Library 2.0: a social network for librarians conceptualized on the topic of Library 2.0.

LinkedIn: a social network for professionals wishing to make business contacts, search for jobs, and find potential clients.

LISWiki: a library and information science encyclopedia built using the Wiki software.

LISZEN: a library and information science search engine.

Livemocha: an online language-learning community.

LucidChart: an online diagramming tool developed to create and publish customized flowcharts and other diagrams.

Lulu: an online self-publishing service.

MARC 21 in Your Library: a series of web-based minicourses (webcasts and self-paced) offered by The MARC of Quality (TMQ).

Meebo: an instant messaging (IM) service that supports multiple IM networks including AIM, Yahoo!, Facebook, Windows Live, MySpace, Google Talk, ICQ, and Jabber.

Mikogo: a web conferencing and desktop sharing service.

Moodle: an open source, web-based Course Management System (CMS) utilized to develop online learning sites.

Movable Type: an online social publishing platform for creating websites, blogs, and social networks.

Myspace: a social networking website empowering its community of users to interact around entertainment and pop culture.

Ning: an online platform for communities to create custom-branded social networks.

OpenID: an online service that offers a secure way to sign in to websites using one login and password.

OpenOffice.org: an open source office software suite used for word processing, spreadsheets, presentations, graphics, and databases.

Orkut: Google's social networking service.

PBworks: a hosted workspace service for creating collaborative wikis.

PDF-to-Word: software for creating editable DOC/RTF files from any PDF document, enabling reuse of original PDF documents in applications such as Microsoft Word, Excel, OpenOffice, and WordPerfect.

Photobucket: a service for hosting and sharing photos, videos, and graphics.

Picasa: Google's photo management and sharing service.

Podcast Alley: one of the largest podcast directories on the internet where subscribers can add new podcasts, search for podcast feeds, and download free podcast software.

Prezi: a web-based presentation application and storytelling tool where disparate concepts are grouped on a single canvas instead of traditional slides to create presentations for conferences, workshops, and collaborative projects.

Project Gutenberg: a digital library hosting one of the largest collections of free electronic books on the internet.

Qwika: a search engine designed specifically for indexing and searching wikis.

Readerjack.com: an online publishing service and ebook store.

Remember the Milk: an application service for web-based task and time management.

Rollyo: a Yahoo!-powered customizable search engine that can be configured to search only specified websites and blogs.

Rondee: a service that provides free conference calls.

Scour: a metasearch engine combining relevant search results from highly ranked search engines Google, Yahoo!, and Bing, and popular social networks Twitter and Digg.

Second Life: a 3D virtual world developed by Linden Lab, which requires download of a free client program (the Viewer) to enable users to interact with each other through their avatars (digital representations of people).

Shelfari: a social cataloging website for users to build virtual bookshelves and share, rate, review, and discuss titles they own or are currently reading.

Skype: a software application that when downloaded to a computer, allows users to make free video and voice calls, send instant messages, and share files with other Skype users.

SlideShare: an online network for sharing slides and other online presentations.

SortFix: a search engine with an intuitive graphical interface developed to boost users' search skills.

Spybot-Search & Destroy: a spyware and adware removal program.

StatCounter: an online web analytics service.

StumbleUpon: a social bookmarking tool for discovering new content based on the collective recommendations of a community of users.

SurveyMonkey: a web-based survey application.

Technorati: a blog search engine.

TripIt: an online service for organizing travel plans that includes assistance with flight, hotel, and rental car reservations regardless of the source site used to make the bookings.

Twitter: a free social networking and microblogging service in which posts (tweets) must be 140 characters or less.

TypeFaster: a free online typing tutor program that teaches users how to touch-type on a simulated keyboard.

Ustream: a web-based video broadcasting platform that allows users with cameras, computers, and internet connections to broadcast live video to a global audience.

Vimeo: a video hosting and sharing site.

VuFind: an open source search and discovery portal developed for libraries to provide integrated access to all of a library's resources (books, journals, audiovisual materials, electronic and digital resources), using a single interface.

Widgets: programming code that can be easily dragged onto desktops or embedded into personal webpages or blogs to enhance the web experience; they often take the form of onscreen tools, and can provide updated information on technology trends, breaking news, the stock market, weather reports, and flight arrivals and departures.

Wikipedia: a web-based, collaborative, multilingual encyclopedia supported by user-contributed content.

Wikis by Wetpaint: Wetpaint is a company that provides a broad range of social publishing services including the wiki hosting service Wikis by Wetpaint.

Wolfram|Alpha: a computational knowledge engine; users enter factual questions or calculations, and Wolfram|Alpha uses its built-in algorithms and a growing collection of curated, structured data to compute the answer.

Wordle: an online tool for generating word clouds or tags from user-supplied text.

WordPress.com: a web-based blog hosting service.

WorldCat.org: OCLC's end-user discovery interface that delivers single-search access to the WorldCat union catalog, which contains bibliographic records and holdings contributed by libraries around the world.

XING: a social network for professionals.

Yahoo! Answers: Yahoo!'s online question-and-answer service.

YouSendIt: an online file management and sharing service.

YouTube: Google's video hosting and sharing online service.

Zoho: a suite of web-based productivity applications.

Zoomerang: a web-based survey application.

Zotero: a citation manager developed to help users collect, manage, cite, and share research resources.

Appendix III

Referenced Websites

Chapter 1
AbiCollab.net, abicollab.net

Chapter 3
Hulu, www.hulu.com

Chapter 4
Centre for Learning and Performance Technologies, www.c4lpt.co.uk/
Top100Tools

Chapter 5
Pennsylvania Library Association College & Research Division Blog,
www.crdpala.org/2011/07/25/adding-spice-to-library-instruction

Chapter 6
Interactive Media Center, University Libraries University at Albany,
SUNY, library.albany.edu/imc

Chapter 7
Google Apps marketplace, www.google.com/enterprise/marketplace/
home
Worth1000.com, www.worth1000.com

Chapter 8
comScore, www.comscore.com

Chapter 9
Duke University Libraries eReaders homepage,
    library.duke.edu/ereaders
Sony Reader Library Program, ebookstore.sony.com/library-program

Chapter 11
Merchant Circle, www.merchantcircle.com/corporate
The Library Success: Best Practices Wiki webpage on RSS feeds,
    www.libsuccess.org/index.php?title=RSS

Chapter 12
Workface Inc., www.workface.com

Chapter 14
Nature Publishing Group, www.nature.com/npg_/index_npg.html

Chapter 16
University of Pennsylvania PennTags, tags.library.upenn.edu

Chapter 17
Reddit, www.reddit.com

Chapter 18
BLINN College Library, www.blinn.edu/library/find/internet/Meta_
    Search_Tools.htm

Chapter 20
Groups.drupal.org, groups.drupal.org/libraries/libraries
Drupalib, drupalib.interoperating.info/library_sites

Chapter 22
Libraries Using Facebook Pages,
    www.facebook.com/group.php?gid=8408315708&ref=ts
Librarians and Facebook,
    www.facebook.com/group.php?gid=2210901334

Chapter 24
Library of Congress' Flickr Photostream,
  www.flickr.com/photos/library_of_congress
Smithsonian Institution's photostream,
  www.flickr.com/photos/smithsonian
The New York Public Library, www.flickr.com/photos/nypl
The U.S. National Archives, www.flickr.com/photos/
  usnationalarchives

Chapter 25
David Lee King blog, www.davidleeking.com
Harvard University Foursquare page, foursquare.com/harvard

Chapter 27
Wikipedia, www.wikipedia.org

Chapter 28
Google Book Settlement, www.googlebooksettlement.com
WorldCat.org, www.worldcat.org
Google Books Partner Program, www.books.google.com/partner
Google ebookstore, books.google.com/ebooks

Chapter 29
Google Docs Blog, googledocs.blogspot.com

Chapter 31
Google Sites webinar, www.steegle.com/websites/google-sites-how-
  tos/basics-gbbo-webinar

Chapter 32
WorldCat Local/HathiTrust Digital Library Prototype Catalog,
  hathitrust.worldcat.org

Chapter 33
Netflix, www.netflix.com

Chapter 34
Library of Congress, www.loc.gov
The Smithsonian, www.si.edu
Alexa, www.alexa.com
Open Directory Project, www.dmoz.org/docs/en/add.html
Etree.org, www.etree.org
Open Library project, openlibrary.org/subjects/accessible_book

Chapter 36
Techsmith, www.techsmith.com

Chapter 39
Nova Southeastern University Libraries CampusGuides,
    www.nova.campusguides.com
Library à la Carte, alacarte.library.oregonstate.edu

Chapter 41
LibraryThing Early Reviewers program,
    www.librarything.com/wiki/index.php/Early_Reviewers
Libraries using LibraryThing for Libraries,
www.librarything.com/wiki/index.php/LTFL:Libraries_using_Library
    Thing_for_Libraries
LibraryThing Local, www.librarything.com/local

Chapter 42
Ning, www.ning.com

Chapter 45
Library Zen & LISZEN wiki,
    libraryzen.com/wiki/index.php?title=LISZEN
Library Zen, libraryzen.com

Chapter 47
LucidChart for educators and students,
    www.lucidchart.com/pages/education

Chapter 48
Rochester Institute of Technology (RIT) Libraries Lulu community,
    connect.lulu.com/t5/Connect/ct-p/en_US

Chapter 49
The MARC of Quality website, www.marcofquality.com
OCLC Training portal, training.oclc.org/home/-
    /courses/details/93221001
MARC and Bibliographic information: the underlying fundamentals
    webinar, www.marcofquality.com/webinars/webm21.html

Chapter 50
Library Success: A Best Practices Wiki Libraries Using MeeboMe for
    Embedded Chat page, www.tinyurl.com/3tlww9n

Chapter 51
BeamYourScreen GmbH,
    www.beamyourscreen.com/EN/welcome.aspx
Dimdim, www.dimdim.com

Chapter 53
University of Minnesota Libraries Uthink blog hosting service,
    blog.lib.umn.edu
TypePad, www.typepad.com

Chapter 54
CrunchBase, www.crunchbase.com/company/myspace
Library Success: A Best Practices Wiki MySpace & Teens page,
    www.libsuccess.org/index.php?title=MySpace_%26_Teens

Chapter 55
Ning Mini for Educators, about.ning.com/pearsonsponsorship
PBS Frontline, www.pbs.org/wgbh/pages/frontline/digitalnation/
    learning/literacy/friending-boo-radley.html

Chapter 56
OpenID Foundation, openid.net/foundation

Chapter 57

OpenOffice.org public wiki, wiki.services.openoffice.org/wiki/
Main_Page

OpenOffice: What Libraries Need to Know webinar, www.info
people.org/training/webcasts/webcast_data/351/index.html

Chapter 59

Using PBworks in Libraries, pbworks.com/content/edu-librarians

The Baltimore County Public Schools Learning 23 Things program,
www.bcps23things.pbworks.com

New Tools for School Librarianship webinar, www.tinyurl.com/
3cmzpra

Chapter 61

Flickr practical workshop, www.slideshare.net/apeoples/flickr-
workshop

Chapter 62

National Library of Egypt photostream on Picasa,
picasaweb.google.com/joseph.ph/LibrariesBibliothecaAlexandrina
Egypt#

Flickr practical workshop, www.slideshare.net/apeoples/flickr-
workshop

Chapter 63

The Library Success wiki list of libraries offering podcasting services,
www.libsuccess.org/index.php?title=Podcasting

Sarah Long's Longshots Podcasts, www.librarybeat.org

Chapter 65

Lexcycle Stanza ebook reader app, www.lexcycle.com/download

Library of Congress E-Resources Online Catalog, eresources.loc.gov

Distributed Proofreaders site, www.pgdp.net/c

LibriVox, librivox.org/volunteer-for-librivox

Chapter 67

Project Gutenberg digital library, www.gutenberg.org

Library and Archives Canada, www.collectionscanada.gc.ca
Readerjack.com Facebook Group,
   www.new.facebook.com/group.php?gid=23353582786

Chapter 68
Google Calendar, www.google.com/calendar

Chapter 69
Learning 2.0 program, plcmcl2-things.blogspot.com

Chapter 71
OneRiot, www.oneriot.com
University of California (Berkeley), www.lib.berkeley.edu/Teaching
   Lib/Guides/Internet/SearchEngines.htm

Chapter 72
Community Virtual Library, infoisland.org

Chapter 73
Libraries and Librarians, www.shelfari.com/groups/10057/
   discussions/67762/Uses-of-Shelfari-in-your-library

Chapter 74
The Ohio University Libraries' Skype a Librarian service,
   www.library.ohiou.edu/ask/skype.html
Library Success: A Best Practices Wiki list of libraries using Skype
   Reference, www.libsuccess.org/index.php?title=Libraries_Offering_
   VoIP_or_Video_Reference

Chapter 76
Phil Bradley's Weblog, philbradley.typepad.com/phil_bradleys_
   weblog/2010/03/SortFix-for-easy-searching.html

Chapter 77
Emory University Office of Information Technology Security
   Awareness FAQs, https://it.emory.edu/getfaqs.cfm?catid=
   1093&fr=1093

Chapter 80
Google Apps Marketplace, www.google.com/enterprise/market
    place/home

Chapter 81
Technorati State of the Blogosphere reports, www.technorati.com/
    state-of-the-blogosphere
Twittorati, www.twittorati.com
Write for Technorati webpage, www.technorati.com/write-for-
    technorati

Chapter 83
Twitter Fan Wiki, twitter.pbworks.com/w/page/1779796/FrontPage
Nebraska Library Commission Ask a Librarian service,
    www.twitter.com/NLC_Reference
Maryland Ask Us Now! online reference service, www.twitter.com/
    askusnow

Chapter 84
SourceForge, sourceforge.net

Chapter 87
Falvey Memorial Library, Villanova University, library.villanova.edu/
    Find/Search/Home

Chapter 88
iGoogle, www.google.com/ig
My Yahoo!, www.my.yahoo.com
University of Texas Libraries LIB Widgets, www.lib.utexas.edu/tools

Chapter 89
Alexa, www.alexa.com

Chapter 90
Go Daddy, www.godaddy.com
Dotster, www.dotster.com
Network Solutions, www.networksolutions.com

Wetpaint Wikis in Education Community forum,
    wikisineducation.wetpaint.com

Chapter 91
Wolfram Demonstrations Project, demonstrations.wolfram.com
Wolfram Mathworld, mathworld.wolfram.com

Chapter 93
Akismet, akismet.com

Chapter 94
Google Books, books.google.com
WorldCat search box widget, www.worldcat.org/affiliate/tools

Chapter 96
LISWiki Chat Reference Libraries,
    liswiki.org/wiki/Chat_reference_libraries

Chapter 99
iLibrarian blog, oedb.org/blogs/ilibrarian
University of Texas Libraries LIB Widgets,
    www.lib.utexas.edu/tools/info.html

Chapter 100
Zoomerang Survey White Papers, www.zoomerang.com/whitepapers

Chapter 101
Harvard Kennedy School Library and Knowledge Services workshop
    on Zotero, www.hks.harvard.edu/library/blog/?p=630

About the Author

Cheryl Ann Peltier-Davis is the archives and digital librarian at the Alvin Sherman Library, Research and Information Technology Center, at Nova Southeastern University in Florida. She is the author of several refereed journal articles on public and national libraries in the Caribbean. In 2007, she collaborated with Shamin Renwick to co-edit the book *Caribbean Libraries in the 21st Century: Changes, Challenges, and Choices,* which was published by Information Today, Inc., and which received the Association of Caribbean Libraries, Research and Institutional Libraries (ACURIL) award for Excellence in Research and Publication.

She has given conference presentations on a diverse array of library-related topics—Web 2.0 and libraries, core competencies for librarians, digitizing library collections, information management, and Caribbean public libraries. She is the author of the blog Caribbean Connector (caribbean-connector.blogspot.com), which was created to connect Caribbean librarians and serve as a clearinghouse to deliver information directly to their desktops.

Her professional association memberships include the Association for Library Collections and Technical Services (an ALA division), the Black Caucus of the American Library Association, and the Association of Caribbean University, Research, and Institutional Library (ACURIL). She has served as co-chair of the ACURIL Special Interest Group on Academic Libraries since 2002.

Cheryl has a BA from the University of the West Indies, St. Augustine, Trinidad and Tobago, and an MLS from the University of the West Indies, Mona, Jamaica. She lives in Fort Lauderdale, Florida.

Index

A

AbiCollab.net web service, 4
AbiWord, 1–4
About.com, 5–8
Academic Earth, 9–13
accessibility of titles to print-disabled, 151
Accessible Version of TypeFaster Typing Tutor, 367
access to eresources. *see* digital libraries
activism and advocacy, using Vimeo for, 376, 378
AdSense program (Google), 42
Akismet, 409
Alexa, 150, 250
Alvin Sherman Library, 95
Amplify, 14–16
Analytics (Google), 116–120
Animoto, 17–20
Answers (Yahoo!), 422–426
antivirus program (Spybot-Search & Destroy), 331–334
Apps marketplace (Google), 28, 347
Arapahoe Library District, 237
Ask.com, 45
Audacity, 21–24
audio archives, 150–151
audio hosting services (iTunes U), 155–159
audio production, recording, and editing services (Audacity), 21–24
Automattic, 407
Aviary, 25–29, 243

B

Baker & Taylor, 35
Ballmer, Steve, 30
Baltimore County Public Schools, 257
Barrier Reef TAFE Library and Information Services, 411
BeamYourScreen GmbH, 222, 223, 225
Benedictine University Library, 410
bibliographic citations
    CiteULike, 54–57
    Connotea, 58–61
    Zotero, 447–452
Bing, 30–33
Birmingham Public Library Teen Summer Reading video, 435
BLINN College Library, 77
Blio, 34–39
Blogger, 40–44
Bloglines, 45–49
blog publishing services
    Blogger, 40–44
    WordPress.com, 407–411
blogs. *see also* content management systems
    academic community and, 232–233
    chat widgets, integrating into, 219
    Digg, 73
    Flickr, 104
    Free Conference Calling, 303
    Google Analytics, 119
    Google Docs, 130
    iLibrarian, 441
    for keeping up with Web 2.0 technologies, 454–455
    LucidChart, 208
    Mikogo, 223

blogs (*cont.*)
  Nitro PDF, 260
  popularity of, 40
  Prezi, 277
  ReadWriteWeb, 383
  StumbleUpon, 341
  Wordle, 406
blog search engines (Technorati),
  349–353
Blowers, Helene, 299
Book Club Blog, 43
bookmarks. *see* social bookmarking
  services
Books (Google), xxiv, 121–125, 139
Boston Public Library, 376, 378
Boyd, Emily, 292
Bradley, Phil, 329
branding libraries with Animoto, 18–19
broadcasting services
  Justin.tv, 164–167
  Ustream, 368–373
Brooklyn College Library, 238
Broward County Library, 38
Brown, Scott, 239
budget cutbacks in libraries, xxiii, 221
BusinessCard2, 50–53
Buytaert, Dries, 83
Buyukkokten, Orkut, 250

C

Calendar (Google), 295
Cameron, Richard, 54
Camtasia Studios, 160
Casey, Michael, 186
cataloging services
  Copac library catalog, 451
  LibraryThing, 180–185
  Shelfari, 312–316
  WorldCat.org, 412–417
cataloging webinars (MARC21 in Your
  Library), 213–216
catalogs, integrating chat widgets into,
  219
Charlotte Mecklenburg Library, 37
chat widgets, integrating, 219
Chen, Steve, 66
CiteULike, 54–57
Clinton, Hillary, 425–426

collections and services. *see also* promotion of library innovations,
  resources, and services
  augmenting with ebooks, 283
  augmenting with streaming content,
    145, 147
  ereaders and, 37–38
Colorado State University Libraries, 382
Columbia University Libraries and
  Google Books, 125
community engagement, fostering
  Foursquare, 110
  WordPress.com, 410–411
Community Virtual Library, 308
computational knowledge engines
  (Wolfram|Alpha), 399–403
Computer Beginners Handbook on
  About.com, 7
comScore market research firm, 30
conference-calling services (Rondee),
  300–303
conference support. *see* presentation and
  workshop support; workshop and
  training support
Connotea, 58–61
content, discovering with StumbleUpon,
  343
Content Management System Library à
  la Carte, 175
content management systems
  Drupal, 83–86
  LibGuides, 172–175
  Movable Type, 230–233
conversion services (Nitro PDF
  Software), 258–261
Copac library catalog, 451
course management systems (Moodle),
  226–229
cross platform tools
  AbiWord, 1
  Audacity, 21–22
  Mikogo, 221–225
  OpenOffice.org, 246–249
Crowley, Dennis, 106
CuePrompter, 62–64
current awareness services
  Amplify, 14–16

Bloglines, 45–49
Digg, 73–74
Google Reader, 133
Library 2.0, 188
Twitter and, 361–362
Current Events and News Blog, 43
cybrarian, definition of, xxv

D

DAISY (Digital Accessible Information
     System) format, 151
data security and Spybot-Search &
     Destroy, 331–334
Delicious, 65–69
democratization of web, xxiii
Denver Public Library, 238
Derriero, David, "Democracy 2.0," 372
design and editing tools (Aviary), 25–29
Desktop widgets (Google), 386
diagramming tools (LucidChart),
     205–208
Digg, 70–74
Digital Accessible Information System
     (DAISY) format, 151
digital libraries
     Google Books, 121–125
     HathiTrust, 139–142
     Internet Archive, 149–154
     Project Gutenberg, 279–284
Dimdim, 225
Docs (Google), 126–130
Dogpile, 75–78
Doodle, 79–82
Dotster, 394
Drew, Bill, 186
Drupal, 83–86
Dublin City Public Libraries, 95
Duke University Libraries, 37

E

ebook readers (Blio), 34–39
ebook repositories (Project Gutenberg),
     279
ebookstores
     Google eBookstore, 125
     Readerjack.com, 288–291

Ecademy, 87–90
economic recovery efforts of libraries,
     xxiii, 221
editing Wikipedia pages, 389–390
educational content on Academic Earth,
     9–13
Emory University Office of Information
     Technology, 333
entries, organization of, xviii–xix
Erving Public Library, 410
Expedia, 354
expert writers and contributing authors
     of About.com, 5, 7

F

Facebook, 91–96, 321
faculty, engaging with Academic Earth,
     12
Fairfax County Public Library, 37
Farkas, Meredith, 176, 178
FaxZero, 97–100
feedback, gathering
     SurveyMonkey, 344–348
     Zoomerang, 443–446
Feher, Gyula, 368
Feinberg, Jonathan, 404, 406
file hosting and sharing services
     (YouSendIt), 427–430
Fitzgerald, Rebecca, "Using Netflix at an
     Academic Library," 145
Flickr, 101–105, 384
Foursquare, 106–111
freelance opportunities
     About.com, 8
     Lulu, 209–212
     Technorati, 352–353
Free Library of Philadelphia, 37
Fritz, Deborah, 213

G

George Mason University, Center for
     History and New Media, 449
Georgia Institute of Technology, 435
GIMP, 112–115
GoDaddy, 394
Goldstein, Eric, 16

Google
    AdSense program, 42
    Analytics, 116–120
    Apps marketplace, 28, 347
    Blogger, 40–44
    Books, xxiv, 121–125, 139
    Calendar, 295
    Desktop widgets, 386
    Docs, 126–130
    eBookstore, 125
    Orkut, 250–253
    Picasa, 266–269
    Reader, 131–134
    Sites, 135–138
graphics editors (GIMP), 112–115

H

Halacsy, Peter, 274
Ham, John, 368
Hamilton, William, 160
Hargadon, Steve, 186, 188
Hart, Michael, 279
Harvard University
    Foursquare and, 110
    Kennedy School Library and
        Knowledge Services, 451
HathiTrust, 139–142
Hayward Public Library Fines-Free Loan
    program, 147
Healy, Ciara, "Netflix in an Academic
    Library," 145
Hertz, 354
The Houston Public Library, 95
The Huffington Post, 353
Hulu, 11–12, 143–148
Hungerford, Garrett, 198, 200
Hunstable, Brad, 368
Hurley, Chad, 66

I

image archives, 150
information literacy, promoting
    Scour, 307
    Wetpaint Wikis in Education
        Community forum, 396–398
InfoSpace, 75

instant messaging services (Meebo),
    217–220
interacting with patrons with Digg,
    73–74
Internet Archive, 139, 149–154
iTunes U, 155–159

J

Jing, 160–163
Justin.tv, 164–167

K

Karim, Jawed, 431
Khan, Salman, 168
Khan Academy, 168–171
Kilani, Omar, 292
Kilar, Jason, 147
Kimball, Spencer, 112
King, David Lee, 109–110
K-NFB Reading Technology, 34
Kolla, Patrick, 331
Kroski, Ellyssa, 441
Kurzweil, Ray, 34–35

L

Lancaster Library, 238
language-learning communities
    (Livemocha), 201–204
Lapitsky, Yakov, 431
Learning 2.0 Program, 299
LibGuides, 172–175
Librarians and Facebook online forum,
    94
libraries. *see also* digital libraries; *specific
    libraries*
    with access to blogs created with
        WordPress, 410–411
    with articles in Wikipedia, 391–392
    with Facebook pages, 95
    with Myspace pages, 237–238
    using Skype, 321
    using YouTube, 433–435
    with VuFind portals, 382
Libraries Using Facebook Pages online
    forum, 94
Library 2.0, 186–188

Library and Archives Canada, 288
library branding with Animoto, 18–19
Library Director Blog, 43
Library of Alexandria, 149
Library of Congress
    Flickr and, 104
    Twitter and, 363
    Wikipedia and, 391
    YouTube Channel, 434
library-related community groups in
        Second Life, 310–311
Library Success: A Best Practices Wiki,
        48, 176–179, 237, 321
LibraryThing, 180–185
LibriVox, 280, 283
LIB Widgets, 385
Linden Lab, 308
LinkedIn, 189–193
LISWiki, 194–197, 425
LISZEN, 198–200
LITA (Library Information Technology
        Association), 372
Livemocha, 201–204
loans of ereaders to patrons, 37
location-based social networks
    Foursquare, 106–111
    Twitter, 361
London School of Economics and
        Political Science Library, 382
Long, Sarah, 145, 147, 272–273
LucidChart, 205–208
Ludlow, Richard, 9
Lulu, 209–212

M

MacManus, Richard, 383
malware programs, Spybot-Search &
        Destroy for, 331–334
Manchester Library and Information
        Services, 95
MARC21 in Your Library, 213–216
marketing library services. *see* promotion
        of library innovations, resources,
        and services
marketing research with SurveyMonkey,
        346–347
Maryland Ask Us Now! online reference
        service, 362

Mashable, 353
Mattis, Peter, 112
McCracken County Public Library, 434
McIntyre, Chris, 270
MediaWiki software, 179, 198
Meebo, 217–220
Menino, Thomas, 376
MerchantCircle online marketing net-
        work, 45
metasearch engines
    Dogpile, 75–78
    Scour, 304–307
microblogging services (Twitter),
        358–363
Mikogo, 221–225
Moodle, 226–229
Movable Type, 230–233
Mozilla Firefox
    SortFix and, 327–328
    Zotero and, 447
music archives, 150
Myspace, 234–238

N

National Library of Ireland, 382
National Library of Scotland, 95
Nature Publishing Group, 58
Nebraska Library Commission, 362
Netflix, 145, 147
networking with Shelfari library groups,
        315
Network Solutions, 394
news and feed aggregators
    Bloglines, 45–49
    Digg, 70–74
    Google Reader, 131–134
    Twitter, 362
New York Public Library
    Flickr and, 105
    Vimeo and, 378
Ning, 186, 239–242
Nitro PDF Reader, 258, 260
Nitro PDF Software, 258
Nova Southeastern University Libraries,
        174, 361–362

O

office applications suites. *see also* word
processing programs
OpenOffice.org, 246–249
Zoho, 436–442
Ohio Public Library Information
Network, 248
Ohio University Libraries
Skype video and internet telephony
pilot reference service,
320–321
Subject Blog on Business, 43
OneRiot search engine, 304
one-stop reference sources. *see* search
engines
Open Directory Project, 150
OpenID, 243–245
Open Library, 151, 153
OpenOffice.org, 246–249
open source, definition of, 21
Orbitz, 354
Oregon State University, Content
Management System Library à la
Carte, 175
Orkut, 250–253
outreach services
Animoto, 19
Flickr, 105

P

partnerships with ereader vendors, 38
patron search experience, simplifying
with Academic Earth, 11–12
PBworks, 254–257
PDF-to-Excel converter, 258, 260
PDF-to-Word converter, 258–261
Pennig, Rachel, 257
PennTags, University of Pennsylvania, 69
Photobucket, 262–265
photo hosting and sharing services
Flickr, 101–105
Photobucket, 262–265
Picasa, 266–269
Picasa, 266–269
Podcast Alley, 270–273
podcasting services
Podcast Alley, 270–273

SlideShare and, 324
presentation and workshop support. *see
also* workshop and training
support
CuePrompter, 62–64
Justin.tv, 167
Mikogo, 223, 225
Picasa, 268–269
Prezi, 274–278
SlideShare, 322–326
Twitter, 362
Ustream, 372
Prezi, 274–278
productivity tools
AbiWord, 1–4
Aviary, 25–29
BusinessCard2, 50–53
CuePrompter, 62–64
Doodle, 79–82
FaxZero, 97–100
GIMP, 112–115
Google Analytics, 116–120
Google Docs, 126–130
Google Sites, 135–138
Jing, 160–163
LucidChart, 205–208
OpenID, 243–245
OpenOffice.org, 246–249
PDF-to-Word, 258–261
Prezi, 274–278
Remember the Milk, 292–295
Rondee, 300–303
Skype, 317–321
SlideShare, 322–326
Spybot-Search & Destroy, 331–334
StatCounter, 335–338
SurveyMonkey, 344–348
TypeFaster, 364–367
Zoho, 436–442
Zoomerang, 443–446
Zotero, 447–452
programming code services (widgets),
383–386
Project Gutenberg, 279–284
promotion of library innovations,
resources, and services
LibGuides, 174–175

Library Success wiki, 177–178
PBworks, 256
Picasa, 268–269
Podcast Alley, 271–273
Widgets, 384–385
Wikipedia, 390–392
Wordle, 406
WordPress.com, 410–411
YouTube and, 433–435
proofreading, volunteer opportunities
    for, 283
publishing opportunities and assistance
    About.com, 8
    CiteULike, 56–57
    Connotea, 61
    LISWiki, 196
    Lulu, 209–212
    Technorati, 352–353
Pyra Labs, 43

Q

question-and-answer services
    Wolfram|Alpha, 399–403
    Yahoo! Answers, 422–426
Qwika, 285–287

R

Reader (Google), 131–134
Readerjack.com, 288–291
Readers'Advisory Blog, 43
recruitment through professional net-
    works, 421
Reddit, 74
reference and research assistance
    About.com, 7
    Academic Earth, 12
    Audacity, 24
    Bing, 32–33
    CiteULike, 56–57
    Connotea, 61
    Google Books, 123–124
    HathiTrust Digital Library, 141–142
    Khan Academy, 170
    Qwika, 287
    Rollyo, 299
    SlideShare, 322–323
    SortFix, 329

Twitter, 362
Wikipedia, 392
Wolfram|Alpha, 401, 403
Yahoo! Answers, 425
Zoho, 441
Zotero, 447–452
Reinhart, Sean, 147
Remember the Milk, 292–295
resources
    authoritative vs. nonauthoritative,
        33–34
    browsing with VuFind, 379–382
    for keeping up with Web 2.0 tech-
        nologies, 454–455
    promotion of with LibGuides,
        174–175
    providing access to online catalog of
        library materials, 416
    sharing with Delicious, 68–69
Rollyo, 296–299
Rondee, 300–303
Rose, Kevin, 70
RSS feeds, popularity of, 48

S

Safer Networking Limited, 331
Sanger, Larry, 387
scheduling and planning services
    Doodle, 79–82
    PBworks, 256
    Remember the Milk, 292–295
Scour, 304–307
screencasting programs (Jing), 160–163
Search (Yahoo!), 30
search-and-discovery portals (VuFind),
    379–382
search engines
    About.com, 5–8
    Bing, 30–33
    Dogpile, 75–78
    LISZEN, 198–200
    Qwika, 285–287
    reviews of, 307
    Rollyo, 296–299
    Scour, 304–307
    SortFix, 327–330
    Technorati, 349–353
    Wolfram|Alpha, 399–403

Second Life, 308–311
self-publishing services
    Lulu, 209–212
    Readerjack.com, 288–291
Selvadurai, Naveen, 106
semantic web, xxiv
SEOmoz list of Web 2.0 Awards, 386
serendipity engines, 340
Shelfari, 312–316
Sifry, Dave, 349
Sinha, Rashmi, 326
Sites (Google), 135–138
Six Apart Limited, 230, 233
Skype, 317–321
SlideShare, 322–326
Smithsonian
    Flickr and, 105
    Ustream and, 372
Snagit, 160
social bookmarking services
    CiteULike, 54–57
    Connotea, 58–61
    Delicious, 65–69
    StumbleUpon, 339–343
social cataloging services
    LibraryThing, 180–185
    Shelfari, 312–316
social networks
    Amplify, 14–16
    benefits of using, xxiii
    Ecademy, 87–90
    Facebook, 91–96
    Foursquare, 106–111
    Library 2.0, 186–188
    LinkedIn, 189–193
    Livemocha, 201–204
    Myspace, 234–238
    Ning, 239–242
    Orkut, 250–253
    Twitter, 358–363
    usage of, xxii
    XING, 418–421
social news services (Digg), 70–74
software archives, 151
Solomon, Laura, 248–249
Somlai-Fischer, Adam, 274
Sony Reader Library Program, 38

SortFix, 327–330
SourceForge website, 364, 382
Spalding, Tim, 181
Spybot-Search & Destroy, 331–334
Standalone Zotero Alpha, 452
StatCounter, 335–338
Steele Creek Library, 238
Stephens, Michael, 186
Stone, Biz, 358
Stoneham Public Library, 238
streaming content
    augmenting physical library collections with, 145, 147
    Justin.tv, 164–167
StumbleUpon, 339–343
Sullivan Library, Dominican College, New York Veritas Blog, 411
SurveyMonkey, 344–348
survey services
    SurveyMonkey, 344–348
    Zoomerang, 443–446
survival in competitive landscape, xxiv

T

tag cloud visualization tools (Wordle), 404–406
task management with Remember the Milk, 292–295
teaching methods and Ning, 242
TechCrunch, 353
Technorati, 40, 349–353
tech-savvy clients, delivery of services to, xxii–xxiii
TechSmith, 160
teleconference services (Rondee), 300–303
teleprompters, 62–64
Tennant, Roy, "Using the Cloud to Please the Crowd," 372
The MARC of Quality (TMQ), 213
third-party applications
    on Facebook, 91–92, 94
    for Twitter, 361
3D virtual world of Second Life, 308–311
travel planning services (TripIt), 354–357
trending topics, tracking with Technorati, 351

TripIt, 354–357
tutorials, hosting with PBworks, 257
Twitter, 32, 358–363
TypeFaster, 364–367
TypePad, 233

U

union catalog and WorldCat.org,
    412–417
University at Albany, SUNY, Interactive
    Media Center, 24
University at Buffalo Libraries, 392
University of California-Berkeley
    Libraries, 307
University of Florida Digital Collections,
    392
University of Georgia Libraries, 382
University of Manchester, John Rylands
    University Library, 411
University of Michigan and digital
    libraries, 141
University of Michigan Libraries, 382
University of Minnesota Libraries,
    232–233
University of Texas Libraries, 134, 385,
    441
University of the West Indies,
    Department of Library and
    Information Studies, 95
University of Washington Information
    School, 435
University of Washington Libraries, 392,
    416
URLs, purchasing, 394
U.S. National Archives and Flickr, 105
Ustream, 368–373

V

vCards, 50–53
vendors of ereaders, partnerships with,
    38, 153
video and voice calls with Skype,
    317–321
video broadcasting services, live
    Justin.tv, 164–167
    Ustream, 368–373

video hosting services
    Flickr, 101–105
    Hulu, 143–148
    iTunes U, 155–159
    Vimeo, 374–378
    YouTube, 431–435
video sharing services
    Academic Earth, 9–13
    Animoto, 17–20
    Khan Academy, 168–171
    Vimeo, 374–378
    YouTube, 431–435
Villanova University, Falvey Memorial
    Library, 379
Vimeo, 374–378
virtual business cards, 50–53
virtual library services, 311
visualization tools (Wordle), 404–406
volunteer opportunities
    Internet Archive, 153
    Project Gutenberg, 283
VuFind, 379–382

W

Wales, Jimmy, 387
Web 2.0
    definition of, xxi
    foundation of, xxi–xxii
Web 2.0 tools
    benefits of using, xxii–xxiv
    criteria used in choosing, xix–xx
    description of, xi
    evaluation of, xxiv–xxv
    keeping up-to-date with, 453–455
Web 3.0, xxiv
web analytics services
    Google Analytics, 116–120
    StatCounter, 335–338
web conferencing services (Mikogo),
    221–225
webinars
    on cataloging, 213–216
    developing with PBworks, 257
    Twitter, 362
webpage creation tools (Google Sites),
    135–138
web portals, building with Drupal, 83–86

websites. *see also* content management
    systems
    archives of, 149, 150
    chat widgets, integrating into, 219
    companion to book, xv
    course management systems, 226–229
    creating, 137–138
    driving traffic to, 342
    Google Books search box for,
        124–125
    OpenID-enabled, 243–245
    usage and design of, improving, 337
    widgets for, 383–386
Wetpaint Entertainment, 394
widgets, 383–386
Widgets (Yahoo!), 385, 386
Wikia, 285
Wikibooks, 388, 392
Wikipedia, 194, 285, 387–393
wikis
    Google Sites, 135–138
    Justin.tv community, 167
    Library Success: A Best Practices
        Wiki, 48, 176–179, 237, 321
    LISWiki, 194–197, 425
    PBworks, 254–257
    Project Gutenberg, 282
    Qwika search engine for, 285–287
    uses of, xxiii
    Wikipedia, 387–393
    Wikis by Wetpaint, 394–398
Wikis by Wetpaint, 394–398
Wiktionary, 388, 392
Winfrey, Oprah, 426
Wolfram, Stephen, 399, 403
Wolfram|Alpha, 399–403
Worcester Polytechnic Institute Gordon
    Library, 95
Wordle, 404–406
Word of the Day widget, 386

WordPress.com, 407–411
word processing programs
    AbiWord, 1–4
    OpenOffice.org, 246–249
    Zoho Writer, 439
Word-to-PDF converter, 258, 260
Workface Inc., 50
workshop and training support. *see also*
    presentation and workshop
    support
    About.com, 7
    Google Reader, 134
    Google Sites, 137–138
    Jing, 162–163
    Mikogo, 223, 225
    Photobucket, 263–264
    Ustream, 372
WorldCat.org, 412–417
WorldCat.org widgets, 386
Worth1000.com online community, 28

X

XING, 418–421

Y

Yahoo!
    Answers, 422–426
    Search, 30
    Widgets, 385, 386
York University Libraries, 382
Young, Bob, 209
YouSendIt, 427–430
YouTube, 143, 431–435

Z

Zoho, 436–442
Zoomerang, 443–446
Zotero, 447–452
Zuckerberg, Mark, 91